BAWLIN'
OUTTA
CONTROL

MAREESE COMER

Marc, I really appreciate your
support. I hope you
enjoy the read. God Bless.

ISBN: 978-1-5356-0679-0

Dedication

Although there is a host of family and friends I am thankful for, this book is dedicated to three women. To my late grandmother Carrie Bell Gooden, who instilled some good qualities in me at a very young age. Still today, the wisdom you shared helps me fight through the toughest situations. I have yet to find someone else who can come close to who you were. To my wonderful mother Shirley Comer, who constantly encouraged me to face my fears and to be a leader. It was you who I watched overcome the most challenging obstacles. In spite of the difficulties you faced, I never once felt you didn't love me. Once you found the strength to overcome those obstacles, you then began to strengthen me. I would not be the man I am today without you. To my late baby sister Darlene Knight, who I only had the pleasure of being with for a couple years before you ascended to heaven. During that short period, I was able to see how much you loved me. And I will never forget us brushing our teeth together every night at the top of the stairs. I love you and miss you. I would also like to dedicate this project to all of the dear family and friends that are mentioned in this book that are no longer with us.

Acknowledgements

My vision to become an author was one that at times seemed impossible. Truth be told, it would have in fact been impossible if not for the amazing people who have helped me along the journey. First, I would like to give an honor to God, who helped me get in the right mental state so that I could convey words that may inspire, excite and heal all readers. I want to thank Denise Waker, who believed in me when I was writing on tablet paper. It was she who took the tablet paper and typed my handwritten pages into Word documents so I could submit them to an editor. I would also like to thank Lynette Hall-Jones for taking time out of her busy schedule to help with typing some of the pages. I want to thank Otis Spears for the powerful cover design and marketing help. Thank you Candace Disher for all the copying and organizing help to more easily bring my manuscript to life. Last but not least, I would like to thank Jessa Claeys for going through my entire book and completing the soft edit in preparation for editing. Because of you all, my vision is now possible.

Contents

BALLIN – PERFORMING AT AN EXTREMELY HIGH LEVEL.
LIVING THE GOOD LIFE. AFFLUENT.

"BAWLIN" – AN OUTWARD CRY. A SEARCH FOR ATTENTION

Chapter One

THE HEIGHTS

Mareese Comer

IT'S IRONIC THAT WE CALLED this place the "Heights" when that was a level very few people from here seemed to reach. Burns Heights was a low-income housing development where I grew up. It was located in a Duquesne, Pennsylvania. Most people would call it the projects. I often wondered if we called it that because of the development itself or because of the people who lived there.

The Heights was full of life by day, but when the streetlights came on, they seemed to turn off any signs of life. After dark was when people were beaten, stabbed, and, even worse, shot. You could be sure all the incidents were repercussions of drugs, alcohol, or some form of domestic violence. It was a time when everyone seemed to walk around freely with their spiritual refreshments in paper bags. Although bad things did often happen during broad daylight, each night was a guarantee that by sunup horror stories would spread through the projects like wildfire.

The neighborhood was run by the Allegheny County Housing Authority. It was established to fulfill their mission statement: To create decent, safe, and affordable living for low-income families.

DECENT - I guess you could say it was decent if that was all you knew. Whether it could be accurately described as decent depended on if you were talking about the people or the living conditions, which were everything opposite of the word. Most of the people who lived there probably believed there was no other world outside of this development.

SAFE - Safety did exist if you could avoid being in the wrong place at the wrong time—or anywhere after dark. Daylight was a source of safety. Another thing that made the Heights really safe was that everyone knew each other. If someone didn't know your name, then they knew your mother or father, or both. Because of this it was hard for anyone to transgress without being exposed. I would go so far as to say that *most* of the residents were very respectable people who just made a choice to live life with the support of government assistance. Often that way of life was handed down from generation to generation.

2

AFFORDABLE - This was the part of Allegheny County's mission statement that definitely held the most credibility. Of course tenants had to meet certain qualifications, or not meet certain qualifications, of the regular working class in order to rent a very small unit for an exceptionally small amount of money. During those times, you could live in a two-bedroom apartment for about $96 a month. The cost depended on your income. For instance, if you happened to have a job (as rare as that may have been), the housing authority would set your rent based on your income. Frequently, the residents who received government assistance were privy to the minimum amount. It is hard for me to imagine a landlord renting a property for its worth of $500 a month. However, since I made a decent income, my landlord charged me more money. But that's how things worked in the Heights, and it seemed to be what made people complacent and not want to strive for more.

You would not believe how often this became a way of life for many families. The children that were raised in these projects ended up raising their kids in the same place. Unless tenants had something within themselves that drove them to seek something better, they became very comfortable with this way of life. Paying $96 a month for rent and nothing for utility bills would allow a person to waste money on alcohol, drugs, or whatever choice habit and still be able to keep a roof over their head. Unfortunately, as low as the rent seemed to be, there were always the irresponsible tenants who allowed their habit to become so bad that even the minimum amount of rent became too much to bear. I later learned that no matter the income and cost of rent, the same principles of responsibility would always apply. It's simple: Just because you can afford something doesn't mean you can afford to neglect the things that should take priority.

My family lived in an "affordable" two-bedroom unit. It was very small in square footage, but very large considering our family. The building was shaped like a huge barn. It was designed with multi-colored reddish brick that only extended halfway up. The top portion of the artificial foundation was constructed of framed plasterboard that was painted white and highlighted with dirty, brown trim. There were about fifty identical buildings within this development. Each one consisted of six units, and therefore about three hundred families occupied the Heights. It was very rare that a family did not have other relatives who also lived in the development. Me? I had several aunts and uncles, and a multitude of cousins who lived there. Both my grandparents, along with extended families that married in, or more frequently, those who became a family without saying any vows, lived there, too.

My best friend was a kid we called Bear. He was more family than a friend, considering how things seemed to work in the Heights. My Uncle Geno and Bear's mother were a couple. They never got married, but were an item throughout my childhood. Geno served in the United States Army for several years. During one of his infrequent trips home, he and Bear's mother had their first biological child together. Neak was a cute little girl who became another link to our families.

When Bear and I were toddlers, we lived across the street from each other. Somehow, even when both of our families moved to other parts of the projects, we still ended up living less than fifty yards away from each other. This made it easy for us to become best friends, and the intertwining of our families sealed the deal. He had an older brother who thought he was a member of the rap group Run-DMC and proudly sported his fancy gold belt. He also had two older sisters. I was the oldest child and only had one younger sister at the time. Her name was Darlene but we called her Dar-Dar, and she was an angel. Of course I was her favorite person in the world. She would follow me around everywhere. Most children would get out of bed and find their way to their parents' bed. But Dar-Dar would find her way to her big brother. Even if we spent the night over at a family member's house, I would still wake up with her next to me.

Mom used to say what a good baby Dar-Dar was because she never cried much. In fact, she really didn't talk too much, either. She just walked around smiling with her two middle fingers in her mouth. Mom made us sit on the top steps every night to brush our teeth together before we went to bed. Although I was a toddler, I felt like a big boy since I had a baby sister that was crazy about me. So in addition to me our house consisted of my mom, Dar-Dar, and her dad Ricky, my mom's boyfriend who she apparently got together with when I was an infant. Ricky seemed to be a good man who treated me very well. My mom would not have accepted anything less. Only time would tell how good of a man he really was. Overall, I would say during that time that my home seemed to have a foundation much stronger than the building that housed us. Mom was a woman of fashion so she made sure that we always looked good. She also made sure that every meal was prepared for us. Dar-Dar and I would sit at the table for hours to finish up our brussel sprouts until I got smart enough to bring a plastic baggie with me to the dinner table and made sure they were disposed of properly. If I hadn't come up with such a brilliant plan, we would have sat there for hours, waiting for those cute little juice cups to hit the table, and there was no way I could let that happen to my baby sis. We didn't have a choice when it came to food, and we weren't asked what we wanted. Whatever Mom cooked is what you ate, and that was the end of the story. I could never forget spending hours doing my homework only to have Mom tell me that I had to do it all over again because it wasn't neat enough for her. Those were the times when I really thought she was possessed.

I was getting a little older and Mom started to let me go outside to play with my buddies. Since our fabulous dwelling and affordable rent did not allow us a yard, we always headed to what we called "the field," which was a big enough yard for all of us. The field was in the back of the development, and it was one place all of us kids really loved, but it wasn't much of a playground. There were never any nets on the bent rims at the hoop court, and the swings always seemed to be broken, so we played Tarzan and just swung on the chains. The sliding board was always leaning to one side, or even worse, resting on the ground, so you would have to scoot along it instead of having the privilege to slide down. We actually did not fool with it much because we were too busy on the grass—or more accurately the patches of dirt – practicing the moves of NFL greats Eric Dickerson, Walter Payton, and Barry Sanders. There was also the Philadelphia Eagles superstar Randall Cunningham, who no matter what, was only imitated by one kid unless he was sick or on punishment. He was my cousin from my father's side of the family. We called him Lump because of the shape of his head, but boy could this kid throw a football.

There always seemed to be two rival running backs who could never be on the same team: me and a kid we called Mo-Joe. Mo-Joe was a very tough kid. He wasn't the fastest, but it seemed like he was invisible at times as he always found a way to avoid tacklers. So the field was where we learned how to play the game of football. We would play every day after our homework was done, and on weekends we met there immediately after a bowl of Fruity Pebbles. We would play for hours and hours until those streetlights kicked on, and then we knew we better be at home before they reached their full power. We would play in the snow, rain, and one hundred degree weather. It didn't matter to us, we just loved to play the game. Besides, there weren't many other things for us to do. Most of us would show up at the field regularly. Only once in a while were we gifted by the presence of my cousin Milik. He was from my mother's side of the family. I'm sure Milik's desire was to always be there, but his stepfather seemed to shelter him and would not let that happen. Although he did not show up often at the field, everyone was always happy to see him when he did. Milik was very tall, but built like a string bean, so playing football was really not his forte.

Bear would always show up, but for some reason we could never figure out, he never wanted to play. We all knew he had blazing speed, and when he did occasionally play, he had hands like Jerry Rice. But he would only play if he felt like playing. Then there was Rodney, who stood on the cement sideline with Ju-Ju, pretending to be Slick Rick and

KRS-One. So as we got our school clothes filthy dirty, Rodney would be the entertainment. He would beat-box and make up raps about whatever was going on that day. We tried to get him to play, but he would say that being a rapper was going to be his career. We knew that he could fight because he would always start them. I can't even count how many times each of us got into fights, but Rodney always seemed to be involved to some extent. Ju-Ju's connection to Rodney was rapping. He was the pretty boy of the bunch. His hair always had to be combed perfectly, and he always had on the freshest sneakers. It was also rumored that he had done things with girls that none of us could even imagine. He claimed that no matter what he did in life, he was going to always look good and have a lot of ladies. Ju-Ju did not live in the Heights, but he would often visit because he had family there. We could never figure out how he kept the flyest gear, because he said his parents didn't work. He did say that they ran a business and were making a fortune selling reefer. Huh! We didn't have a clue what that was, but Ju-Ju seemed to know what he was talking about. This was the regular audience hanging out at the field most of the time. There was nothing more that we liked to do except, of course, when Damien came to get us.

This kid was incredible. He probably was one of the reasons that I would never trade my childhood, no matter how horrific living in the Heights was. Damien was by far every neighborhood kid's favorite person to be around. He always had some fun adventure for us to go on. When he arrived, as much as we loved to play football, we would always end the game immediately. It was as if he had a compass installed in his head, because he knew how to get everywhere and always knew the fastest way to get there. We would go on dangerous survival missions down the mountainous hill in the back of the projects. Although its peak was the Heights, the valley below was made up of 60 mph traffic that bordered the Monongahela River. Each kid would be in line with Damien leading the way. We would slip and slide on parts of the mountain, but if we stayed behind our fearless leader, we knew he would guide us to safety.

Once we got to the bottom, we would wait for his signal, and then it was time to put our football moves to work as we raced across the highway, praying that a car would not tackle us. But that's why we had so much faith in him. We always made it across.

Once we did, it was a pretty short distance to the edge of the river. That's where the fun began. Sometimes we would swim, but mostly we caught lizards, frogs, crayfish, and pretty much anything that dwelled in the shallow water that we did not need a fishing pole to catch. We would take them back to the Heights and play with them as long as we could keep them alive. It was a very dangerous adventure to the river and back, but I don't recall a time when harm was in our way. Either Damien was just that good, or the good Lord was watching over us. We would argue that it was the skills of Damien even though it was most likely the latter.

If it was Halloween, everyone wanted to go trick-or-treating with Damien. He seemed to have some inside information as to what houses gave out the most candy. He usually took us to neighborhoods beyond the Heights. If we did go to any houses inside the projects, you could bet your bottom dollar that we would hit the jackpot. We took pillowcases and garbage bags to collect all the candy. Damien would end up with two bags because we all gave him a handful of candy to show our appreciation for the tour. This kid was already an entrepreneur and hadn't even reached middle school. If it was Christmas season, he would gather us all together and convince us to go door to door to sing Christmas carols. He thought it was a brilliant idea, and of course he was right. The people that did open their doors for us always gave us some really charitable gifts. We figured they had to have felt sorry for us because we couldn't sing a lick. And as good as Rodney could rap, he would always forget the words to "Silent Night" —the favorite song of the rest of the choir. People gave us candy canes, cookies, chocolate, and most of all, money. When we had enough of people feeling sorry for us, or we began to lose our voices, Damien would gather us up and divide all the earnings. He would not keep an extra penny. We would split everything dead even down to the chocolate and cookies. He would joke that he was going to deduct a quarter from Rodney for every time he messed up, but Damien never did. We insisted that he take extra, but he always refused. He would say with his forehead wrinkled, "I don't deserve more than any of you, but make sure you get some nice gifts for your family."

That was why we all loved him. Damien was such a fair kid. Fair and very considerate, but you did not want to cross him. Some kids were beginning to call him Grip because it was said that one day after school he had chastised a middle school kid twice his size for teasing his little brother. Bear said that Damien put this kid in a sleeper hold and not even the teachers could get him to loosen his grip. So we intentionally stayed on his good side, not necessarily because we were afraid, but because we respected him and accepted him as our leader.

When it was summertime, we still played ball, but we always took a break to eat a free lunch. It was a phrase that I would later learn did not exist in the real world. But in the Heights there was a government program that provided food during the summer for the kids in the projects.

We would be gone for most of the day and somehow, at some point, end up riding our bikes across the bridge that lead to our famous amusement park called "Kennywood." We got to go inside once a year during our school picnic day. It was usually at the end of the school year, and therefore was the only other time bedsides Easter and the first day of school that I got new clothes. On our adventures we would ride past the park and say how much we loved to ride the scariest ride there, and how our parents would let us run loose as long as we met back at our designated picnic table a few times during the day.

I will never forget a day the crew and I had just gotten back to the Heights from one of our bike adventures. As soon as we entered the main entrance, we heard a bunch of yelling. The loudest yell came from Ms. Marlene, Bear's mom, who was directing us to come inside her house. Mr. Willie yelled out profanities as he chased his target, an older black man who had no shirt or shoes on. We were just in time to capture what Ms. Marlene did not want our young eyes to see. Mr. Willie reached down in the front part of his pants and pulled out a gun. He obviously had no concern for his surroundings, or his anger made everything invisible except his target. This target had to be faster than any NFL running back that we often imitated down at the field. He was moving almost at lightning speed, weaving from left to right, likely to prevent Mr. Willie from getting a clear shot. His Barry Sanders moves proved futile, as Mr. Willie seemed to have the concentration of John Wayne. He squinted one of his eyes and pulled the trigger. It seemed as if hours passed as the bullet traveled the length of three buildings and eventually reached the intended destination. The target let out an echoing scream and began to hold his leg. His injury was not life threatening, but you couldn't say the same for Mr. Willie. He was sent away to prison for a very long time, leaving his family behind to survive without his financial or emotional support.

The funny thing about life is that presence doesn't necessarily translate into someone being there. As odd as this story may seem to a suburban family, this was the norm in the Heights. So many mothers were greatly appreciated as they were forced to play the role of both parents. Or in my case, you did have two parents as the man accepted the role of father because he was dating your mother, but was not a biological relative.

Grade school was a lot of fun. Most of the kids from the Heights went to the same school. There were no buses so we had to walk about two miles to and from school each day. We really didn't mind at all as it gave us extra time to hang out with each other. At this point, school was just a part of our lives. We had no choice whether to go or not, but we were probably more interested in socializing than what was in the textbooks. Rodney and I seemed to always end up in the same class every year during grade school. I'm sure it had to be some kind of mistake—whoever was in charge of assigning classes was brave to put us together. We didn't compete against each other down at the field in football, but we did have a fierce competition going at school. Our challenge was to see who could be the biggest class clown. Rodney would make the absolute funniest faces and it was my job not to laugh, which proved impossible. That was if we were not in Mr. Linen's class. For some reason, I was always able to keep my composure while he was teaching. The politically correct reason would have been that I really enjoyed learning from him, but I think it had more to do with having to write whatever behavior you had an issue with about a thousand times on paper—or worse the chalkboard—during recess. I believe I wrote, "I will not chew gum," so many times that it forced me to lose my taste for it indefinitely. Mr. Linen was the first person I met that really did have eyes in the back of his head. He could also seemingly hear you in class even if you were mouthing words silently. He must have been reading our lips. Making each other laugh was one thing, but the problem was that our comedy usually affected the entire classroom. This would ultimately get us a first-class ticket to the principal's office. There was no doubt that we were tough kids, but no one wanted to visit Mr. Archie D's office. He believed in the old-fashioned way of discipline, the paddle. I guess he figured keeping us kids in school as much as possible was the right thing to do, so a suspension was not his first choice. This "act right stick" of his had to have been designed by a high-class architect. It was made of light-colored wood with tiny rows of holes in the center. Its length was equivalent to the height of our shoulders and wide enough to cover the whole territory of our backside. I would imagine that if Mr. Archie D had traded in his paddle for a golf club (which I wish he would have), Tiger Woods would be no match for him. His form was perfect and his swing was an all-in-one motion with the power of a home run hitter. The worst part of getting a swat in his office was that it was usually just the pregame warm up until you got home and had to deal with the real punishment. Although punishments seemed to be quite frequent, Mom made sure that she was somehow able to mix in surprises even when I wasn't deserving of them.

Mareese Comer

I will never forget when Mom walked through the front door with a battleship hoagie that was too big for her to carry. She yelled for me to come downstairs as she had a surprise for me. I came down, smiled at what I saw, and remembered thinking that I was not even hungry. She put it across the table as she told me that she had just signed me up for football. I looked at her with an unappreciative smirk and said, "Mom, we do that every day." She then explained that a couple of older guys from the neighborhood had reestablished the little league football program. She said that she had already paid my fees and I would be receiving my football equipment. This was at the point in my life that I had decided I was ready to make a name for myself. I mean, I did have respect down at the field, but putting on equipment would take me to the next level!

Our practices were held behind John F. Kennedy Elementary School. I will never forget showing up to practice on the first day. I walked with my shoulders held high, and even deepened my voice when the coach asked me my name. It was like the equipment made me into a different person. I now understood how Superman felt after he came out of the booth. To my surprise, this was totally different from the field. We had to do all kinds of exercises before we even touched the football. That didn't make sense to me at all. Why would we exhaust ourselves before we got a chance to show our skills? I would later understand that the exercises were the most important part of practice. Our bodies would only perform as well as we conditioned them to perform. We would also do all kinds of drills that I couldn't quite understand, but I always gave my very best. One drill was called the "Oklahoma." My opponent and I would lay on our backs with the top of our heads against each other and legs facing the opposite way. As soon as we heard the whistle, we had to get to our feet as fast as our opponent and then avoid or make the tackle. My favorite drill was "bull in the ring." For this one, the whole team would stand in a circle and one player would get in the middle and spin, waiting for the coach to call a number, and then a player would charge full speed at you. Every kid hated when my number was called because they knew I had no fear when I charged toward them. A short time before this, I thought I knew everything about football, but I quickly realized that I really didn't know much at all. For the first time, I was actually learning how to play the game. Huh, a life lesson. I learned that you can be more effective working together as a team. I learned that although you thought you had everything figured out, you still had a lot to learn.

Mom and Grandma were my cheerleaders. They showed up to every single game unless it was scheduled for early Sunday morning. Then none of us went. Grandma was serious about putting church before everything. Thankfully, most of the games were in the afternoon.

We had practiced for about a month and it was finally time for the first big game. I could not wait to put on that red and white jersey with the number sixty-seven on the back. I really had no concern with what number they gave me. I just wanted to play the game. I was physically and mentally ready. There was only one obstacle in my way. The game started at 2:00 p.m. and Grandma was not feeling the idea of me missing church for my first game. The church service was long and sometimes went past 2:00 p.m. First game, first year playing or not, it was just not an option. The real problem was that there was no way I could really know what time the service would end. Bishop Mitchell would get hit with the spirit and we might be there until the night service began. Today my prayer was that God would quickly give him the revelation to Shadrack, Meshack, and Obendigo. That was the day I felt that God really hears us. We got out of church about 1:40 p.m., and Mom started up the old Plymouth Gremlin and we were headed to the field where the Dukes played. She had already put my uniform in the trunk so I just had to get dressed in the back of the hatch while she raced toward the field. We got there while my team was still stretching. Coach Steve yelled at me, telling me to hurry up. I thought, "It's not my fault I don't drive. And he really doesn't understand Bishop Mitchell."

I jumped in the circle on the last set of neck rolls and we closed the warm up with a huddle, chanting who we were. They called for the coin toss and I could not believe my eyes. There were men dressed like the same men that I saw on TV who seemed to control the games. They had on black and white striped shirts and everything. Man, this was the real deal. Mom and Grandma were headed toward their seats—still wearing their church clothes—with hands full of popcorn and fountain drinks. I looked up at them with a little irritation since Coach Steve wouldn't let me start since I was late. I sat patiently throughout the whole first quarter with my helmet strapped on and my mouthpiece filled with Bubblicious gum. It wasn't until the second quarter that my heart almost jumped out of my chest. There was a shout coming from Coach Steve. "Number sixty-seven," he yelled with that exact same tone he used when calling me during "bull in the ring" at practice. I was so excited that I didn't even stop to ask him where he wanted me to play or what he wanted me to do.

I raced onto the field and Sweet Pea, the captain of the football team, had to put me in place at linebacker. The only break I got for the rest of the game was at halftime and between quarters. It was in a huddle during the fourth quarter when one of my teammates made an observation that would stick with me forever. He smacked me on my helmet and said, "Man, you are playing like an animal today. It must be those church socks you have on." Everyone in the huddle looked down toward my cleats and immediately busted out laughing. I quickly realized I had changed all my clothes in the back of the hatch except my socks. From that day forward I was stuck with the nickname "Church Socks," and continued to wear them every single game.

I was having the time of my life. Since Mo-Joe was the only one of my friends who played football with me, I didn't get a chance to hang out with the fellas too much. That was until the end of the season when it was announced that the league would be canceled due to the mismanagement of funds. That was typical in a neighborhood like ours. So it was going to be back to the field after all. I loved the experience of playing the real game, but what us kids learned in the Heights, no game could ever teach.

Chapter Two

RED-EYE TO HEAVEN

Mareese Comer

I sat out the next year of football, and just when I thought my football dreams were over, Mom found a league across the McKeesport Bridge. My cousin Lump was already playing there. The team was called the Tigers, and I was prepared to live up to the name of the mascot. I had learned a secret when playing for the Dukes: You had to make a name for yourself at practice. So I quickly made a name for myself by playing every snap as if I were in a real game. Coach Bill took notice of my hard work and rewarded me with a starting job as running back. The other starting running back was my cousin Lump. I was quite surprised by this because he could throw a football better than any other kid I knew. But there was a kid name Hueby from McKeesport who already had the quarterback position.

I seemed to dominate every single practice. That was unless we scrimmaged this team where the players were about two years older than us. They had this kid name Curtis Martin who would run all over us every time he touched the ball. He was so fast that I don't think we were ever able to touch his jersey, or it may have been that he was so strong that we stayed out of his way. The season went great and I learned so much more about the game. When it was over, I was all schoolwork and hanging with the crew.

Today was a very special day. Mom bought me a brand new outfit and some new sneakers. Showers did not exist in our apartment so I usually did just a quick wipe down from the bathroom sink, but on this occasion it was imperative that I run some bath water. Mom went out quite a bit at night, but tonight she was taking me on a date. I was going to my very first concert. I had never seen the group Run-D.M.C, who Bear's brother often imitated, and had never heard of LL Cool J. It probably wouldn't have mattered if we were going to see an opera. I was just so happy to be spending the day with Mom. We arrived at the Civic Arena and I could not believe how many people were standing in line to get a ticket for the performance.

It was at this very moment that I realized my mother was a warrior. People were pushing and shoving, trying to force their way to the front of the line. Mom grabbed my hand and pulled me closer to her. I thought, "If Mom was the fullback who blocked for me on my football team, I would score every time I touched the ball." She used her strength to force her way to the front of the line. I saw another side of her when this tall man with his hat turned backward bumped her. She looked at him with fury in her eyes as she yelled that if any part of his body touched her son, he would regret it for the rest of his life. I had always felt like a mother's love centered on being a provider, but I now understood love also meant being a protector.

We made it inside the arena. I could not see where we were going, so I just had to trust Mom as she led the way. By the time we reached our seats, all I could hear was loud music blaring from the speakers. I couldn't figure out if it was coming from the arena or the giant boom box on the stage. The guy who was performing said he likes his radio loud. In the next song, he said he was bad. I could not believe all the people screaming along with the words to his songs. Then all of a sudden, everyone seemed to calm down as he started whispering about being alone in his room, staring at a wall, and saying that he needed love. I was so hypnotized by his performance—Mom was even moving to every beat. I didn't notice the sign on stage that said "LL Cool J" until he was done. Although I could feel the excitement, I stood there like a deer in the headlights with my mouth wide open.

The next performance was quite different, but the crowd was just as excited. I had no idea what a freak was, but this group kept singing that they came out at night. Mom told me later that the group was called Whodini. The whole experience was frightening. I was with my favorite person in the world, though, so I found a way to adjust.

On the way home I asked Mom to turn down the music because I had to tell her something. She turned it down immediately and said, "What's up, baby?"

I looked up to the front seat and said, "THANK YOU!"

Those were the special moments that I would always remember. Mom made a point to take time out for us to go on dates. Sometimes my mom, stepdad, Dar-Dar, and I would all go out together. No matter where we went, Dar-Dar would always want to hold my hand. I could not believe how attached she was to me. It was probably because I could make the funniest faces, which would make her laugh every single time. I also knew where Mom hid the snacks, and I often treated my baby sis.

Things seemed to be going really well with my family. Mom and my stepfather appeared to be very happy together. Tonight they were going out, so Dar-Dar and I were going to spend the night at my grandmother's. She was my other favorite person in the world. Since I was her first grandchild, she treated me as if I meant the world to her. She would always take me with her when she went to the grocery store, and, of course, to church. She let us watch TV as long as we wanted, and she always had snacks waiting for us. My two youngest aunts, Ron and Bam, who seemed to be more like my sisters, always took time to play games with us. They always seemed to be conducting a talent show or imitating how people danced at church when the spirit hit them.

My stepfather dropped us off and Grandma had already ordered pizza for us. We stayed up as late as we could watching TV with Grandma. Dar-Dar fell asleep first, so Aunt Ron carried her to her bed. I lay there on Grandma's lap while she played cassette tapes of church services. She noticed me nodding off and told me to get up and get in my uncle's bed. Little did I know how much my world would change when I woke up.

When I opened my eyes the next morning, I was not surprised to see Dar-Dar lying next to me. What surprised me was that she was very cold. I was sure Aunt Ron had put her in her bed, but she still found a way to come lie next to her big brother. I got out of bed, put the covers over her, and went downstairs to see who was awake. Both of my aunts were in the kitchen trying to cook up a homemade snack made out of Kix cereal, butter, and a ton of sugar. They turned on cartoons for me and gave me a bowl of their homemade delicacy. A few hours later, the whole house would be in an uproar.

One of my aunts asked where Dar-Dar was. I told her that she was still asleep, and cold, so I put the blanket over her before I came downstairs. I thought it was a little odd since Dar-Dar was always the one waking up to get some milk. Although she didn't say much, I knew what it meant when she was standing over me with her cute little sippy cup. But that was not the case this morning. She seemed to be really tired and still peacefully asleep. Aunt Ron went up to check on her. Suddenly, I heard a loud scream from the top of the steps. I wasn't quite sure what was wrong. I had heard similar screams come from Aunt Ron when she saw a mouse in the house, or from Aunt Bam when she tried to plug in the iron while her hand was wet, but this particular scream was a thunderous roar unlike any I had ever heard from Aunt Ron, especially since she was the most peaceful of the family. Then came a demanding yell of the word "mommy," prompting my grandma to come right away. I was so into *The Flintstones* and did not want to move, but I went over by the steps to peek upstairs. I could see Grandma rushing into the room where my baby sister was sleeping.

It seemed like my grandma's house was full of people within a matter of minutes. I tried my best to get upstairs to see what was going on, but Aunt Bam would not allow it. When Mom came in, I knew that something had to be really wrong because I had never seen her move that fast in my life. She rushed past everyone in the house, pushing over anyone in her path. My stepfather was a step behind her. They raced up about twelve steps in three strides. I was still a little shook up from Aunt Ron's scream, but the next scream I heard made Aunt Ron's seem like a whisper in comparison. As Mom screamed, "Nooooooooooo, my baby!" I was sure that the walls were shaking and the picture frames were about to fall off the nails.

Shortly after, I heard sirens outside and a couple of medical people were rushing in through the door. I loved my Aunt Bam a whole lot, but this was the first time that I remember really being disgusted with her. She grabbed my hand, pulled me to the door, and said we had to go to another building in the Heights to a friend's house. I could not understand why I had to leave. I had the right to know what was wrong. I was already crying my little heart out and didn't even know why. All I knew was that hearing my mother scream and cry automatically made me sad and terrified at the same time. I cried out, "I want my mommy," as Aunt Bam dragged me across the project's sidewalks. When we got to the friend's house, her friend and my aunt were being extra nice to me. They told me that I could have any snack I wanted. They even offered to take me to the store. Ivan's, as the store was called, was actually a house by the entrance of the projects that had a small store set up in the would-be living room. It was also the corner that every kid rushed to when we heard the musical chimes coming from Alex's truck.

Alex was an older white man who kind of reminded me of a taller version of Archie Bunker. He owned an ice cream truck and drove through the projects every day during the summer selling ice cream cones. What us kids liked the most was that he would pick two of us out of the crowd to work for him that day. Those kids would receive free ice cream for their hard work. Once in a while, Rodney and Damien would jump on the back of his truck to get a free ride, not caring about the free ice cream. Ju-Ju used to say that he didn't need to be to be chosen by Alex as he always had money to buy what he wanted.

I ended up going to the corner to get something from the store that day. When we arrived, my aunt asked me what I wanted. I looked her in her face, started crying, and said that I just wanted my mom. It felt strange that Aunt Bam was being so nice to me. She always treated me pretty well, but this was the first time that she told me to get whatever I wanted. On a normal day, she would tell me exactly what I was allowed to get. We went back to her friend's house empty-handed. I asked why we couldn't go back to Grandma's house. She just looked at me and said, "We can't right now."

After sitting over there for hours, which seemed like years, Aunt Bam finally said Grandma was coming to get me. I thought, "What don't they understand about me wanting my mommy?" Grandma arrived soon after. I couldn't tell if she was treating me a certain way, because she always treated me so well. She explained to me that I would be staying with her because my mother was not feeling well. At first, I thought she meant I'd stay with her for a few hours. Later, I learned that she was referring to me staying there for weeks or maybe even months. Upon realizing that my mother would not be coming, I then asked the million-dollar question. "Where is Dar-Dar?"

Grandma looked at me, her eyes peaceful, and calmly said, "Baby, your mother will explain it to you better, but the best thing I can do is tell you the truth. Your baby sister went to heaven."

What? That didn't make any sense to me at all, so I looked at her strangely and asked, "Why did she get to go? Can I go with her?"

Grandma looked at me with a comfortable smile and said, "Baby, you sure can go to heaven." She then explained that God would only let me go there when He's ready for me. I could not go when I wanted to. *Thanks, Grandma!* I was now even more confused.

As the days passed, I began to understand things a little better. I was clear about one thing. My baby sister was not coming back. Two days later, Mom came to Grandma's and took me into a room to talk. Her eyes were bloodshot, and she looked like she had taken a couple of jabs from Muhammad Ali. She sat in silence for quite a while before she finally spoke. She looked me in the eye and said, "Baby, your little sister is dead."

The room went silent. Mom grabbed me and hugged me tighter than she ever had before. She told me how much she loved me as tears began to run down both of our faces. She went on to explain that I would be going to a funeral in a couple of days. After that, I would have to stay with Grandma for a while, but she promised to check on me. She kissed me, got up, and grabbed my hand to lead me downstairs to the kitchen. Then she left to go to the funeral home.

I sat there staring at my food. I tried to eat a french fry, but it didn't taste as good with snot. I was still crying about the horrible news. So many things were racing through my little brain, and every single thought was as irritating as a bee sting. The fact that my baby sister would not be coming back was a devastating blow to me. I would miss her standing over me with her sippy cup. I would miss her being glued to me on the couch and watching cartoons while Mom was still asleep. Yeah, I enjoyed hanging out with the fellas, but this was my little buddy. Sitting on the steps and brushing my teeth by myself was going to be extremely lonely. Plus, not only did I lose my baby sister, but I was also staying with Grandma for a while and would be losing my mother as well.

Although those thoughts were very painful, they didn't hurt as badly as me realizing that when I got up to put a blanket over my sister's cold body, she had already taken a red-eye flight to heaven. I couldn't help but wonder if there was anything I could have done to delay that flight. With that thought came the most excruciating pain to the front of my forehead and a series of stomach flutters. Had I done something wrong? Had I rolled over on her accidentally? *God, if you can hear me, please tell me that it's not my fault.* I was not asked one single question about my sister or if I remembered anything, so at least my family didn't make me feel like I had done anything wrong. They had not asked how I was feeling, either.

Over the next few days, Grandma seemed to pay more attention to me. She would pray with me, and we had long talks about God's love. She also took the time to play board games with me. I really enjoyed it, even though it wasn't fair when Grandma would nod off to sleep with her Big Gulp cup in her hand right before she went bankrupt in Monopoly. As competitive as I was, this was not really about winning. Playing games with Grandma brought me a small amount of happiness in an otherwise dark time. Losing my baby sister was almost too hard for me to swallow. It was even worse than the brussel sprouts that Mom made me eat at the dinner table (or at least thought she made me eat).

Grandma and my aunts took me shopping to buy a new suit and shoes. I already had church clothes, but they were adamant that I get a black suit. The very next day was the funeral, or "going home service" as Grandma called it. I then understood why I needed to wear a black suit—everyone seemed to be wearing that color. We were picked up in a long black limousine and escorted to the church, where I would be seeing my baby sister for the very last time.

Unlike the concert Mom had taken me to, this event was the saddest thing I had ever experienced. Before we could even get to our seats, the whole church seemed to be flooding with tears—my own included. Most of my tears came from watching how sad everyone was. Mom literally had to be carried to her seat. Her tears seemed infinite.

My stepfather had a stoic look on his face as he hugged Mom as close as he could. I imagined that if he were a hose, the water was turned on, but he was waiting for the trigger to be released so that water could burst out with force. Maybe that moment would be when he found some time alone. As for now, he had to represent the strength that Mom needed.

Grandma cried a bit, but overall had the look of peace on her face. Maybe God had given her an explanation as to why it was time for my baby sister to go to heaven.

After the service and the devastating trip to the graveyard, everyone went to Grandma's for dinner. It's amazing how many people could fit in a small project apartment. Most of the people who attended the funeral came to the dinner. Even people who did not attend the "going home" service came to show their respect. Everyone seemed to be feeling a little better, giving each other hugs and warm smiles. I overheard conversations of how sweet a baby my sister was, and how she never cried much and always listened so well.

I was sitting on Grandma's lap and she cradled me as if I were an infant. As sad as a day like today was, she sure knew how to make me feel okay. I just lay there, content in my comfort zone, and watched everyone. I slowly scanned the room from left to right. That's when it happened.

It was as if something came over my mother. All of a sudden, she erupted. She had been sitting and talking to my aunts and seemed to be really calm one moment, but the next moment she was yelling at the top of her lungs, and pushing people away who were trying to restrain her and calm her down. As hard as they tried, they were not successful in their attempts. Tables were pushed over, pictures were knocked off the walls, and food seemed to be everywhere. It was like a mini tornado had swept through the small project apartment. By the time Grandma and my stepfather were able to calm her down, everyone had left the apartment. Now it was Mom's turn to be cradled like an infant as Grandma rocked her back and forth, telling her that everything was going to be all right. God knew what He was doing.

From that point on, the mother that I knew before seemed to have been buried in the grave with my baby sister. Mom was true to her word about me staying with Grandma for a while, as days turned to weeks, and weeks to months and months. Let's just say that I finished a few grades in school while living at Grandma's house.

Mom did come around from time to time, and when she did, it was just to drop off food or some clothes for me. I was hoping that one day she would show up and say we were going on a date again. But that never happened. She always gave me a brief hug—like the kind people gave each other at church, touching at the shoulders and connecting each other's cheek while kissing the air. That was very different for me. I had always loved it when she almost squeezed the life out of me when we hugged. That was a true embrace.

The other thing that was impossible for me to ignore was the strong smell of smoke. I had never seen Mom smoke a cigarette before. And that smell was overpowered by the stench of alcohol. This was so different than the sweet smell of perfume that Mom used to spray on herself before leaving the house every day. I also noticed that she wore the same black sweat suit and tam hat every time I saw her. She had this look in her eyes that I could not figure out. Although her face was looking toward me, her eyes seemed to be going so much further. It was like I was looking at a total stranger. I couldn't understand how a person who was once so full of life now seemed to be walking around dead, her spirit broken.

God, please bring back my old mother!

Each time Mom arrived, Grandma would force her into another room to talk with her. I could never quite hear the words, but I was able to hear my grandmother raising her voice at my mother. When Mom had had enough, she would burst out of the room with tearful eyes. Grandma would yell, "I love you!" as my mom walked out the door.

I had not seen my stepfather for some time, but was too afraid to ask Mom about it. One of my aunts told me that he was sent off to prison. I wondered if it had anything to do with the small yellow envelopes that he kept in his purple Crown Royal bag. So many people came to our house to get them. I had no idea what was inside of them, but I did notice that people were willing to give him money for them. My Aunt Bam explained that after the death of my sister, his mother and sister died within a matter of months. This made it almost impossible for him and my mother to coexist. I had only seen him a few times since Dar-Dar passed, and then all of a sudden, he just seemed to vanish into thin air.

I was getting a little older and more eager to understand this word called "life," and also the dark moment called "death." I felt it was time that I got some answers to the questions I had about my baby sister. When I arrived home after school one day, I decided that I would ask Grandma what really happened. I understood Dar-Dar's spirit had ascended up to heaven. Today I was more concerned with the natural event. I walked inside as Grandma was pulling a pan of roasted peanuts out of the oven. I immediately sat at the kitchen table, putting both of my elbows on the tabletop and resting my chin in the palms of my hands. Grandma put the hot pan on the top of the stove, and without even looking at me, said, "Hey, baby. What's wrong?"

"Wow," I thought. I had not said one word but she knew something was on my mind. She was either a psychic or just knew me that well. I sat for a few seconds to gather my courage. Then I looked her in the eye and asked Grams what really happened to my sister.

The question was deep enough for her to give me all of her attention. She turned off the stove and quieted the blaring voice of Shirley Caesar on the stereo. Then she sat across from me and slowly started to explain. Grandma said she wanted me to understand that I had the right to question her, but I should never question the hand of God. She went on to say that the doctors said the cause of my sister's death was SIDS (sudden infant death syndrome), something that a lot of young children die from. It was a term used to describe the sudden death of a normal and healthy child. In other words, they could not really find a cause of death, and had no logical explanation as to what might have happened. Darlene was definitely a normal and healthy baby, and had never showed any signs that something was wrong with her. In fact, I couldn't even remember her ever going to the doctor except for a regular checkup, where she left happy and was given a sticker. For this reason, I struggled with the fact that she was suddenly dead.

Grandma continued in a very soft voice, saying I was a great big brother to my sister and took really good care of her while she was here. "She is now in the best care that she could ever be in with God," Grams said. She ended the conversation by getting up from the table, coming around to kiss me on my forehead, and giving me a big hug. Then Grandma said she had a surprise for me—but only after I finished all my homework and helped her clean up.

I thought, "Cool. Grams always knows how to make me feel better." I had only a little homework to do, but I was very nervous about helping her "clean up," as cleaning up could actually mean changing around the whole apartment. Oh well, I was sure the surprise would be worth doing my assignments.

Chapter Three

DEAR MAMA

"LA DI DA DI, WE like to party. We do cause trouble and bother everybody." Rodney had changed around Slick Rick's rap lyrics to fit his own personality. Then Ju-Ju chimed in. "Fresh dressed like a million bucks." I guess that was the only part he knew, but that was all he needed to know. Damien paid no attention as he walked fast and warned us that we were going to be late for school. He also reminded Rodney and Ju-Ju that being a troublemaker and having a new outfit wasn't going to help them with their grades.

It was the first day of school. Yup! We were headed to the second grade. I was always excited for the first day of school—mostly because I could show off my new clothes. We would compare our new sneakers and talk about the clothes we planned to wear for the rest of the week. After the first week, it was pretty much a dead issue as our new clothes became frivolous.

By now I was getting used to this routine, and it was something all of us kids had in common. It didn't matter how smart we were or if we had passed the previous grade. The parents in our neighborhood made sure you had something new for the start of the school year. I'm not sure if getting a good education was on everyone's list of priorities, but going to school on the first day with old clothes seemed to be forbidden. And since most of our parents didn't have college experience, educational goals probably didn't extend past a high school diploma.

I was really looking forward to this school year. Summer seemed to get boring at times. Our summer vacations consisted of hanging out in the Heights, and getting cups of water and splashing each other with them—not going to an exotic beach. We were privileged to have a blow-up pool from the local grocery store, which seemed heavenly if that was all you knew. And kids from the Heights knew how to get their money's worth out of the pool. By the time we were done, we would be using it as a Slip'N Slide.

Our journey to school that morning was as fun as expected, but I had no idea my year would start off with an even bigger bang. I had made it through half the day, but by the time lunch arrived, I decided that this was the worst day I had ever had at school. I sat in the office of Mr. Archie D with both cheeks tearstained and my mouth poked out. I had fury in my eyes. I selected a few specks on his light brown carpet and channeled my focus there until Grandma arrived to pick me up.

Mr. Archie D's office made me want to go to the bathroom every time I entered it. He was a principal with zero tolerance. Detentions and extra writing assignments for bad behavior were one thing, but if you were sent to his office, you just knew you were in big trouble. I could not remember leaving his office with a smile on my face. In fact, my face would always look exactly how it was looking right now, with tear marks and a poked-out mouth. What was so odd about today? Why did these tears seem to hurt more than any of the others that had fallen from my face?

Another odd thing about this day was the fact that Mr. Archie D was actually being extremely nice to me, considering that I had just been in a fight. Grandma arrived about an hour after she received the call. She barged into the office with her large purse on her shoulder, ignoring the secretary and marching directly over to me. She told me to stop crying. Her warning only seemed to release the flood of tears that I was apparently holding back. After she rubbed my head, she went inside the inner office with Mr. Archie D and closed the door. I sat there impatiently and wondered why I had to wait outside. I assumed he was giving her the full story, all the information he had gathered from my teacher and the other kids. I knew he couldn't give her the whole story as I never told him why I had really snapped. I was also sure that no one from our little crew would've told him.

After about twenty minutes, which seemed like hours, Grandma opened the door and prompted me to come inside. I slowly walked in and took a seat next to her. Mr. Archie D started talking first. He informed me that I would be suspended for a whole week and that Grandma had to bring me back when I returned to school. He went on to say that he had never seen me act this way as long as he had known me. He asked again if I wanted to tell him why. I put my head down and shook it from side to side. He had already tried to force this out of me earlier, but he was not successful. I guess he felt the need to try again since Grandma was there. He then turned his attention to my grandmother and thanked her for coming right away. He said that he appreciated how well she was raising me. She then stood and shook his hand, and we were on our way.

On our way out of the school, I was trying to read Grandma's mood to see if she was really upset, but it was impossible for me to tell as she greeted every person we encountered with a huge smile and hello. She hadn't spoken many words to me except to say we had to go to the grocery store before going home. Much to my surprise, she was not treating me like she was mad at me. In fact, she was acting as if everything was normal.

I helped put anything in the buggy that she pointed to as we moved through the store. It amazed me that every single person we saw seemed to be so happy to see Grams when we got to the checkout counter. She looked at me and said, "Baby, pick our something that you want." Huh? Now this was starting to feel really weird. I was suspended from school, but she was treating me as if I just made the honor roll.

When we got home, I still found it strange that Grandma had not mentioned what I did at school. I helped unload the groceries. She turned on her gospel music and I knew then that she was ready to talk with me. After pouring me a glass of milk, Grandma sat down at the table across from me and started by asking if I was okay. She then went on to say that she knew me well enough to know there was a reason for me to lash out the way I did—especially against one of the kids who I played with almost every day. Of course, she was right. She went on to say that I could take my time and it was okay to tell her whatever the case might have been. She continued talking when suddenly, for the first time in my life, I felt that I had disrespected my grandmother. But I could not hold it back any longer. She was in the middle of a sentence when I looked at her and said, "Grams, what is a crackhead?" There had never been a question that was too hard for her to answer, but this one seemed to turn her into a mannequin. She instantly froze with her right hand on her face as if I had cast some kind of spell on her.

The room became silent, and she calculated her thoughts before she spoke. Grandma obviously knew the answer, yet was hesitant to share it with me. My question also seemed to answer all of her questions about why I was home with her right now in the first place. I then noticed a melancholy expression come across her face. When she finally looked up, she said, "Baby, there is no such thing." She went on to explain that the term referred to someone who was on drugs. She argued, however, that no one should be called anything but their name. She also told me that people on drugs were bound and waiting to be set free by God.

I sat there trying to digest her explanation, and figured that my question had been sufficient enough after such a tumultuous day. As if Grandma were reading my mind, she said she wanted me to tell her what happened. I took a deep breath and began talking.

We had all met on the hoop court as soon as we were released for lunch. It was our normal crew: Bear, Rodney, Damien, Ju-Ju, and me. We were having a lot of fun and disregarding the instruction to not get our new clothes messed up. Instead of playing touch football, we decided to play "it tag," where you had to catch someone and tag them. Then they would become the person who chases everyone else until they've caught someone. It was Rodney's turn to chase. For some reason, I became the person he wanted to hunt. I ran near the other kids so that he could chase them, too, but he would not change his target. He was getting closer to me. That's when I had to put into play the Barry Sanders moves I had practiced so much down at the field. I faked left and darted to the right, and Rodney fell flat on his face. The rest of the guys thought this was hilarious and busted out laughing. By the time Rodney got to his feet, I could see in his eyes that our game of "it tag" was over.

He immediately tried to attack, but Bear and Damien grabbed him before he could get to me. Damien told him to chill out or we would get in trouble. That advice seemed to calm him down, at least for the moment. As they let Rodney go, he started to walk in the other direction but looked back me and said, "That's why your mom is a crackhead." I had no idea what that meant, but I knew, considering what had just happened, that he was not giving my mother a compliment. Rodney had finally completed his mission. He tagged me harder than I had ever been while playing "it tag." And since it was my turn to hunt then, I had to complete my mission—except my hunt was definitely not a game. I immediately charged after him. Bear and Damien tried to stop me, but I somehow had more strength than I had ever felt before. I pushed through them with ease. To my surprise, Rodney started to run away, but I quickly caught him. By the time I came to my senses, I was being led to Mr. Archie D's office.

Grandma kept quiet during my entire story. She waited until I was finished before she began to speak. She told me that it was not nice of Rodney to say mean things about my mother, but that gave me no reason to act the way I did. She went on to say that Rodney did not even understand what he was saying. He was just repeating something he might have heard. She also pointed out that he was only retaliating for the embarrassment he probably felt from falling on his face.

In my mind, I knew she was right, but she had no idea the embarrassment I felt when someone said the "M" word. You could talk about anyone in the world, but talking about someone's mother was a cardinal sin.

Grandma told me that Rodney didn't mean anything by it and I had to forgive him. More importantly, she said, I owed him, along with Mr. Archie D, an apology. However, Mr. Archie D's needed to be written. I responded, "Yes, ma'am."

As I started to get up from the table, she smiled really wide and said, "Not so fast, little guy." She explained that there were going to be many times in my life when people would say things I would not like, but that still would not make it okay for me to act out. She went on to say that she was sorry that I had to deal with humiliation regarding my mother, and that I should remember that Mom was in God's hands so I shouldn't worry about her. As for the way I acted and getting suspended, I would have to be on punishment because she wanted me to understand that there were consequences to all of my actions.

The next couple of days seemed more like years to me. I tried my best to read a book Grandma had given me, but it was rather difficult. The only place that I was allowed to go to was church, so I tried to make the best of it. I never understood how serious Grandma was at church. She would be singing happily one minute and in the blink of an eye she would be in tears. This swing of emotions happened every time we went. However, Grandma was also happy and peaceful by the time we left.

Soon enough I was back at school, and boy, was I happy. It almost felt like the first day of school all over again—except for the fact that Grandma was going with me. Mr. Archie D was appreciative of the letter that Grandma made me read to him. He told me that he thought I was a good kid, but warned me about getting caught up with the wrong crowd. He thanked my grandmother, and I was off to class.

When I walked in, the whole room seemed to go silent. I knew for sure it was because of me. I then also noticed that it was quiz time. Mr. Linen brought me up to speed. I looked toward Rodney's seat and he seemed to be really into the quiz. What was funny to me was the fact that it didn't matter if it was a quiz or a final exam, Rodney and I were never able to give our full attention to it. We always found time to make each other laugh and see what we could get away with in class. Today was different. I made several *psst* sounds, but Rodney would not look my way. I even did our secret code where I made a certain beat with my pencil, and still no Rodney. I got a little frustrated. Why should he be mad at me? He was the one who used the "M" word. I noticed that he had some bruises on the left side of his face. Was that from the fall that started the whole thing? Oh, wow! No wonder I couldn't get his attention.

The bell finally rang, and Rodney jumped out of his seat and raced to the door before I had the chance to talk with him. "Jeez," I thought, "I was just trying to say I was sorry." It was no use, so I slowly walked toward my locker. As soon as I turned the corner, my mouth immediately dropped, and so did the books in my hands. What in the world was going on? I took some steps backward and that's when Damien called me over. All of my friends were standing in front of my locker with Rodney standing in front of them. I thought, "Boy, they are really mad at me. This is not going to be fun at all."

I approached unhurriedly while looking for a clear path to run away if what I thought was going to happen started to actually happen. By the time I reached Rodney, he had already put his arms around me. He gave me a big hug, looked me in the face, and said he was sorry for saying that about my mother. I let out the breath that I had been holding for the past minute and immediately said, "I forgive you, but I also need you to forgive me for snapping on you." We both forgave each other. Bear picked up my books off the floor and we seemed to forget everything that had happened. Everything went back to normal. We had a blast on the way home to the Heights after school that day.

I had not seen my mother for a couple of days. She stopped by on my second day of suspension to drop off some snacks for me. She didn't have much to say except that I better behave in school. She had only been there for a few minutes when a horn started to blow outside. She looked at me and said she had to go. I was wondering if it was actually the horn that made her leave, or if she was trying to get away before my grandmother came downstairs. In any case,, she was out of there in a flash. A part of me was upset that she had left so quickly, but a bigger part of me was happy that I had seen her even if it was only for a few minutes. I thought about the words Grandma had spoken a few days ago, "Don't worry, baby. She's in God's hands."

I woke up the next morning very excited because it was Saturday, and that's when the fellas and I met down at the field to play some football—unless Damien showed up with some great adventures in mind. The other reason I was happy was that it was the day I was finally off of punishment. I struggled to open up the old pickle jar that Grandma kept the Kix cereal in so that it stayed fresh. It took bending on my knees over the top of it to get it to open, but I eventually got the job done. I decided that since it was only half full, I would get only one bowl (just in case my aunt wanted to put some sugar, cinnamon, and butter with the rest so we could have a good snack later).

I poured the cereal, sprinkled about ten spoonfuls of sugar over it, and I was ready to go. I went to the refrigerator and the only milk I saw was the disgusting buttermilk that Grams drank with her cookies. There was no way I was pouring that on my cereal, but then there was no way I was going down to the field on an empty stomach. "Oh well, I guess I have to improvise," I thought.

I held the bowl over the sink and turned the cold water on. It wasn't the first time and I was sure it wouldn't be the last. After I finished my gluten-free cereal, I went upstairs to let Grandma know that I was headed down to the field. She looked up at me and said, "Boy, it is only eight o'clock in the morning." I said that I knew that, but I had to get there early to practice a few moves since I had been on the injured reserve the last couple of weeks. She chuckled and then told me to have fun and to check in with her.

Grams may have had a good point as the streetlights in the Heights were just starting to dim. I was only halfway to the field—just about in front of Aunt Rose's house—when I heard a scream. Aunt Rose was my biological father's sister who treated me like family despite me not having a relationship with my father. Since she lived right by the field, I decided to use her house as a locker room when we needed a halftime snack. Every single time I showed up, she would welcome me with open arms, and have a snack and something to drink for me. She didn't even mind that I brought the crew with me. She was such a sweetheart.

The scream was coming from the side of the building where she lived. For a moment, I considered turning around and going back home. Instead, I decided to walk really fast. Hopefully, I would not be noticed! I also thought that if I was in danger, I could go knock on Aunt Rose's door. The only problem was that she was probably asleep. Oh well, I decided to look straight toward the field. I would start running if I was in danger. I took about five sneaky steps before I saw a man standing over a lady and throwing a punch with every curse word that came out of his mouth. He suddenly stopped when he noticed me and yelled, "What are you looking at?"

I quickly responded, "N-n-nothing, sir. I am looking at the field." My sneaky steps immediately turned into the same walk that I used when I had to urgently use the restroom. When the couple was out of sight, I heard the same scream that I had heard during my initial approach. I paused for a moment and wondered if I should go and tell someone what was happening. Then I quickly remembered a phrase that was often quoted in the Heights, "Mind your own business."

The phrase was definitely an oxymoron, as it seemed like everything that happened in the Heights became everyone's business. In fact, the couple that I had just seen was often in the news headlines or current events of the Heights—even us kids knew that they were alcoholics who always seemed to be fighting. The question in my youthful brain was what was so bad at eight o'clock in the morning that had caused them to fight? I guessed that they had probably been up all night drinking and the alcohol had finally gotten the best of them. It was amazing that their fighting was so expected that most of the time people didn't even bother calling the police. The police probably didn't even want to show up because they were so tired of breaking up their drunken fights.

Yup, so I kept on walking toward the field and didn't think about looking back. I was old enough to understand that these kinds of things took place in the projects every day. When things repeatedly happened around you, you began to think it was just a part of normal life. Huh. There had to be a better life outside of this development. "The question is how do I find my way out?" I thought.

By the time I got to the top of the small dirt hill that led down to the field, I was in for another big surprise. I had planned on getting an early jump on my moves, but all the fellas were already there. In fact, Mo-Joe was breaking loose for a long touchdown. His personal trainer and coach, Billy Barber, was yelling for him to go. I ran down the hill with excitement and told them that the MVP was back now. Mo-Joe just smirked and said, "I'm already here."

That was how it was. We always seemed to compete against each other when we stepped on the field. Anywhere else, we loved each other and were definitely on the same team.

Chapter Four

Boys Club

WE HAD BEEN PLAYING FOOTBALL for hours, but it seemed as if we had just arrived. Everyone was still full of energy. We even had a little audience at this point. Billy Barber was coaching Mo-Joe's team and "Man Daddy" was coaching my team. Man Daddy was a high school superstar who hoped to go on to play in college and maybe even the NFL. His roadblock would prove to be the very projects where we lived. We had music to motivate us as we were playing that day. It was coming from a few high school kids. Ken Hicks, Boojie, and E.T. sat in a brand new Saab with the doors wide open, blasting "Love's Gonna Get'cha" by KRS-One. I could never quite catch the words, but the beat was so hypnotizing. Later, when I had the privilege to really listen to the song in my uncle's car, I understood exactly what it was about.

The rapper was explaining how a love of material things would eventually get you, meaning that it would result in the police knocking at your door. The lyrics also talked about the struggles of poor families and how growing up in the projects tempted young men to sell drugs. I had seen kids around the Heights who were able to drive brand new cars before they got out of high school. They would also have a lot of jewelry, along with the nicest clothes. I couldn't figure out how they did it.

We were still playing football when Ju-Ju drifted over to the Saab and was bobbing his head to the music. The rest of us then decided it was time to take a break. I told everyone to follow me to Aunt Rose's so we could get some snacks. Just as we were headed off the field, one of the guys in the Saab yelled for us to come over. We slowly walked toward the car. Boojie stepped out and handed Mo-Joe and me a twenty-dollar bill. I looked at him with a puzzled expression and asked him what the money was for. He said to buy everyone a snack from Ivan's corner store. He also said that he thought Mo-Joe and I were young superstars, and that when we go to the NFL, we better remember him. He gave us high fives and told us to do well in school and to stay out of trouble.

As we headed up the dirt hill, I thought, "Should I tell Grandma that I received a twenty-dollar bill?" I remembered her clear instructions: Don't ask anyone for money, and be careful when taking money from anyone.

The guys must have been reading my mind, because as soon as we reached the top of the hill, Damien said, "Let's have a party."

Our version of a party was to go to Ivan's corner store, buy a ton of junk food and drinks, and sit around talking about our crazy adolescent life and what we were going to be when we grew up. No matter what profession each person chose, one thing was clear and we agreed on it. Someday we were not going to live in the Heights.

We aborted our mission to Aunt Rose's and headed straight for the store. We bought so much junk food that it was a sure thing that all of us would probably get sick to our stomachs. We didn't care. It was a party! We had to enjoy the food and drinks. I had heard grownups say that it wasn't a party without the food and drinks.

We sat on the steps listening to Rodney and Ju-Ju rap. Milik was trying his best to beatbox when Rodney ordered him to stop because it was throwing him off. He stated he was better off a cappella because Milik was so off and all he was doing was spitting on us. After we grew tired of all of the rap impressions, we spent time making each other laugh. We talked about each other's clothes. We talked about how nappy Milik's hair was. We even talked about each other's family members. However, no one's mother became part of our comedy show. We also discussed which girls we wanted to marry. Little did we know that someday we'd reflect back on times like these as "the good ole days." We were a group of project kids who were oblivious to our surroundings, and found a way, in spite of everything, to enjoy and love one another. We also shared an unspoken expectation that none of us would grow up to be like the adults we saw every day in the Heights.

As we picked up the wrappers from all the snacks we had eaten, we noticed a parade of cars entering the playground area. It seemed pretty odd, so we sat and watched. Each car pulled in and parked, and then all the passengers began to unload chairs from the cars. Within an hour, the whole basketball court was lined neatly with chairs.

We still couldn't quite figure out what was taking place, but when my grandmother walked up behind us with her Bible in hand, I had a good idea what they were setting up for. She asked me what I was doing. I quickly told her that it was halftime and we were about to finish our game. She smiled and confirmed that she was attending a church service on the basketball court. She said the congregation came from a church called Soul Saving Station and they were having a revival here today. I had no clue what that meant.

We went back to playing football, and within minutes we were playing to some music again. Instead of the booming beat of KRS-One, this music came from live instruments that the congregation had set up on the playground. And instead of the hypnotizing rhythm of rap, now it was the hypnotizing voices of gospel music.

As I was trying to break the tackles from my friends, I could hear my grandmother's tambourine in perfect unison with the singers and the band. We continued to play despite the parade of people headed to the field's basketball court. I had just tackled Mo-Joe and was beginning to taunt him when I suddenly saw my grandmother headed right toward us. I thought, "Oh, boy. She's going to make me go to the service."

40

I knew she was coming for me, so I shortened her chase and began to walk toward her. By the time I reached her—with my head down and my lip poked out—she had a smile on her face. She then said, "Baby, I need you to do me a big favor. I know you are having fun playing football, but I need you to go to the house and get an extension cord for me. The church needs it to plug in some of their equipment. And bring that lamp that is on the end table by the door so that they can use it for light when it starts to get dark." She assured me that when I brought her the items, I could go back to playing football with my friends. I instantly lifted my head up and turned my poked out lip into a smile. I was happy that I was going to be able to continue playing football. Plus, I would happily do anything for my grandmother. I loved that woman so much.

I sprinted off full speed toward the house before she had even stopped speaking. As I ran past the fellas, I yelled that I would be back. Within minutes, I arrived at the house, grabbed the lamp and extension cord, and headed back to the field. In the distance I could see my friends, and Mo-Joe was running all over them. I had to get back to put a stop to that. But when I arrived at the basketball court, all I could do was stand still with my mouth wide open. Everyone was dancing, jumping, and singing. I was kind of confused. Although the majority of people seemed to be really happy, there were others whose expressions seemed contrary. Instead, they were crying with their hands lifted up in the air. There was a man in front of the chairs who was screaming into a microphone. I had been to church many times with my grandmother, but I had never seen a service like this.

I peeked over at my friends and Mo-Joe was running another touchdown. But I was stuck like a deer in the headlights. I could not figure out what was taking place, so I just stood there with the lamp in one hand and the extension cord in the other. Suddenly, Aunt Ron's fingers were snapping in front of my eyes and I heard, "Earth to Church Socks. Earth to Church Socks." I smirked, pushing her hands away from my face. She started laughing, then grabbed the items from my hands and said, "Thanks."

Aunt Ron handed off the lamp and extension cord to one of the ladies at the front of the congregation. I looked toward my grandmother and she was dancing to the band. The funny thing was that she was not dancing to the beat at all. In fact, it seemed as if she was purposely trying to stay offbeat as she hopped up and down, losing control over her body.

My mind wanted to go play football with my friends, but my body did not cooperate. I continued to stand there in amazement. Just when I thought I had seen it all, the band suddenly changed the dancing music to a soft, slow beat. A lady began singing, "God is So Good." All at once, the man who had been screaming earlier changed his tone and was now talking softly. The woman continued to sing in a whisper, and the man asked people to come to the front with the promise that all of their problems would be forgotten. It didn't seem like anyone was paying him any attention at first, but all of a sudden, a man stood and grabbed the hand of the woman next to him and pulled her up to the front of the chairs. After they got up, it seemed like several other people felt comfortable following suit as the front of the basketball court was full of people. At that moment, something dawned on me. Wasn't that the same couple that I had seen fighting earlier that morning? I could not believe it. They were both crying, and the man had his arm around the woman, seemingly holding her up as her whole body appeared to be limp.

I decided that I could play football with my friends another day and I slid into one of the empty seats. I was so mesmerized by what was taking place. How could some people seem so sad, yet at the very same event others seemed so full of joy? All I could do was sit there with my mouth wide open. I then realized that I was probably the only person occupying a chair, so I quietly headed up to the front in stealth mode. Others may have gone up front because the man who was speaking beckoned them, but I was just curious (or as my aunt would say, just plain nosy). As I made my way up, I saw the couple again, crying and hugging each other.

I was amazed how this woman was crying the same way that I had seen earlier that morning, but somehow I was able to recognize that these tears were totally different. It was the first time I had ever seen that couple together when they were not arguing or fighting. I looked over to the right and I could see my grandmother. She kept repeating the words, "Thank you. Thank you. Thank you." It didn't seem like she was talking to anyone in particular.

Things were really starting to get weird. Just when I thought I had seen enough and decided to head over to play football with my friends, something happened. When I turned and started to walk away, I heard the preacher say, "Hey, young man." I kept walking until I heard him say it again. I turned around to figure out whom he was talking to. Sure enough, he was trying to get my attention. I raised my eyebrows and pointed to myself to make sure, and he said, "Yes, you. Come here, please."

I walked back to the front. He looked at me and said that I was a special young man and that God was going to help me do some great things. He also said that I was called. *Called?* He had to know that I had absolutely no idea what he was talking about because he went on to say that he was impressed that all of the kids seemed to be playing, but I was there at the service. Huh! I wanted to tell him that I was only there by default, but I just stood there silently. He then asked where my mother was. At that point, I really didn't have a voice, so I just shook my head side to side and pushed my palms to the air. That's when the man said he was going to pray for her. As soon as the words left his mouth, they seemed to invoke in me an avalanche of tears to fall. Within seconds, Grandma was behind me, putting her arms around me. She then ushered me to some nearby seats and I sat through the rest of the service. I couldn't explain what was going on in my head, but I knew that I had never felt that way before. In fact, I hadn't cried that hard since Dar-Dar's funeral.

As the service was coming to an end, a white man got up and started talking into the microphone. He said his name was Danny Mangrum and he was starting a Boys Club at the church. He invited all the parents to allow their kids to participate. He said there would be games and snacks, but most importantly, he wanted to teach the children about God.

I looked over at my Grandma and she was already writing down the information. After the service, Grandma prompted me to help put the chairs back into a truck. Meanwhile, she stood talking to the man who was starting the Boys Club. I imagined that she was asking him a billion questions, but I also imagined that she was signing me up for something that I had no choice about.

On the walk back to our apartment it was confirmed. Grandma told me that I would be going to the Boys Club on Wednesday nights after school. She also told me that she was glad that I made the choice to stay at the service, and that she already knew all the things the man had said to me. She then told me that she noticed how I started crying when he mentioned my mother. Grams again assured me that God was going to take care of Mom. She told me not to worry and that she prayed for my mom every day.

Wednesday seemed to come in a flash. I had a great day at school. On the way home, my friends asked me if I was coming out to play football after my homework was done. I immediately answered, "Yeah! Oh, wait…I think my grandmother is going to make me go to this Boys Club that she verbally signed me up for." I told the fellas they were welcome to come with me, but they all declined my invitation.

Later that evening, a gray van pulled up in front of our apartment. I watched out the window as the white man who had made the announcement at the service was headed to our door. Grams told me to go get my coat. She sat at the table with the man and asked him several more questions. I came downstairs and was ready to go. She stopped me by the door, looked me in the eye, and said that I had better be on my best behavior. I got into the van and set off toward the unknown. I sat quietly as we picked up a couple more kids. After we left the Heights, we went down to the other projects called Cochran Dale. This housing development was smaller than the Heights, but it was the same when it came to living conditions and the presence of hazardous activities. There was only one way in and one way out. Although most people who lived there were born there, everyone hoped that death would not be their only way out.

Cochran Dale had two long red brick buildings. All activity took place in the center of these buildings—parking, playing, cookouts, drugs, fights, everything. We pulled in and immediately a couple of men ran to the window of the van screaming, "What you need? I got whatever you need."

One of the men pushed that man away and said, "It's my turn. You got the last lick."

The white man looked at them with poise and said, "I don't want anything you have, but I do have something for you." He reached out of his window and handed one of the men a Bible. He tried to give one to the other man, but the other man refused, saying he had one at home already. The two men told the Boys Club man to have a nice day as they hurried away from the van. It was as if they were afraid of something.

We continued driving into the projects. By the time the white man parked, there was a lady standing with her two sons waiting for us. I immediately notice that these kids went to the same school as me. Their names were Sam and David Barlow. The Boys Club man got out and talked with their mom for a few seconds. Then we were off to our destination.

We pulled up to the church and it seemed like something out of a scary movie. It looked more like an old castle instead of a church. The brick was very old, and the building had two giant red doors. By the time I walked up what felt like a million steps, I thought, "I probably don't have any more energy for games." The other kids and I quietly followed the man who drove us in the van. When we got inside, we were instructed to go to the basement. Man, this was really starting to feel weird. I also noticed the smell of a very old building. At that point, the only comfort I had was knowing that I really trusted my grandmother. There was no way she would have trusted this man to take me if it was not going to be safe. When we got downstairs, all my worries seemed to dissipate as I instantly noticed a bunch of kids playing dodgeball. The stomach flutters then turned into excitement. There was only one big problem: Mikey Taylor.

I was by no means a saint, but this boy was the baddest kid in the school… No, the baddest kid in the projects… No, the baddest kid in the whole city of Duquesne. Why in the world would they invite him to this Boys Club? Mikey was so bad that I knew for sure we would be fighting by the time this was over. I wished my friends were with me.

I took off my coat and headed toward the competition. To my surprise there wasn't one single fight the entire night. When Mikey started fussing with one of the other kids, the man who brought us to the church took him off to the side. After a short talk, he began to play fair. It really looked like he was enjoying himself.

As for me, I was having the time of my life. I usually played with the same group of kids from the Heights, but this was actually fun. Everyone seemed to be playing fair for a change. We played for a while, and then they brought us together and gave us hot dogs and something to drink. We all rushed to eat so we could get back to dodgeball. To our surprise, we were told it was time for Bible study. Wow! I knew there was a catch. I spent enough time studying at school and did not need to do it here. We all sat in a circle and that's when Mr. Danny Mangrum began to speak. He told us that he was originally from Colorado, and after going to Southwestern Christian College for ministry, he felt that he was led by God to this area. I thought, "Wow! God must be mad at you to send you to a place like Duquesne."

He went on to tell us about his missionary trip to Haiti and how fortunate we were compared to the kids there. He told us that they barely had any food to eat, and that most of them walked around barefoot. He also wanted us to know that his purpose for starting the Boys Club was to give kids something fun to do. But most importantly, he wanted us to learn about God.

I raised my hand and said, "Excuse me, sir, but my grandma always takes me to church."

Mr. Mangrum told me that going to church with Grandma was phenomenal, but I still needed to form a relationship with God for myself. He opened his Bible and read a story to us about Christ dying on the cross for our sins. I could not believe that this man had the attention of every single one of us. After he finished the lesson, Mr. Mangrum told us that he hoped we had fun, and that we were welcome to come every Wednesday if we wanted. Then we loaded up in the van. He planned to drop the Barlow boys off first before heading to the Heights.

We were driving up the street to the Cochran Dale projects when we noticed the police cars. One of the cops came up to the van and told us that we could not drive in. As he was talking, Ms. Barlow rushed to the van and told the officer that her kids were in there. The cop told her that she could walk back to her apartment with her kids, but no cars were allowed inside Cochran Dale.

Later I found out that shortly after we picked up the Barlows for the Boys Club, someone was murdered in broad daylight. My grandmother said it was the boyfriend of a distant cousin of mine who pulled the trigger, and he would probably be off to prison for a long time if not for the rest of his life.

After the Barlow kids jumped out of the van, we headed to the Heights. Mr. Mangrum drove off, shaking his head from side to side. I wanted to ask him if he still thought that the kids in Haiti had it worse than us, but I kept my silence instead. As strange as this may have been to him, I had seen the projects blocked off many times. And each time the news had been intense or even fatal. We were just taught to mind our own business and go inside before the streetlights came on. In this case, however, the streetlights were not a factor as someone was shot in cold blood in the middle of the day.

We approached our apartment and Grandma was waiting with the door wide open. I looked over at Mr. Mangrum and said, "Thank you."

"No problem," he responded, adding that I was a good kid and he hoped I would be back on Wednesdays.

Not only did I start going every Wednesday, but I also started going to the church on Sunday mornings. To my surprise, Ms. Barlow was actually the Sunday school teacher. She looked totally different in her church clothes than she did when she was standing outside in the projects. She was really a nice lady, and she had the same smile that my grandma often wore. I really liked her class because she always made us laugh. But what I liked the most was that she had candy bars for us if we were paying attention to what she was teaching. If I could pay attention to Mr. Linen at school, I could definitely pay attention to Ms. Barlow.

From that point on, Mr. Mangrum, or Brother Danny as he requested that we call him, started to pick me up quite often to take me to church as well as events that I was not privileged enough to go to with my family. I then started to learn that this was a man who really loved God. He also really had a desire to help us poverty-stricken kids have a better life. Up until this point, I had never encountered any men who had a positive influence on my life, so I began to grow a great respect for him.

Brother Danny made sure that I began to really understand whom God was. He had me listen to cassette tapes while at his house. One story, which was my favorite, was about a talking donkey and a man on his way to Jericho. The man asked the question, "Who is my neighbor?"

It turned out that this man was an angel from God who helped me focus beyond my environment.

Chapter Five

REAL DAD?

A COUPLE YEARS PASSED AND I was now going into the fourth grade. So much had taken place in such a short time. I continued to go to the Boys Club on Wednesdays, and I alternated between my grandmother's church and Brother Danny's church on Sundays. One Sunday I would get the energetic message from Bishop George Mitchell, and the other Sunday the ever-so-powerful voice of Reverend Carter. No matter which service I attended, one thing was always consistent: Jesus Christ was Lord and He was crucified.

I still made time to hang out with my friends, but none of them really liked going to church. Ju-Ju had moved away to a nearby town called Whitaker and would sometimes come around on the weekends. When he did, he would still have on the newest sneakers and the nicest clothes. The last weekend I was with him, he had a funny look in his eyes. I asked him if he was okay and he just immediately started laughing. I said, "What's funny?"

He responded, "Nothing, man. I'm coooool."

I knew he always talked about his family and their involvement with reefer. Maybe he was now using what his parents were selling. Ju-Ju wanted me to listen to a rap he had written, so I stood there and listened, bobbing my head to the rhythm.

The rest of the crew seemed to be doing the same old things, playing football at the field or following Damien on adventurous excursions. The last time we were about to go on an adventure, we were stopped by the yells of his older brother J.R., who was saying Damien's mom wanted him home right away. Later on that evening, my grandmother told me that Damien's little brother Brandon had been hit by a car. One of my grandmother's favorite sermons to preach to me was to stay out of the streets. I received her message then, but wondered if I would remember that sermon when I became an adult.

I had been attending church for a while now. I prayed for my mother every time I went. I realized that God must have had a really long wait list, but I finally started to believe in prayer when my number was called. It was unbelievable. My mother was actually getting her life together. She had even convinced Grandma to let me move back in with her. She was pregnant with a girl, and I had already been blessed with another sister about a year earlier. Her name was Raquel. She was soooo cute, and it was super easy to make her smile. Wow! I was a big brother again, and soon I would have two sisters. I missed Darlene so much and never quite understood why God had taken her away from me. Now He was giving me double for my troubles.

Mom seemed clothed in her right mind and was taking care of us as well. My stepfather was released from prison about a year and a half earlier. He and my mother got back together and they seemed to be really happy. I liked him a lot because he treated me as if I were his real son. He was also very helpful to Mom. He loved to clean the house.

We had moved to another apartment in the Heights. Bear and his family lived right down the hill from me. Lump, Damien, and I actually lived in the same building, and Rodney only lived about two buildings down. We were all pretty much inseparable and played together regularly. Grams had also moved. She now lived in the same building as Bear. Although I had moved back in with Mom, I still spent a lot of time at my grandma's. She still took me with her every time she went shopping, and once in a while, we would all get together and play a game of Monopoly. On holidays, the entire family would end up at her house. Lump and I continued to play football for the Tigers, and during the summer, we would all get together for our annual bike ride around the city of Duquesne. That's until one summer when everything I deemed fun seemed to come to a halt.

We all met down at the field with our bikes where we waited for Damien to be our tour guide. An older kid named Tone B showed up on his bike. He wanted to know what we were doing, and we told him that we were just taking a ride but going nowhere in particular. (Huh, that sounded like something those high school kids in the Saab said to me one day. They were "taking a ride but going nowhere in particular." I figured they were talking about riding in a car, but I would later learn that they were describing their lifestyle.) Tone said he wanted to come with us. There was no way I was telling this kid no. I just looked at the ground and said, "Ooooh-kay."

I figured if anyone could stand up to Tone, it would be Damien. Well, I was definitely wrong about that. When Damien showed up, he didn't look Tone's way. In fact, he acted as if he was part of our crew. He verbalized our itinerary and we were off to the races. We rode for hours and ended up riding across the bridge that led toward Kennywood Park. We rode past the stadium where our high school football team played. Then Tone spoke up for the first time. He suggested that we ride to Kmart. I found the courage to use my voice and asked, "Why?" I knew that we would be lucky to scrounge up enough money to buy a bag of chips to share, let alone buy something else from Kmart. He said that he had seen some new G.I. Joe action figures on a TV commercial and he wanted us to see them. He said his cousin Jeremy had gotten the full collection already. "Well, why we can't just look at his?" I asked.

His answer was simple, and it showed what he thought of me. He said five words. "Shut up and come on."

Mareese Comer

He sped up on his bike and took the lead. Everyone seemed to follow. *Oh, wait a minute. Didn't my mother tell me to always be a leader and never a follower?* I could actually hear her voice in my head. For whatever reason, Tone's voice was overpowering hers. I continued to pedal my bike and follow after him. Maybe it was because the rest of my friends had followed as well. What happened next made me realize that it wasn't always such a bad thing to renege. If only we were playing a simple game of spades.

We arrived at Kmart. I put down the kickstand, took my backpack off my shoulders, and hung it on the handlebars of my bike. We all went in together, but within minutes seemed to be attracted to different aisles of toys. Bear, Milik, and I headed toward the wrestling aisle. As I was walking away, I saw Tone whispering to the rest of the guys. It looked as if he was in a huddle and calling a play. He had everyone's attention. After looking at Hulk Hogan and the rest of the action figures, I told Milik and Bear that I had to use the restroom. I asked them to wait there for me. I wouldn't be long.

When I got to the restroom, the door was locked. I stood there doing a dance called the Running Man so that I didn't go on myself. After a few minutes, an old man walked out slowly with his cane and I rushed inside. Whew, I felt so relieved! I had no idea that that feeling in my stomach would come back shortly. But this time it would have nothing to do with using the restroom.

I pushed open the door and headed toward the wrestling aisle. I took a couple of wrong turns but eventually made it. To my surprise, none of my friends were there. I ran through the store but never found them. I thought for a minute that they were playing a joke on me. Finally, I checked outside, and my bike was standing alone. The thing that I was sure of was that we always stuck together. Damien always made sure that we got home safely. So why had they left me? As soon as I put my hand on the handlebars, I had an answer to this enigma.

A large white man touched my shoulder and said he needed me to come with him. He then grabbed my backpack off of my bike and led me to a small office inside the store. Within minutes, a security guard showed up. He started to ask me questions, and I responded by saying I didn't know what he was talking about. He asked where my friends went, and again I told him I didn't know. When he opened my backpack, which was only half-zipped, my mouth just dropped open. Inside were several packages of G.I. Joe figures. Tears filled my eyes as I hysterically explained that I had no idea how they had gotten there. My argument seemed futile as he asked for my information and called my mother to come get me. I sat quietly until Mom got there. She showed up with my stepfather. If looks could kill, then my obituary was already being printed. She stormed in and talked with the security guard. He informed her that I would not be allowed in the store anymore.

I never told the security guard who my friends were, but I could not withhold the entire story from my mother. When we got home, she called every one of my friend's parents, and I was on punishment for the rest of the summer. I wasn't even allowed to play football that year with Lump. My stepfather tried to talk her into cutting me some slack, but she did not go for it at all. This was not fair. I lost all my privileges and had not done anything wrong. I reminded Mom of this about a thousand times. Why didn't she believe me?

I told Grandma, and she said she believed I was telling her the truth. She explained to me that the lesson I needed to learn was that being with the wrong people could get you in trouble even if you were innocent. She also reminded me that I had the opportunity to not follow Tone when he suggested that we go there in the first place. Therefore, I had no choice but to deal with the consequences. To add insult to injury, all of my friends were mad at me. Since we were not allowed to hang out with each other, I was stuck walking home from school by myself.

About three days after this incident, I was quickly reminded that not only were my close friends mad at me, but I had also created an enemy.

Was I the next victim of a bloody nose? As soon as I entered the Heights, Tone spotted me. At first I thought he was ignoring me like the rest of my friends, but it took him just a minute to focus in and realize that his prey was right in front of him. My instincts kicked in. I immediately dropped my book bag and took off running. I would worry about the books later. I was only two project buildings away from my apartment. He started to chase me, but my football career was paying off. I was about fifteen yards ahead of him. I approached the small dirt hill that led to my back door. Halfway up the hill, I could see that my door was cracked open. At that point, I felt safe. I was ready to start doing my Deon Sanders dance. I even started taunting him by saying, "He's gone! He's to the 50, to the 40, to the 30, to the 20, to the 10-yard line and touch–" *Bam!* I smashed into my back door. What in the world was going on? I knew this door was cracked open seconds ago, but now I saw my mother looking out the window at me. She had obviously seen me running up the hill. Why would she close and lock the door right before I got there? *This is insane.*

Unfortunately, I didn't have much time to figure out her reasoning as I had Tone's arm wrapped around my neck. All of a sudden, I could not breathe and my vision was getting blurry. *Why would she do this to me?* I was sure I was about to die, so I had to do something. With all the strength I had left, I hunched over a bit, and as hard as I could, I elbowed Tone right in his gut. To my satisfaction he was now hunched over and holding his stomach. I took a couple of quick breaths of relief, but I knew if he stood back up, there was no way that I would survive—especially after what I had done to him.

Again, I had to think fast. I quickly thought about my cousin's nose that Tone had bloodied, and how he had taken my lunch tickets last year. I balled my fist and swung with everything in me and it landed on the right side of his head. For some reason, I had closed my eyes while swinging. By the time I opened them, Tone was crawling back up to his feet. I held my breath as he got up. I could not believe my eyes. Instead of him charging at me, he actually took off running in the opposite direction. I looked in the window and I could see my stepfather standing with his arms folded and the biggest smile on his face. I went to grab my book bag, and when I got back to the door, it was mysteriously cracked open again.

I walked in, my eyes squinting with anger. I was so mad at my mother that I just looked at the floor and wanted to head to my room. When my foot hit the first step, I heard her say, "Come here and sit down." I walked slowly toward the worn couch and slid down onto the ripped cushion. She began with the million-dollar question. "Do you know why I locked you out?"

I wanted to yell, "You tell me why!" but I had enough sense to know that disrespecting Mom was like driving off a cliff, so I sat silently and just shook my head from side to side. Her next words would stick with me for the rest of my life. She looked me straight in the eye and said that I could not turn away from my fears. She said that if she had not locked the door on me, then I would have had to run home from school for the rest of the year. She had seen me from the window the very moment I had taken off running. She was aware that this kid was bigger than me, and she also figured that he was mad because we had gotten into trouble. She went on to explain that I would have many challenges in my life and would have to face them with the same courage. If I ran away from my problems, they would continue to chase me.

By being forced to deal with this fear, I actually did something that I didn't even know I could do. She called me a warrior and a leader. She struggled to get up off the couch to hug me, her stomach as big as a watermelon. Within that same week she gave birth to my second sister, Ashley. I had gotten a lot of practice with Raquel so I was ready to take care of my new baby sister.

A little time had passed and things seemed to be going well. Then Mom started to act differently all of a sudden. I couldn't figure out what was going on. She seemed to be very irritated. Both of my sisters were getting older, but I made sure that I helped out as much as I could. One thing I noticed that may have been the reason for her moods was the fact that I hadn't seen my stepfather in the last couple of weeks. I wanted to ask Mom where he was, but I was too scared since she had been in a recent funk. He had treated me so well, and seemed happy to be there, so I was wondering if his absence was beyond his control—yet a result of his decisions. In other words, was he back in the slammer?

If I wanted the 411, the one person I could count on was my Aunt Bam. She always knew what was going on. And the next time I went to my grandmother's house, my theory was confirmed. Yup, my stepfather was back in prison. So that's why Mom was acting like she was! Once I knew he was gone, I made up my mind that I had to pick up the slack. I started cleaning the house more. I was even learning how to cook quick meals for my sisters and me. I spent less time playing, but Mom still allowed Brother Danny to pick me up for church and the Boys Club.

School was going pretty well. My friends and I were finally able to forgive each other. Even Tone spoke to me when I saw him in the halls. The end of the school year was approaching and I was excited to be getting past the fourth grade. The year had gone relatively smoothly, but my, oh my, did it end with a bang!

There were very few white families that lived in the Heights. One of those happened to live in the same building as me. The family included a mother and three children, but I never noticed the presence of a father. Although they were different in ethnicity, the fact that the family was missing a male influence made them blend in very well with everyone else in the projects. The older daughter was in the same class as me. In fact, she actually sat next to me in the second row of our class. Ms. Bush would always keep an eye on me since we both got the exact same grade percentage on a few tests. In my mind, I wanted to believe that Ms. Bush thought this girl was cheating off of my paper. But in my heart, I felt she had to know who was guilty.

It was the week of final exams and I was not prepared at all. Being unprepared was a normal routine, but I was totally caught off guard by what took place next. Ms. Bush handed out the exams. I looked to my left at an empty seat. In the past, the white girl's dusty blond hair would sometimes get in the way of my seeing her paper, but I would wait until she lifted her head so I could get a peek at her answers. Today, however, I couldn't even do that. She was by far the smartest student in our class and had never missed a single day of school. Why was she not here? And when I really needed her! Oh well, I guess I would have to wing it. To my surprise, I actually knew some of the answers, which meant that I relied on my neighbor so much that I usually didn't even try on my own. The class finished the test and Ms. Bush gave us a recess.

I immediately noticed that Rodney and a few other kids had huddled in a small group. I approached the group and all the whispers instantly stopped. I looked at Rodney and said, "What?" He did not respond. In fact, all the kids just looked at me with an empty stare. I started to get frustrated and began to walk away. I had taken two steps when I heard one of the kids say the word "rapist." I turned back and looked, and they busted out laughing. I obviously did not get the joke, and they apparently wouldn't tell me why I was the object of their humor.

I went to my seat and kept to myself the rest of the day. I figured that Rodney was in one of his moods and was just trying to get under my skin. After school I quickly realized that it was not just a joke at all. I put my books in my locker, and as I headed down the hall, something grabbed my attention. Was it just me, or was every kid looking at me strangely? And why were they whispering when I walked past? Just as I was walking out the front door of the school, I heard another kid yell the word "rapist." At this point, my eyes were squinting and my forehead looked like one of those shar-pei puppies. I was frustrated and most of all confused. I saw my friends standing on the sidewalk across the street so I did a beeline toward them. "Thank God," I thought, "at least I have my friends."

As soon as I approached, they started to walk off. I quickly tried to follow, but Rodney spoke up and said, "Church Socks, we are not walking home with you today because we don't want to be embarrassed."

"What?" I said in a very hostile tone.

There was no response as they slowly walked off. For some reason, my body just stood still and my mouth dropped open. I could not believe what was happening. *What in the world is going on?* In the middle of my thought, I heard Bear tell the rest of the crew to go ahead. He was going to walk home from school with me.

As we began to walk, I kept quiet. I really did not know what to say. I was totally oblivious to my surroundings. I just kept walking. Finally, Bear spoke up. He started by saying that he didn't know how to tell me, and was surprised that I didn't know.

I cut him off. "What? Just tell me, for Christ's sake." He looked over and said that my father was all over the news last night and this morning. The newsman said that he was arrested and faced charges for rape. Now only the left side of my face was squinting as I wondered, "I thought he was in jail."

Bear must have been reading my mind. He said, "Not your mom's boyfriend, but your real dad."

Real dad? I gathered that he was referring to my biological father, but that man was not real to me at all. In fact, all I knew was his name. I had no idea who he really was as a person. I could not believe what I was hearing. My stomach began to turn and I could feel the blood rushing to my head. This man had not done a thing for me and had not given me anything—not even his last name—but I get the privilege of getting a worse reputation at school? "Rapist." I couldn't say that I had a dislike for my biological father, because I simply did not know him. However, the taste in my mouth at this point was not sweet at all.

We were almost to the Heights and I thought I'd heard the worst of it. Then Bear said, "Oh! One more thing." I gave him an inquisitive look and he continued. "You know that white family that lives in your building?"

I didn't speak, but I slowly nodded my head.

"Well, that's the house that they said your dad broke into and tried to rape someone."

I said, "Oh." Then, "Ohhhhh!" So that was why there was no dusty blond hair to look through to get some answers for my test. As it all was coming back to me, I started to get more frustrated. I tried to hold back but a few tears escaped my eyes. That's when I knew Bear was my best friend.

He put his arm across my shoulders and said, "Don't worry, Church Socks. It is not your fault and you did nothing wrong." He said that he could not wait to talk to the rest of the guys and tell them that it was wrong to turn their backs on me.

I wiped my eyes with the inside of my forearm and elbow and just kept silent. By the time I got close to my building, I heard a voice that could soothe even the worst stomach pains. It was Grandma, yelling for me to come to her apartment. When I got there, she had already baked some cookies and poured a glass of milk for me. She said she had already told my mother that she wanted me to come over for a while after school. I had not said a word to her, but I never had to. Somehow she had this sixth sense that told her when something was wrong with me. She turned on her gospel music softly. I heard a man singing "I Don't Believe You Brought Me This Far to Leave Me." I think it was her favorite as she always played that song. She sat across from me and asked if I had heard about my father. I slowly nodded yes and looked down inside my glass of milk. Then she spoke with the voice of an angel and said, "Baby, don't worry. Everything will be okay. God has his hand on you, and you have a calling that one day will be fulfilled. Everything that happens to you will turn out for the good. Your dad is also in the hands of God, and although you don't really know him, still pray for him. One day he will be delivered."

She also told me that he was bound by drugs. She said his addiction was one that people shot in their veins. I soaked everything in that she had to say. By the time I dunked my last cookie in the milk, I felt so much better. I got up and gave Grams the biggest hug. Then I went out her back door and headed to my apartment.

Chapter Six

THE VOW

FAKE DAD, REAL DAD. THE prefix didn't really matter. The fact was that Dad was in jail, no matter which one of them I picked. Mr. Mangrum, or Brother Danny as he was called, was a true godsend. He was the only positive male role model in my life. He picked us kids up faithfully every week to take us to the Boys Club.

There were probably a lot of regular people who were afraid to come to the Heights, but Brother Danny had no problem driving his gray van there to pick us kids up and talk to people about God. I thought that maybe he just didn't realize that he was coming to very dangerous projects. Although there were a few white families that lived there, most of the white people that came to the Heights were either buying drugs, or working for the state and coming to see about the "welfare" of the children.

But Brother Danny was different. He had this quiet confidence when he came to get us. And every time he was approached or solicited by the world of substance abuse, he would begin to talk to the solicitors about the Bible. That alone would force them to back away as if Brother Danny was pointing a weapon at them. I would later learn that he was pointing a weapon, "a sword," which was the word of God. Eventually, people just left Brother Danny alone and accepted him as a regular visitor. Plus, they probably realized that he was a good man who was trying to help the children gain a different outlook or perspective than they normally would growing up in the projects. I began to open up and talk to him a bit about my family. I began to have trust in this man.

Then one day on the way home I was really thrown off guard. I had mentioned my real dad to Brother Danny a few times. I expressed how he didn't care about me and that I had never had a real conversation with him, but I followed Grandma's instructions and prayed for him every day. Well, one night when Mr. Mangrum was dropping me off, and right before we got to the Heights, he started talking. He said that he spoke with my grandmother and told her how much I talked about my real dad. He said that she gave him permission to take me to visit him if I wanted.

"In jail?" I immediately asked.

I had no doubts as to his whereabouts, but I believed I had asked because I was surprised—and I was also buying some time to answer a very difficult question. There was no paper that I could look at to cheat on this one. This question had to be answered by me. I had heard that on certain tests you aren't penalized as much if you leave the question blank instead of answering it wrong. Since I really didn't know the answer, I figured that I would just leave this one blank. Without taking my focus off the dark gray carpet, I calmly responded and said that I didn't know. He said he understood and whatever I decided was okay. He was available to take me if I decided that I wanted to go. After thinking about it for a few days and asking Grandma a million questions, I finally decided that I wanted to go.

The next time thst I was picked up by Mr. Mangrum for Boys Club, I told him that I would like to go if he was still willing to take me. Even though Gram had answered all of my questions, I still couldn't envision what jail actually looked like.

The next Saturday the gray van pulled up to our apartment. Mom wiped lotion on my face and asked me if I was sure I wanted to do this.

I looked away from her but answered, "Yeah, I'm ready." The drive there seemed to take forever, but the voices of BeBe and CeCe Winans seemed to calm my nerves.

After crossing a long, yellow bridge, Mr. Mangrum looked over and asked, "Are you okay?" I responded by saying I was cool, and realized that was the first word I had spoken since we left the Heights. Although my mouth was saying I was okay, my heart was saying something totally different.

The truth was I had never been more terrified. For one thing, I was scared that I was actually going to a jail. I kept telling myself that I was only a visitor (with the hope that one day I wouldn't become a permanent resident). The other thing that bothered me even more was that I didn't really know what to say to the man I was about to visit. Would I tell him how mad I was for the embarrassment he had caused me? Or would I tell him that I prayed for him every day? Oh well, there wasn't any more time to think as we pulled up to the ugliest building that I had ever seen. It actually looked like this haunted castle that I had seen in a scary movie. The bricks looked like they were ancient as the dirt overpowered their original color. I noticed the sign that said Allegheny County Jail.

We got out of the van and entered the "haunted house." I was already scared and hadn't even seen a ghost yet. Will the ghost be the man who I was coming to visit? We walked up the never-ending steps only to see a long line of people waiting to see the security guard to fill out some paperwork. I was amazed that there were white, black, short, tall, young, and old people standing in this line. The majority was the same color as me, but the mix of visitors told me that it didn't matter what race you were to end up a resident of this place. After a 30-minute wait, they finally called our names. We were escorted through a metal door that locked behind us. We were then told to sit at booth number thirteen. Mr. Mangrum asked me to stand for a minute as he sat and waited for my dad to arrive.

Within minutes, Dad came through a larger metal door. He had a weird look on his face as he sat down. Mr. Mangrum instantly put the phone to his ear and began to speak. He started by telling my dad he was the leader of the Boys Club at the local church in Duquesne and that's how I met him. He went on to say how great of a kid I was and that I had talked about my father a whole lot. He let him know that he had gotten the okay from my mother and grandmother to bring me to visit. Mr. Mangrum ended by telling my dad that he didn't know exactly why he was in jail, but he wanted him to know that God forgives. He said, "God Bless," and stood up, trying to hand the phone to me.

It took me a second to snap out of it. I was still mesmerized by my surroundings. My trance was broken by a lady arguing on the phone next to us. I then noticed that Mr. Mangrum was holding out the phone to me. I reluctantly grabbed hold of it and slowly sat down on the metal stool. I had rehearsed my speech a thousand times over the last few days and now it was showtime. I was ready to tell my dad how upset I was, and how I was embarrassed at school because of him. I was ready to tell him that I was disappointed that he had never taken the time to get to know me. I was ready to tell him that I was tired of hearing all the negative things about his life of drug abuse.

Yes, I was finally ready. I put the receiver to my ear and I couldn't believe what was happening. I had the speech down pat, but I never thought about the possibility of experiencing stage fright. I felt as if I were standing in front of hundreds of people with a microphone in my hand. My mouth was wide open, but the only word I could think of was, "Uhhhhhhhh!" I took a deep breath and gathered myself. By the time I started to remember parts of my speech, I was interrupted by the words, "Hello, son."

I looked through the glass at a man who was partly responsible for my existence, but so irresponsible when it came to my well-being. I responded by saying, "Hi." At that point, only three words had been spoken. I had totally lost the courage to say the things that had been troubling me for so long, so my plans for big talk automatically became small talk. He asked about school and my mother, and yada, yada, yada. He thanked me for wanting to visit him, and said he knew he didn't deserve it. He promised me that he was going to get his life together and that he would have a long talk with me when I was a little older. He said a few more things, and then I heard the loud intercom announce that visiting was now over.

He asked me to give the phone to Mr. Mangrum. I assumed he was thanking him as Mr. Mangum said, "You're welcome. No problem." The problem was that I was leaving with a lot of unanswered questions. Oh well, I guess time reveals all, and I had to be patient in understanding this part of my life.

We left the jail. I was a little more conversational on the way home. I must have said thank you a billion times. I could not believe that this man had taken the time to help me get a load off my chest. Although that load was not totally lifted, my attempt made me feel just as good. Mr. Mangrum dropped me off at Grandma's and said that he would see me in a few days for Boys Club. I went in and told Grandma about the whole thing. I told her that I didn't know what to say. She smiled and said that I had said enough just by showing up there, and now it was up to my dad to respond.

It took a couple of weeks but everything went back to normal at school. My friends apologized to me, and my father was never brought up again. My blond-haired answer key never showed up at school for the remainder of the year. I also noticed that her family's apartment was now as vacant as the empty space in my mind that was starving for answers.

A big part of me wanted to ignore my father's life—just as he had done mine. But I had a real issue. His choices were somehow starting to affect me despite him not being present. No matter what he did with his life, everyone in the Heights knew that he was my biological father. Oh well, I guess I would have to wait on the promise of the talk when I got a little older.

Mr. Mangrum continued to be a very positive influence in my life. I began to attend his church even more than Grandma's. The church took us underprivileged kids to many events. I even got a chance to go to New York City and see the Statue of Liberty on a field trip. Although I had an absentee father and no male role model at home, God had sent someone to the rough neighborhood of Duquesne to help instill some good qualities in me. Most of all, through Mr. Mangrum I was able to learn more about Him.

Everything seemed to be going okay, although Mom was starting to spend a lot more time away from home. There were times when I couldn't go to Boys Club because I had to keep an eye on my little sisters. To me it wasn't all that bad, as I loved them dearly. I had already promised myself that I would take good care of them, especially after losing Dar-Dar.

My only irritation came from not being able to participate in the things to which I had become accustomed. Mr. Mangrum told me not to worry about it. He said to talk to God about anything that bothered me and He wouldn't let me down. Grandma said the same thing. She would also take pressure off of me by allowing my sisters to come over to her apartment so I could go to Boys Club. I was pretty confident Mr. Mangrum and Grandma were right. God wouldn't let me down. However, I was not prepared for the letdown I was about to receive.

One day Mr. Mangrum was dropping me off after Boys Club. When he pulled up to my apartment, I opened the door of the van, but he stopped me before I jumped out. He said, "There is something I need to tell you."

I closed the van door and said, "Okay."

He then informed me that Mr. Ray would be continuing with the Boys Club as he was moving back to Colorado to take care of his mother.

"Oh, wow," I thought.

Mr. Ray was cool, but I had never really gotten used to him. Mr. Mangrum seemed to make sure everything ran smoothly—not to mention that he really cared about us kids from the projects. He had taught us so much about God, and he gave us an escape from the Heights. He must have read my mind because he said he would make sure Mr. Ray came to pick us up every Wednesday. He said he would be around a little while longer but had to move really soon. Before I knew it, he was off to the Rocky Mountains.

Mr. Ray did pick us up a few times, but the Boys Club eventually vanished into thin air. And that probably wasn't such a bad thing. I realized that I was really needed at home. Mom started to disappear more and more, and I was starting to notice some of the things that I had first seen a few years back.

Mom was wearing the same sweat suit for a couple of days and putting on a hat instead of doing her hair. The strong stench of alcohol was hard to ignore as well. But just like when I was down at the field and Mo-Joe was scoring more touchdowns than me, it was time to step up my game. I started cleaning the house more, and making meals from canned goods and the little that was in the refrigerator. Whether it was boiling eggs, cutting a couple of pieces of cheese off the long rectangular brown box that we always seemed to have, or making bowls of stale cereal with sugar and water, it really didn't matter to me. But one thing was for sure. I had to make sure that my baby sisters had something to eat.

I would also make sure that they were never bored. I would watch cartoons with them and play with them most of the day. Ashley would bring her fake plastic eggs to me and just say, "Uhh, uhh." She could not form a word, but I knew exactly what she was trying to communicate to me. It was all my fault why they thought their big brother was magic. Not just because I had taken good care of them, but also because one day I decided that I wanted to show them a trick. I boiled a couple of eggs while they were upstairs. When they were done and all cooled off, I called my sisters downstairs for the trick. I had a few pieces of candy, so I grabbed their plastic toy eggs and pretended to turn them into real eggs and pieces of candy. From that point on, they were always urging me to do that same trick. I loved entertaining them, especially since I felt I was responsible for them—which I was the majority of the time.

Mom progressively got worse. She would show up and be mad at me for no particular reason. One day, I decided that I would get up early and clean the entire house. I had recently noticed that dishes were being left in the sink, and a small pot was being left on the stove with a little bit of water in it. But I hadn't seen Mom cook anything in quite a while so it was a mystery. Maybe one day my mind would be privy to what she was really cooking. There was no dish soap, so I poured some of the laundry detergent in the sink and made some dishwater. I washed every single dish in the house, even the ones that had dust on them. When my sisters got up, I made them a bowl of cereal and put on *The Flintstones*. I told them to watch TV while I cleaned up the house. It took me all day, but I finally finished every single room in the house except Mom's. I could not wait until she got home so she could see my surprise. I was sure that this would put her in a good mood.

After I finished cleaning, I found a couple of potpies and made them for my sisters. Then I sat patiently waiting for Mom to come through the door. I looked out the window. It was now dark outside and both of my little princesses were spread out on the floor in a deep sleep. Oh well, I guess it was time for bed. I carried them one by one up to their beds and tucked them in. I wiped my neck of the slobber that Ashley had blessed me with while I was carrying her upstairs. I was afraid Mom would yell at me if I stayed downstairs to wait for her, so I turned off the light and TV and went to my room.

I turned down the volume on my TV and turned on the Atari game system I had gotten for Christmas. I was trying really hard to stay awake. I did not realize that I had lost the battle until I was awakened by a couple of voices. They were coming from downstairs. One was Mom's and the other was a deep male voice. I put the controller on the dresser as I realized I had fallen asleep with it glued to my hand. I had no idea what time it was. It was still dark outside, but I could hear birds singing.

I slightly cracked open my door and I could hear Mom cursing and screaming at someone. I could hear the other voice warning her that she had better stop talking to him in that manner. I did not have the courage to go downstairs to see what was going on, so instead I jumped on my bed and put the pillow over my head. I was somehow able to fall back to sleep.

When I woke up, I noticed it was now light outside so I quietly went to Mom's door. She was not in her bed. I began to worry. Had that deep voice done something to my mother? I was upset with myself for putting the pillow over my head like a coward instead of walking downstairs to make sure she was okay. *Lord, please let my mother be okay. If something happened to her, it would be on my conscience forever.* I quickly peeked into my baby sisters' room to make sure they were all right. Raquel was not in her bed, so I went into the room only to find her fast asleep on the floor beside it. After putting her back in bed, I continued looking for Mom. As I walked down the steps, I could hear the TV, which gave me some relief. But when I got downstairs, there was no sign of Mom. Just as panic was about to set in, the back door opened. Mom walked in, and I was so happy to see her. I greeted her immediately before she was even able to close the door behind her. "Hey, Mom!" I said with excitement in my voice.

She barely acknowledged me with an almost silent, "Hey."

After throwing her coat on the couch, she jogged up the steps in slow motion. I heard the toilet flush a few times and the door slam to her room. There was no sign of her for the rest of the day. I was very disappointed that I would be spending another day in the house as I could not leave my sisters alone while Mom was asleep, but I was very happy that my mother was safe. Although she was in her room in REM mode, at least she was home with us. But I was disappointed she had not noticed that I had cleaned the entire house. I had done it for her. A bigger part of me understood that it was now my duty whether she recognized my kind gesture or not, and it actually made me feel good.

She woke up later that evening in a much better mood. I heard the bath water upstairs. After about an hour, she came down the steps and gave me the biggest hug. I was so in shock that I stood with my arms limp for a second. My delayed reaction was to reach up and hug her back, but my mind began to wander. Mom was able to read my thoughts. She looked at me and said, "Thank you for cleaning the house. You are such a little man." So she had noticed! I just smiled and said it was easy. The truth was there were several times while I was cleaning that I wanted to give up, but I pushed myself to get the job done. She also thanked me for taking such good care of the girls. I was on cloud nine. It felt so good to know that my hard work had not been in vain. Another part of my excitement was due to the fact that Mom had come downstairs in her socks, which meant she was not leaving anytime soon.

She instructed Raquel to get the bucket of beads so that she could do her hair. These were the moments that had me so confused. That night Mom was being the mother that we needed her to be, but the last couple of days she had been a total stranger. What was changing her into this other person, and more importantly, how can I get the woman that we needed to stay? This was way too hard for me to figure out, so I just asked God to please get rid of that stranger. My thoughts were interrupted by Mom asking me to hand her the phone. She put it to her ear and began to place an order. "Cool. Pizza!" I thought.

Although the refrigerator wasn't always full, and sometimes it was hard to find something to eat, Mom would order us food during the times when she was home. She turned on some music, and one of my little sisters began to run around and dance. Today we looked like the happy family that was in the picture we had taken on Easter Sunday. Unfortunately, that smile was one moment, and was only consistent on the wall.

Mom was almost done with Raquel's hair when there was a knock on the door. A voice yelled, "Pizza man!" Mom looked at me and told me to go look in her top right drawer. She said there was a twenty-dollar bill under the clothes. I pretended to put a football in my right hand, did a spin move around the table, and sprinted up the steps. I got to Mom's room and went directly to the drawer. I opened it and moved around an assortment of wrinkled-up clothing. I could not find the twenty-dollar bill. Just when I was about to give up, my hand grazed over a hard object. I was well aware that it was not the twenty-dollar bill that I had been searching for. However, my curiosity got the better of me and I gripped the object. It fit in my hand like a light bulb. "Oh!" I thought. "A light bulb." I pulled the object out of the drawer and I quickly noticed that, although it had a lot of similarities to a light bulb, like its shape and color, there were some distinct differences. For instance, there was a long, skinny stem coming out of the center of it. I also noticed that if it was a light bulb, then it was definitely blown out, as there were dark, smoke-like marks throughout the entire thing. I stood there hypnotized by the object.

I had heard a lot of things about drugs but had no idea what they looked like or how people used them. I remembered Rodney's comment about my mother being a crackhead. At the time, my fury caused my mind to go blank. I thought of Rodney, however, as I stood there looking at this object. I also remembered him saying that my mother was "on the pipe." I thought, "Is this what brings the stranger alive in my mother? Is this why she forgets that we exist? Is this why she goes days without interacting with us?" The very thought made me want to destroy the glass object right then and there. "Should I hide it somewhere else? No, maybe she would find it again," I thought. So I made a choice. I was going to destroy it. I would take it outside tomorrow, far away from our apartment, and smash it with the soles of my feet. Once I did that, I figured maybe our mother would stay present.

Right then, as I was standing in my mother's room, I decided to make a vow. I held the evil object in front of my face as I pledged that I would never use drugs. But what I didn't vow was that I would never allow drugs to use me! I was shaken out of my trance by a loud yell.

"What are you doing up there? Hurry up and get down here. The pizza man is waiting," Mom demanded. I sucked my teeth, shook my head, and quickly put the object back in the drawer. I would have to come back later to get it. After burying it in the clothes, I realized that the twenty-dollar bill was right in front of my face. I grabbed it, rushed downstairs, and handed it to Mom. She asked what took so long, and I replied that I could not find it at first.

We listened to music and stuffed our faces with pizza. The next morning, I awoke and Mom was not there. I immediately thought about the light bulb-looking object and headed toward her room. I opened the drawer to look through it and could not find the glass object. I even took out all the clothes in the drawer. It was not there. It was now clear to me why Mom would do her disappearing acts. That day was proof positive. The object disappeared from the drawer and so did she. "Well, I will keep checking this drawer, and when I find it, I will make sure it disappears for good," I promised myself.

Chapter Seven

My Heritage

I HAD TO HAVE SEARCHED that dresser drawer about a hundred times over the next couple of weeks, but there was no sign of the blown out light bulb-looking object. Mom still did her disappearing acts, but they seemed to be less frequent. She would be around for weeks at a time, and then all of a sudden, it would be just my little sisters and me for a couple of days. When I noticed her absence, I would instinctively go into protective mode.

After one of Mom's mini vacations, I got up early to check if she was back in her bed (I seemed to do this every single morning then). I saw that she was passed out with half her body on the bed and her feet on the floor as if she had fallen asleep praying. I quickly thought about trying to lift her legs onto the bed, but immediately dismissed the thought. I knew that I was pretty strong, but it still would have been rather difficult. More importantly, I wasn't quite sure what reaction I would get from her. Instead, I walked on my tiptoes across the old hardwood floor and gently tapped Mom on her arm. She didn't even budge. I started to back away slowly, and then I thought that I had better make sure she was okay. Her light snore provided some comfort, but I wouldn't feel good unless I got a response from her. I took two tiptoes forward again, tapped

Mareese Comer

Mom a little harder, and called her name in a light whisper. She suddenly jerked her head up as if I had scared her. I said, "Are you okay, Mom?"

She looked at me through squinty eyes and said she was fine. She then crawled all the way onto the bed and mumbled something that I could not understand. I didn't even try to interpret her language. I was just happy that I had accomplished my goals. One, she had gotten into a comfortable position, and two, she was okay. No matter how rough the last couple of days might have been, somehow when she was inside our tiny project apartment, it gave me peace. Plus, I really did believe Grandma when she said my mother was in God's hands. So I gently closed the bedroom door and came up with an excellent idea.

I peeked into my baby sisters' room to make sure they were okay. Raquel was sound asleep, but Ashley was wide awake, staring at me with a look that dared me to shut the door without coming to get her. I gave in to the look and went over to her. Then I took her downstairs with me so that I could carry out my big surprise for Mom. I quickly made Ashley a bottle and laid her on her back in her playpen, and she gave me a little smile as if she was saying thanks.

I went to the kitchen and realized that in order for me to make this happen, I had first better wash the dirty dishes in the sink. After I was done, I looked through the refrigerator and cabinets to find something I could cook Mom for breakfast. A thorough search produced half a container of oatmeal and two slices of bread (one was the end piece). I put my hands on my head and let out a long sigh, "Ohhh, God!" As soon as I said the word "God," I actually came up with a solution. I ran, picked up the phone, and dialed Grandma's house. My Aunt Ron answered on the second ring. I quickly told her I had a serious problem. She responded by saying she'd get Grandma on the phone. "Wait, wait! You may be able to help," I said, and explained that my mom wasn't feeling too well. "I want to make her breakfast." I told Aunt Ron my first problem was that I was staring at a half empty box of oatmeal and two slices of bread—and one was the end piece. My second problem was that I couldn't leave my baby sisters to come get whatever they had in their fridge.

Aunt Ron immediately chuckled into the receiver and said, "Boy, I thought you had a serious problem!" She said she would be right there. She showed up with eggs, bacon, bread, and half a container of orange juice. I looked at her with the biggest smile and told her she had saved the day. She started putting the items on the table and asked if I wanted help.

I smiled and said, "Ohhh, no!" I had seen Aunt Ron burn enough eggs and toast. I had more confidence in myself than in her to cook this meal. She gave me a funny look, and then went to pick Ashley up out of the playpen and played with her while she watched me prepare the meal.

Aunt Ron stayed until I was completely finished. She congratulated me on a fine job and said she had to go. Just as she closed the back door, I heard my other sister creeping down the steps. I was already prepared as I had made her a plate and had it sitting on the table with a napkin over it. She came over and hugged my leg, and I sat her on the chair at the table. Now that I had gotten both of my sisters situated, it was time to serve breakfast in bed to Mom. I wiped off the serving tray that had been tucked behind the refrigerator and began to neatly set the food on it. I had a big bowl of oatmeal, and bacon and eggs. I put butter on the toast and even poured a cup of orange juice.

I took a deep breath, picked up the tray, and slowly walked upstairs to Mom's room. By the time I got to the door, I realized that I could not open it as both of my hands were occupied holding the tray. Just as I was about to set it down on the floor, I noticed my little sister Raquel right behind me with a piece of toast in her mouth. After a sigh of relief, I directed her to open the door for me so I could deliver the room service.

As I got to the edge of the bed, I called out "Mom!" a few times. Raquel climbed onto the mattress and Mom stirred. Then all of a sudden, the air in my body seemed to deflate as my mother picked her head up and yelled, "What are y'all doing?"

I quickly spoke up and said, "Mom, I made you breakfast." I lifted the tray up a bit so she could see. My arms were burning from its weight. She surveyed the tray, and then looked at me and said that she was not hungry and didn't even like oatmeal. I stood there speechless and wanted to drop the tray right there on her bedroom floor, but I knew that would make things worse. Instead, I slowly walked out of her room with my head down and my eyes full of tears, trying not to spill the orange juice.

There were many moments when I could see that Mom really loved me. This was clearly not one of them. I went downstairs and poured the orange juice in the sink and dumped the food in the garbage can. I had even lost my appetite for the plate I had made for myself. I put it in the empty refrigerator. Then the phone rang. It was my Aunt Ron calling to see how things went. I just told her that I really didn't feel like talking about it. She must have told my Grams, because shortly afterward they showed up with my Aunt Bam. They got my sisters ready and told me that I could go play with my friends. Grams was going to cook dinner for us later in the day. Before we left my house, Grams went in my mom's room. I heard her say a few words and then we all left. Grams cooked dinner that night like it was a holiday. We ate and then played board games until she started to nod off.

The next morning Mom was back to normal. The first thing she did was apologize for being so mean to me. She promised that things were going to change really soon, and I actually believed her. There wasn't a day that went by that I had not prayed for her, so I knew God was going to eventually answer my prayers. The question was when was he going to do it?

Mom seemed to be true to her word as she did not leave the house except to go to the store or visit Grandma. She either cooked or ordered food almost every day. The past weekend she had even made it down to Robert Wholey's in the strip district so that we could have a seafood feast. She bought her favorite, live crabs. And that was exactly how I would describe our project apartment. It was finally alive. It would also become a little more exciting in the next couple of weeks as Mom told me that my Uncle Mee-Mee was moving in with us.

The next day was a very big day for me. We finally went to another concert. This time it was a little different. It was our annual middle school talent show. Mom brought most of the family along. Although Grandma didn't care for anything other than church, she was even a part of the group.

I stood by the boy's bathroom in the hallway with my cousin Nooter next to me. We heard a deep voice announce in the microphone that the next performance would be Eric B. and Rakim. "Oh no!" I thought. The show was about to begin. The problem was that we were standing by the boy's bathroom and we were the show. I looked at my cousin and asked, "Are you ready?"

He responded with confidence. "I was born ready." I grabbed his arm and pulled him toward the stage.

Nooter was my Aunt Mary's son, and Aunt Mary was Grandma's sister. Nooter and his family—Aunt Mary, Nooter's dad, and Nooter's two sisters Toni and Nee-Nee—had just recently moved back from Florida, which was where our family originated. Nooter looked like he was actually ready, and to be quite honest, I only asked him because my stomach felt like I had to throw up. Oh well, there wasn't much time left, so I took a deep breath and we hit the stage. The crowd seemed to erupt. I grabbed the microphone and Noot was set up on his homemade turntables that we had spent three days making out of cardboard. I looked over at the lady controlling the sound and motioned her to start.

The beat came through the speakers and Noot was rocking side to side as if he were controlling the music through his cardboard turntables. I walked back and forth across the stage, bobbing my head with my fake gold chain and black leather tam hat. I was dressed just like Rakim, so this performance had better be just as good. I grabbed the mic, put it to my mouth, and went off. "A pen and a paper, a stereo, a tape of/Me and Eric B, and nice big plate of/Fish, which is my favorite dish/But without no money it's still a wish/ 'Cuz I don't like to dream about gettin' paid/ So I dig into the books of the rhymes that I made/So now to test to see if I got pull/Hit the studio, 'cuz I'm paid in full."

It seemed every single person in the audience was out of their chair. I even had Grandma doing a different dance than she did at church. I had done my thing, now it was Noot's turn as he had the grand finale and had to tear up the turntables. He began to scratch, and I moved out of the way so everyone could see him. He was ready! He was tearing those cardboard turntables up and dancing to the beat as he was scratching. He got so caught up in the moment that the cardboard flew off the table it was on and out into the audience. The crowd immediately burst into laughter, and then everyone began to whistle and clap their hands for a very long time.

Noot and I then went to the edge of the stage, took our bows, and walked off. As soon as we were out of sight, I looked at my cousin and said, "Man, you really messed up by letting that cardboard slip out of your hands." Noot smiled at me and said the crowd loved it. He said he had planned it but just didn't tell me. I thought, "Yeah, right!" Whether he was being truthful or not, the crowd must have loved it. We won first place in our middle school talent show.

Rodney and Ju-Ju were the first ones to meet me after the show. Instead of congratulating me, they both criticized that I had to lip sync as opposed to writing my own original rap. I just looked at both of them with a smirk and said, "Well, why didn't you enter the show?" The question was interrupted by the rest of the fellas as Bear was the first one to almost tackle me. Damien looked at me and said, "Way to represent the Heights!"

I then went over by my mom and grandmother, and they were all smiles. I had a feeling inside that could not be described. I really didn't understand the words to the song I was singing, but I did like the sound of it. I wasn't quite sure how I was going to make the song "Paid in Full" a reality, but I had made up my mind that it was going to happen.

The next morning I woke up with a hangover. I wasn't sure if it was from my big concert or from a couple of Hi-C juice boxes I had drank. Nevertheless, there were only a couple of weeks left of the school year, and I had woken up extremely late. I knew that my crew was long gone, so I hurried to brush my teeth and do a quick wipe down. I threw on my wrinkled clothes and was out the door. This wasn't the first time I was late for school, but I had forgotten how much longer it took to walk with the fellas.

I was turning the corner of the local bar called Union Grill, and Reverend Caldwell's candy store when a black IROC pulled up next to me. I noticed it slow down, so that was a sign for me to speed up my steps. I looked straight ahead and gripped the straps on my book bag in preparation to take off running if the car made a sudden stop. I had been warned many times not to talk to strangers, so there was no way I was even looking in the direction of the car. It kept moving slowly beside me. My heart began to beat fast. All of a sudden, the horn blew a couple times. As the window rolled down, I took off running. I didn't stop until I heard a voice yell out, "Church Socks!"

The voice kind of sounded familiar, so I pumped my breaks and did a complete stop. I looked over at the car and noticed that it was the Duquesne High School basketball superstar we called Dirty-Meech. In our neighborhood, nicknames had nothing to do with being unclean—at least from a physical stand point. Some said he earned the name because of how good he was in basketball. Others in the projects would say it was because of his lifestyle. Dirty-Meech always came to the Heights, but he was from the other projects called Cochran Dale. I wanted to believe that his nickname did come from his basketball skills, as he was set to break the all-time scoring record that year. My gut, however, told me that the other assumptions of how he got his nickname did have some validity. I believe that was confirmed when he prompted me to get in the car so he could give me a ride to school. As I was getting in the car, I first noticed that he was holding his stomach with one hand and bursting out in laughter. I sat on the seat, closed the door, and asked him what was so funny. He said while still laughing, "I really scared you, didn't I?"

I smirked and said, "Yeah, you did, but I don't think it's funny at all."

He eventually stopped laughing and asked if I was going to the game that week against the Clairton Bears. He said he was going to dunk all over them and try to score fifty points. He reached in the glove box, grabbed a few tickets, and gave them to me for my crew and me. I took them and said thanks. Then I noticed there were all kinds of wires in every color sticking out from under the steering wheel. I also noticed that the car was running without a key in the ignition. I was smart enough not ask too many questions, and I was also smart enough to know that something just wasn't right with this picture.

I appreciated the ride but was now in a hurry to get to class. He pulled into an alley close to the school and told me to get out there. I opened my mouth and was about to ask why, but then thought I had better not. I opened the passenger door. Before I jumped out, there was a question that I just had to ask. I looked over at him and said, "Is it real?"

He looked back at me and said, "What are you talking about?"

I put my head down and thought about my words carefully. Then I mustered up the courage to ask the question, "Is the gun real in the glove box where the tickets were?"

He looked at me and quickly responded, "Boy, you better get out and get your butt to school. And stop being nosy!"

His answer was good enough for me. I jumped out of the car and hurried down the yellow brick road that led to the school. As I entered the building, I thought about Dirty-Meech. This was a kid that everyone in the town loved. He had such an amazing personality, and he was one of the greatest basketball players that we had ever seen. But I wondered if his glove box and the loose wires would prevent him from becoming an honest, productive, and successful man.

The school year ended. Grandma had already told me a few weeks earlier that she was taking me on vacation. Yup, we were going to Florida.

When most people think of Florida, they immediately think of tall palm trees and exotic beaches, but the part we were going to was the complete opposite of that. We came from a town called Jacob, Florida. It was more like killer mosquitoes and long dirt roads than palm trees and beaches. But that's where my family originated. While Miami was movie stars and paparazzi, Jacob was boring and desolate.

Mom went to Kmart and bought me a couple of short sets. She gave me a little cash, and then we were on our way south. We had all loaded up in a van, and Uncle June Bug, Nooter's dad, was the designated driver. It seemed like it took us forever. I think we stopped at every single exit for soda and snacks. Grams played her church music all the way down the interstate. Almost thirty hours later, we finally reached our destination. As soon as I saw the dirt roads, I knew we were really close to my great-grandmother's house.

Jacob was so different from living in the city. Not only did people dress differently, but their names also seemed different from people who lived the city life. We had family there named Maple, Molly, Lady, Sweet Pea, Aunt Edna, Uncle Willie-D, and many more. When they spoke, they sounded as if they were from the country.

As out of place as we may have felt, after a few days Noot and I seemed to find our way around just fine. Our family treated us like royalty. My great-grandmother was named Lu La Bell. She was the sweetest person I had ever met. She had to be approaching her eighties, yet she would still be in the kitchen cooking and humming her spirituals.

Over the next few days, I was really caught by surprise. Grandma announced that we were going to work with her. I thought I might have just misunderstood her. *Work? Why would I be going to work on my vacation?* She couldn't be talking to me as I wasn't even old enough to work. Sure enough, she was definitely talking to me. She got Noot and me up early the next morning and told us we were going to the fields to pick peas. She then told us that we needed to learn about our heritage and what our people had to go through. She said the good part was that we were even going to get paid for it. Our ancestors didn't get that privilege.

I was not excited about the idea, but there was no way I would think of refusing Grandma's order, so we were off to the fields. They gave us huge wooden baskets and said we would be paid for every basket we filled up with peas. "Well," I thought, "I hope they pay something for effort because there is no way I am filling up this large wooden basket with little, tiny peas."

It had to be about 120 degrees as I was dripping sweat and practicing karate with the mosquitoes. This was complete torture. I looked over at Grams. She had already filled up two wooden baskets and was working on her third. This was one hardworking lady. After we finished, she handed me a twenty-dollar bill and Noot a ten. She said he threw more peas in the field at people than he had put in the baskets. On the way back, she gave a long lesson about how hard her mother and father had to work in the fields just to put food on their table. She said she only took us so that we would never forget that experience. I spoke up quickly and said with a smirk, "Oh, believe me, Grams, I will never forget this."

She went on to say that I had to be willing to work hard for whatever I wanted in life. She said some things might seem unbearable, but I would be paving the way for generations to come. I also figured that she wanted me to understand my heritage and how she was raised. Years ago she had migrated up north to Pittsburgh after my mother and Uncle Geno were born. Apparently, my grandfather, who was Eugene Comer Sr., had died when they were infants. So she moved up North to find a better way of life. Grandma took a couple of her sisters with her when she left. Yup, Aunt Gussie, Aunt Jackie, and Aunt Mary followed suit. They all started families, and those were the roots that sprouted our family tree in the city of Pittsburgh.

Grandma met my grandfather John Gooden and went on to have five more children. Her marriage lasted for quite some time, but eventually ended in a separation that was due to Granddad's long struggle with alcohol and many other normal relationship issues. Although they physically separated and lived in different houses, they never seemed to separate spiritually and emotionally. The strange thing about it was, when they were together, they were partiers—a lifestyle destined to tear any marriage apart. However, when they separated, both of them gravitated toward a lifestyle that would have kept them together. He and my grandmother were members of different churches, but believers of the same faith. They both became devout Christians and dedicated their lives to the service of God. I would always hear Grandma talking on the phone with my grandfather as if they had never separated. And there were times when I would hear him fussing through the receiver at her like they were still together. Truth be told, they were still together. Their bodies had separated, but their hearts were still attached.

Granddad was actually a great man. He was a really good example of what a real man looked like. He worked very hard at McKeesport Hospital where I was born, and he ended up retiring from there. Although he wasn't my mother's biological father, you would never be able to tell. He treated every one of my grandmother's children the same. I used to stay the weekends at his house sometimes, and I really enjoyed eating all the Little Debbie snack cakes that he always had at home. Another sign that they had never separated was the fact that neither of them was able to move forward in a new marriage.

When I looked at Grandma, I could see strength in her hands and determination in her eyes, as well as compassion and love for others in all of her actions. I had so much respect for this amazing woman. I had already known that she was a hard worker before I saw her fill the wooden baskets with peas. She would spend hours and hours changing around the whole house. When she asked me to help her clean up, I usually just canceled my plans for the entire day, as I knew wiping a table or two would not be enough for her. She would have me polish all her knickknacks (of which there seemed to be hundreds), and she would always want to rearrange the furniture so that the house looked different.

She would change around the pictures on the wall as if she were just moving in. Her gospel music would be playing, and she would not sit down until everything was complete.

As we headed back to my great-grandmother's house from the fields, I told my grandmother that I now understood, and her lesson was so strong that I probably didn't need to go back to the fields the next day. She immediately started to laugh and told me that I didn't have to go if I didn't want to, but she was going back the next day. At that point, my mind was set. I wasn't going. But by the time morning came, I had changed it. I got up ready to go with Grams to the fields. There was no way I was letting her go by herself. We were partners whether we were at the grocery store, cleaning the house, or working in the fields. We had to be a team.

We stayed in Florida for about a week. During that time, I really got a chance to know another part of my family—better yet, the original side of my family. I fell in love with my Uncle Jimmy, who was my grandmother's youngest brother. He was born with Down syndrome, but you could only tell by the look in his eyes and his slurred speech. Otherwise, he was pretty normal to the rest of the family. He spent a lot of time by himself in his room, listening to music and playing cards. Although we couldn't understand what game he was playing, he seemed to know exactly what he was doing. It is very difficult to understand any of God's creations. We may perceive a person one way, yet that person's perception of himself or herself may be totally different. That is the beauty of God. Everyone—regardless of disability, race, or creed—has the opportunity to be happy. Uncle Jimmy never seemed to be upset unless you messed with my grandmother. She was dear to his heart. He also had a thing for the ladies and would take any opportunity to steal yours if you brought her around. He would secretly blow kisses at her and then put his pointer finger to his mouth as if to warn her to keep it a secret. When you looked at him, he would smile and look the other way as if nothing had happened. It's amazing how we view someone as mentally disabled who is physically able to bring a smile to so many people, yet there are many people that have all of their mental faculties but do not possess the same power. God is amazing!

We were loading up the van and ready to return to the Northeast. Grandma packed up all kinds of fresh produce that she had picked from the fields. She had peas, peanuts, collard greens, and corn, as well as sticks of sugar cane. These were things that you could not get at a Giant Eagle grocery store.

It seemed like the trip back was a little faster than when we came. Uncle June Bug had warned everyone to get everything they needed on the first stop. We arrived back home and pulled into the Heights in front of Grandma's apartment. I helped her unload everything, and then immediately took off running toward my apartment. I couldn't wait to see my baby sisters and to give Mom a big hug. I hadn't been away from them much before and I really missed them.

I ran up the hill and the back door was cracked open. This time it didn't suddenly close on me before I got there. I pushed open the door as if I were running through one of the dummy pads at football practice and fell right on my face onto the worn-out carpet. It actually felt worse than the worn-out grass down at the field, but the pain was overshadowed by my excitement to be home. Both of my little princesses were in the living room playing. I immediately gave them both the biggest hugs and about three kisses each. I peeked in the kitchen and didn't see Mom, so I put another imaginary football in my hand and did a juke move around my sisters. I hurdled over Ashley's walker and did high knees up the steps to Mom's room.

I opened the door but she was not there. The bathroom door was wide open, so I knew she wasn't in there. I checked every room in the house and yelled out "Mom" a couple of times. There was no sign of her. *Oh no, God. Please tell me that my baby sisters weren't left in the house by themselves. And if so, God, I want to thank you that they are okay. Last but not least, I am thankful that I made it home in time to take care of them.*

Just as I finished my prayer, the front door opened and Mom came in with her slippers on. She had been out front talking. I acted as if I had heard the whistle for kickoff and immediately took off toward her. I slammed into her with my arms wide open and she just laughed and said, "Boy, what's wrong with you?" I kept my arms around her legs and ran in place like one of our practice drills. She reached down, hugged me, and said, "You must have really missed me."

I sat at the table and told her all about the trip. She said she was happy that I enjoyed myself. Things seemed to be pretty normal as my sisters both had their hair done and there was food in the refrigerator. Maybe Mom was starting to evolve. Or maybe God was starting to answer some of my prayers. She then told me to look in the living room closet. I opened it up and lying on the floor was a brand new Huffy Freestyle bike. "Man, this summer is the best!" I thought. I looked up at the closet ceiling and whispered, "Thank you, Lord!"

Chapter Eight

THE YUM YUM TREE

I HAD TAKEN THE VACATION with Grandma and now it was time to spend the weekend with my grandfather. I couldn't say it was all that exciting as there were no other kids to play with and I really didn't go outside unless I went to the store with Granddad. It felt like I was at training camp. I could never forget the plethora of steps you had to walk up inside of his apartment door.

Granddad walked with a limp, but he still had a confident gait as if he was sure of where he was going. He knew I was coming over for the weekend, so he had already loaded up with a ton of snacks. I just fed my face and watched TV. It was kind of a getaway from all the madness that went on in the Heights. He really didn't bother me too much except that he had one rule that I had to follow, and that was the same rule that grandma had. I had to go to church on Sunday morning. One time I had purposely left my church clothes home and brought some bright shorts that looked like swim trunks. I thought maybe he would let it slide and allow me to stay home and watch football. Instead he laughed at my shorts, shook his head, and said that I was still going. He said that stunt might be a sign I needed to get baptized. From that point on, I didn't play any games with him and made sure my church clothes were the first things that I packed.

Mareese Comer

This Sunday Granddad was performing with the men's choir. He always seemed excited about doing that and would rock from side to side with his head held high while singing praises to the Lord. I even got out of my seat and clapped for him as he sang. Granddad did an excellent job and I was proud of him, but the men's choir was not what really grabbed my attention.

The children's choir was up next, and instead of clapping to their song, I just stood there in a daze with my mouth open. Yes, there was a group of kids singing, but I only saw one angel in the whole choir. She was the prettiest little girl I had ever laid eyes on. She had long pretty hair that looked like silk. She was light skinned with a slight tint to her complexion. The truth was that I had never been really excited to go to Granddad's church, but right there at that very moment I wanted to find out how I could join. I had not heard one word of their whole song, but when they finished, I clapped my hands as if it was the greatest song I had ever heard. I spent the rest of the service trying to get her attention. I wondered if she had seen me staring, but she had not even looked in my direction. She seemed to be focused on the sermon. Either she was really into this message, or she was just trying to send me the same message that most of the pretty girls sent: "I'm going to ignore you until you beg me to pay you some attention." I wasn't really sure which she meant, but I was determined to find out after the service.

When it ended, I could see that she was headed downstairs. I could also see Granddad doing a beeline toward me. His limp wasn't even noticeable. When he got to me, he said we had to hurry because the Steelers game was coming on soon. I had to think fast, so right there in Payne Chapel I lied to my grandfather's face. "Lord, please forgive me," I thought. I looked up at him with my eyes as wide as I could open them and started moving side to side. I said, "Granddad, I have to go to the restroom reaaaally bad."

He looked down in disgust and said, "Boy, hurry up."

I replied, "Yes, sir," and made my way down the steps of the church. I hadn't thought about all the grown-ups that were down there. How was I supposed to talk to her without getting in trouble? When I got downstairs, there was no sign of her. I weaved through all the people and I could not find her. Maybe she was in the ladies room? Oh well. My grandfather would kill me if I didn't hurry up. Just as I was about to give up and was walking toward the stairs, I heard the cutest voice say, "Looking for me?"

I sucked my teeth, squinted my eyes, and said, "No, I was looking for the restroom."

"Uhhh hmmm," she replied. "Well, you passed it when you first got down the steps. And why were you staring at me during the whole service?"

So she did see me looking at her. Since I was already busted, I cut to the chase. "So, what's your name?"

She said her name was Dwan and she lived in West Mifflin. West Mifflin was north of the Heights. It was considered the suburbs compared to the projects, and it was more like a middle-class neighborhood, too. She then asked me where I lived and I said I was from the Heights. She immediately turned her nose up at me and asked, "Isn't that place pretty bad?"

I quickly responded, "Yeah, but I'm pretty good."

"Whatever," she said smartly and turned to walk away.

I grabbed her arm and said, "So you're not going to give me your number?"

She stood there thinking about it for a minute, and then finally said, "I hope you have a good memory because I'm not writing it down. And if you do call, let the phone ring one time, hang up, call right back, and I'll answer it." She recited her number, and I repeated it over and over again on the way to Granddad. I was determined to remember this number.

By the time we got to Granddad's house, the Steelers were just kicking off. At the start of the second quarter, my mother arrived to get me. I gave Granddad a hug and told him that I would be back soon, and that I was really starting to like his church. He said, "Good," but did not turn his attention away from the game.

Mom grabbed some Kentucky Fried Chicken and we were on our way home. After we ate, I asked Mom if it was okay to take my new bike for a spin. She said my friends had come by earlier to see if I was home. I said, "Okay, cool," but I had no intention of meeting up with them that day. I was on a completely different mission. I had written Dwan's number down as soon as I got to Granddad's, but there was no way I could call her the same day she gave me her number as that would make me seem desperate (as my uncle Mee-Mee would say). I could hear his voice now: "Never call a girl on the first day."

Calling was definitely out of the question, but I had an even better idea. I needed to break in my new bike, so I headed north to West Mifflin. As I was pulling out of the Heights, I realized that I didn't even know her address. This was insane. But West Mifflin wasn't that big, so I decided to just ride down the streets in hopes that I'd see her playing outside somewhere.

West Mifflin seemed to be peaceful as I did not see many people outside. I could not believe I was riding my bike through the neighborhood singing a love song that I'd heard on a radio station called WAMO. At that moment, I realized the power that women have over men. Yup, I had been bitten by a lovebug, but didn't yet have a clue as to what love was. It had me riding alone on my bike through a town with no clue where I was going. I was just hoping I would get lucky.

My hopeful adventure was cut short by day turning into night, and I was definitely going to make it home before those streetlights came on. I did an illegal U-turn in the middle of the street and headed back to the Heights with my head down. Oh well! I guess I would have to try that one ring code and talk to her on the phone.

We talked on the phone a couple of times and seemed to run out of words after a few conversations. You see, we lived in the same general area, but we were so very different. She was a smart kid that came from a working family, and I was a kid from the projects who came from a family where living was work in itself.

During the next couple of days, I decided to pay a visit to my other grandma who lived in the same projects. Although I didn't have much contact with my real dad, the rest of the family seemed to accept me. I pulled my bike close to her door so I could see it while I was inside. I knocked pretty hard on the screen door although the main door was open. She had always told me, "My door is always open to you."

She motioned for me to come inside and immediately poured me something to drink. She also sliced me a piece of her famous pound cake. I sat at the table as she picked up the phone and said a few words. Minutes later, my Auntie Rose was coming through the door. She prompted me to get up from the table and gave me the biggest hug. She said that I was her baby. Both of them threatened that they were going to give me a "beatin'." I looked at them with confusion. Then my grandma said it was because I didn't come and visit them enough.

Aunt Rose had a soft, sweet voice, but when she spoke to my grandmother, her voice would almost raise to a yell. My grandmother had a hearing problem and wore hearing aids. Everyone who came around her knew that, so they would speak very loudly. She understood everything that was said, but she was probably also reading lips. As hard as it may have been for her to hear us, there was no problem with anyone hearing what she would say. When she spoke, people moved. She commanded respect from everyone around her at all times. Every time I went to her house, it was spotless and smelled so good, as she always had something cooking.

My Auntie Rose sat across the table from me and talked about my real dad. She said he was finally getting his life together. She went on to say that he had moved to Detroit, gotten married, and been clean of drugs for quite a while. She then told me that I had another sister whose name was Ebony, and a little brother named Randy, and I would be meeting them when they came for the holidays. I sat quietly and tried to let everything soak in. I really didn't have any emotional reaction to the information, as I really didn't know this man at all.

I stayed a little while longer before I got up, hugged them both, and was out the door. I picked up my bike and began to cruise toward my apartment. After I pedaled past one project building, there it was to the right of me. It was the biggest tree in the whole entire development. In fact, it may have been the only tree within the development. It stood almost in the center of the Heights, which was fitting because it always seemed to be the center of attention. I thought about the message I had recently heard at church where the preacher was teaching about the Garden of Eden. God said that the fruit of the tree in the midst of the garden you shall not eat, nor shall you touch, or you will surely die. My mother and grandmother made it clear to me that this tree was forbidden, and I was not allowed to go near it. But what was the forbidden fruit of this tree?

I had noticed leaves on the tree, but I had never seen a piece of fruit grow on it. What I did see was that it always had a lot of people hanging around it—no matter the time of day. Under the tree, people seemed to drink whatever refreshments they chose: forty bottles, half pints of gin, even a silver barrel-looking object from which they would squirt beer into their cups. And although no fruit grew on this tree, whatever the people who hung around it had, people were eager to get ahold of it. Cars waited in line to pull up to this tree. When one reached the front of the line, a guy would run up to the car, lean in the window, and exchange the forbidden fruit for money. And even though this was clearly a drive-thru, people were also allowed to walk up to get their order. I had even seen the high school kids with the new Saab (Boojie, E.T., and Ken Hicks) under the tree.

As I was passing the tree that day, one of the guys standing under it yelled out, "Hey, Church Socks! How is your mom? Tell her that we haven't seen her at the Yum Yum Tree for a while and she should come see us."

I hadn't said a curse word in all of my life up to this point as Grandma preached that we should always use respectable language. I don't know what came over me, but I put up my middle finger and started to pedal fast because I knew he would chase me. I had a little lead, but he was gaining on me and I was going as fast as I could. "Oh no!" I thought. Maybe that was a bad idea. He was just behind my back wheel when a white man pulled up to the Yum Yum Tree. The guy who was chasing me immediately stopped and yelled toward the tree that it was his turn to "hit a lick"—whatever that meant. I was just happy that the white man had showed up. The man who was chasing me called me a little punk and said he would see me later. I yelled back that he would be seeing my uncle later.

I couldn't say I was a straight A student, but I was wise enough to figure that this forbidden fruit that they were giving out had everything to do with what was wrong with my mother. I had actually seen her a few times talking to the people under the tree, and the fact that the guy said he hadn't seen her for a while explained why things had been so normal lately. I wasn't going to relay his message, of course. If I had had an electric saw, I would have tried to cut the tree down.

Again, I had no idea what drugs looked like or why people liked them so much, but I could see the effect they had on so many people in my neighborhood. The fact that I didn't have to look any further than my own apartment to see these effects really bothered me.

Rodney was on my front porch by the time I made it home. He laid his bike in the grass and was sitting on the steps waiting for me to arrive. I jumped off my bike, went over to him, and said, "What's up?" He took a few moments to answer. When he did, all I could do was keep silent and just listen to him. He began by telling me how he wanted to run away. He said his mother was never home, and when she was home, all she did was fuss at him. He went on to say that he had spied on her a few times when she was under the Yum Yum Tree. He saw her handing money to a guy in exchange for something that he could not see. I looked at my friend as his eyes began to fill with tears. I sat next to him and put my arm around his shoulders. We had fought many times, but when we really needed each other, we were there.

I gave him the chance to get everything off his chest before I spoke. I started by saying that everything he had mentioned had been happening to me. I reminded him of the fight we had at school, and said that the things he said about my mother seemed to be happening to his mother. I told him I knew that he didn't know what he was saying at the time and was just repeating something he had heard. I said our mothers are going through something very serious. I then went on to tell him how normal things had been lately and I was ready to tell him my secret. His eyes lit up and he gave me his full attention. I just said the word "prayer." He squinted his left eye, which was his favorite thing to do when he didn't like or understand something. I noticed the confusion so I explained a little further.

I revealed to him that I had been going to church a lot lately, and it was also something he should start doing. I told him that my grandmother said if I wanted something to change, then I needed to pray and God would answer my prayer. Therefore, every day I said a prayer for my mother. I didn't know if the job was complete yet, but I could tell that God was working on her.

Rodney looked down at his feet and said, "Are you sure that this works?"

I looked at him with confidence and said I was positive, and added that the key to praying was to believe it was going to happen. I told him that it was called faith. He then said he didn't even know how to pray. I told him that he should tell God everything he told me and ask Him to change things. Right there on my step, I grabbed Rodney's hand and he began to talk to God. When he finished, I gave him a hug and we slapped five. He said we would see each other at school the next day. That night I went to bed in peace, knowing that I had really helped my friend. I really believed that one day both of our mothers would be delivered.

The school year had started again, so I knew I had to get to bed early. I fell asleep for a few hours but woke up to get something to drink. Since I was the man of the house, I thought I'd better check to see if everyone was okay. I first checked my sisters' room, and they were sound asleep. Then I peeked into Mom's room, but she was not there. After checking the whole apartment, I realized that she was gone. I began to panic, thinking she would be gone a couple of days and I would probably have to miss school until I was able to talk to Grams.

I went back to my bed, put the pillow over my head, and started to whine to God. I told him that I thought He had answered my prayer, and that I even got Rodney to believe that it worked. My tears must have put me back to sleep. By the time I pulled the pillow off my head, my mom was yelling about how I hadn't left for school yet. I jumped up quickly, ran in the bathroom, wiped my face, and brushed my teeth. Oh well, wrinkled clothes once again! I was quickly out the door.

Mom had me thinking everything was normal because she had seemingly been home. What she was really doing was leaving while we were asleep. After a little more thought, I realized that God was working on her, but the work was not yet complete. I thought about how the refrigerator was now always full. Although Mom may have been sneaking out at night, she had not disappeared for days in a very long time. So right there on the way to school, I thanked God for what He had done so far, and I believed that He would complete it.

That day at school seemed to be pretty routine. Rodney was happy to see me since I had been a good friend. There's one thing we'd never forget about our neighborhood: It may have lacked many things, but one thing it didn't lack was the love we all had for each other. We stopped at Swamp's on the way home from school. It was another local candy store, owned by a short black man who wore a big apple cap like Super Fly. I also overheard that it was the place to go if you wanted to win the lottery. He was very nice to us kids and often gave us free stuff.

As smooth as the day had been, I should have known that would change by the time we got to the Heights. There were police cars everywhere, accompanied by a couple of ambulance trucks. If you saw an ambulance escorted by one or two cop cars, you could assume someone was sick or got hurt accidentally. However, when the ambulance was escorted by five or ten cop cars, then you knew automatically that someone was hurt really badly and it was probably on purpose. That was exactly the case now.

Before we could get up the hill by Ivan's corner store, my Aunt Bam and grandmother were approaching. Grams led me away from the scene and we went the long way to get to her apartment. When we got there, we could still see all the police cars and ambulances. I knew something really bad had happened when I saw the Channel 4 News trucks. They did not come around for anything good.

We went inside the apartment and Mom showed up shortly afterward. My Aunt Ron was crying, saying that he was a friend that she went to school with and was a good kid. I had no clue what was going on and the suspense was starting to kill me, so I finally asked, "What happened?" I had noticed that all the sirens and lights seemed to be surrounding the tree of forbidden fruit. I should have known that if something bad happened in the Heights, it wouldn't be far from the Yum Yum Tree.

My mom spoke up and said, "A high school kid named Jamont Neil was shot and killed."

"Mont Neil," I kept saying to myself until it finally registered. "Wait a minute," I said in a high-pitched voice, "isn't that our high school quarterback?"

My aunt responded, "Yeah," after blowing her nose.

"Oh, my," I thought. He was one of my favorite high school guys. He was always so nice to us middle school kids. Although he was from Second Street, he would always come to the Heights and throw footballs with us. Why in the world would someone kill him? In a town like ours, sports meant everything. Going to a Duquesne Dukes football game was everybody's highlight of the week. And if you were quarterback of the team, then you were like a god in the city of Duquesne.

I remembered that a few weeks earlier a couple of us kids didn't feel like walking to the Heights during our lunch break, so we just went to downtown Duquesne's famous diner called Richy's. Richy's had the best food in town and everyone went for their famous cheese fries. If you were a high school superstar, you ate free at Richy's. One day, my crew and I went down there hoping to run into one of our family members so they would buy us lunch. Mont Neil saw us standing in front of Richy's and told us to follow him inside. He whispered something to the lady working there, who looked like Flo from Mel's Diner. She told all of us to sit down and order whatever we wanted—it was on the house. Mont knew us from the Heights and probably knew that we didn't have any money, so he used his superstar power to get us free food. The kid always had a smile on his face. Why would someone do that to him? I would later find out that someone started shooting by the Yum Yum Tree and one of the bullets found its way to Mont. He probably wasn't even the target, they said. Mont took off running, and by the time they found him, it was already too late.

Things were already bad in the Heights, but they seemed to be getting worse. Now this kid, who was an all-American quarterback with so much potential, had his life taken over nothing. His whole childhood he had enjoyed running with a football in his hand and probably never imagined that he would be running his last sprint with a bullet inside of him. I could only hope that it was just being in the wrong place at the wrong time and had nothing to do with the forbidden fruit. But I had a question: Does a wrong place and a wrong time really exist with God? Jamont Neal was all over the news. He had the biggest funeral I had ever seen. His number 12 jersey was celebrated all over town. His death had nothing to do with that, because when he had life, he was already celebrated as a superstar.

Mareese Comer

As my mom had warned me weeks ago, my Uncle Mee-Mee finally moved in. He was my mother's youngest brother and they seemed to be pretty close. She had two other brothers, the oldest was Uncle Geno, who was away serving in the military, and the other was Uncle John, who was away serving time mandated by our judicial system.

Mee-Mee was the youngest, and he actually seemed to be very smart and responsible. He had graduated high school with honors, but instead of going off to college, he landed a job with Castriota Dodge. He was very proud of his job and would come home in his uniform with his real name "Eric" embroidered on the top left of his jacket. Now this may not have been a Fortune 500 career, but considering what most men in the Heights did for a living, Uncle Mee-Mee was living the life. He had worked so hard at his job that he started to get jobs there for some of his friends.

He drove a small Pinto that happened to be the same color tan as the pinto bean. Its paint job seemed to be closer to wall paint than one that was done in a spray booth. He didn't really seem to care. He just wanted to get back and forth to work. One thing I liked was that he always came home from work with a bag of groceries. And when he wasn't working, he had three guys that he always hung out with: Cornell, Earl, and Andre. Cornell was actually my other uncle. He was my real dad's brother. He was the neighborhood barber and could dance to any song that you played. Earl and Andre were also family. They were my grandmother's sister Gussie's two sons. Earl went off to the Navy, and Andre just seemed to hang around the Yum Yum Tree. But that was Uncle Mee-Mee's crew, and since he had moved in, I saw a lot more of them. It was funny that most people in the Heights were related in some way. If you weren't related by blood, everyone knew that everyone who lived in the Heights was like family anyway.

While my Uncle Mee-Mee made an honest living, Cornell made money cutting hair, and Earl was away in the service. Yet somehow, Andre seemed to have more money than all of them. He would always come around, as he and my mother seemed to be very close as well. He would pull out a wad of cash and hand me a twenty-dollar bill for no particular reason at all. Every time I saw him, he had on a brand new pair of tennis shoes with an outfit to match. I really couldn't understand his life, as he seemed to be free to do whatever he wanted and buy whatever he felt like. My Uncle Mee-Mee, on the other hand, got up at five in the morning to go to work and didn't get home until after seven. By the time he returned, all he felt like doing was grabbing a snack and sitting down on the couch until he nodded off. He eventually just went to bed to get ready for the same routine the next day.

I was so confused. I had heard the phrase "hard work pays off," but my uncle's and Andre's roles seemed to be reversed. Uncle Mee-Mee was working hard, but Andre seemed to be the one that was getting paid. I would hear Andre teasing my uncle sometimes, saying that he made his whole paycheck in one day and that he didn't have to answer to anyone. My uncle would pay him no mind and respond by saying, "Oh, you'll have to answer to more people than you think." Andre would laugh and offer my uncle a job to work for him under the Yum Yum Tree. He said he would triple the salary of what the Dodge dealership was paying him. My uncle would joke and ask him if he would give him benefits such as insurance, dental, and a 401k. Andre would just say, "Who needs all that when you could just purchase whatever you wanted with cash?" My uncle would then change the subject as if Andre did not bother him at all. I knew he was pretty strong-minded, but I could tell that Andre's words did have an effect on him. How long would he be able to withstand the temptation?

Mee-Mee dated a beautiful girl named Lolita from our rival town in sports called Clairton. She had the prettiest eyes—but those eyes also said she wasn't to be played with. She eventually moved in with us while she and my uncle waited for a vacant unit in the Heights. She had a brother named Omar who was a little older than me, so Mom allowed me to spend weekends over in Clairton. The more I went over there, the more I wanted to go back again.

Although Omar and I lived in different towns, we both lived in a housing project. Mine was Burns Heights and his was Millvue Acres. His project was a lot smaller than the Heights, but it was the exact same size when it came to activities. No, it didn't have a Yum Yum Tree, but it still had a drive-thru, and my guess was that their product was still the forbidden fruit.

I was introduced to some new friends, Joe Joe, Kenny Man, Terrill, and Jay Jay. While Burns Heights kids were still riding bikes and going on adventures, these Millvue kids had a different adventure in mind: Girls! We would sit in Omar's room and listen to the Beastie Boys. When the sun went down, we were off to the house of a girl named Nickyshell. Nickyshell would always be with her girl Cher and a few other girls. Her mom was always at work, so we would hang out there until it got pretty late. I enjoyed going over there as it was always filled with thrills and feels. Yeah, I had a lot of crushes on girls, but this was another level.

Omar and I became really good friends, and his mother Ms. Angela was exactly what her named spelled without the "A" on the end—an absolute angel. She treated me just like she treated her kids when I was there, and welcomed me to stay anytime I wanted. So, of course I took advantage of it.

My Uncle Mee-Mee was holding pretty strong to his word and was still working hard every day. Then one day it happened. He came home from work and slammed his jacket on the couch, complaining about how the white man was treating him. He said he had broken his back for his company for almost two years and they brought someone else in and gave him a higher position. He felt he was really deserving of that promotion. Just like clockwork, Andre walked in the door during his rant. He tried to kill the conversation, but Andre had already noticed something was going on. He walked over to Mee-Mee and asked him what was wrong. My uncle dismissed him, but Andre was way too persistent. Eventually my uncle gave in and told him what had happened.

I sat there on the couch pretending to watch *Heathcliff*, but I was paying attention to every word. Was he going to give in? Then Andre put his arm around my uncle's neck and said, "Come outside and take a walk with me so we can have a real talk." When I saw my uncle agree to go with him, I knew that nothing good would come of it.

Chapter Nine

The Move

"ALL I HAVE IN THIS world, all I have in this world," were the lyrics that could be heard from the music blasting in Uncle Mee-Mee's car. "I started small time, dope game, cocaine/Pushin' rocks on the block, I'm never broke mane/Sportin' jewelry and the s**t they came with rollin' hard/You try to serve me you'll get served, with no regard."

Yup, my Uncle Mee-Mee had given in to the temptation. As I was riding in his car with him, listening to a song by Scarface, I noticed some things. He had totally changed his image. He had traded in his work boots for some Timberlands, his work uniform for Karl Kani baggy jeans with pockets big enough to hold knots of money, and his work hat for a fitted Chicago Bulls cap. Last but not least, he traded in his pinto bean car for a royal blue Cutlass with candy paint so shiny that you could see your face in it. I was wondering if he had also traded in his soul. He had chrome rims that were so bright they flickered like one of those disco balls when he was driving. And now that he didn't have to leave the Heights to go to work, he and Andre were inseparable.

My other uncle traded in his nickname Corn-Peas for Corn-Waves, perfected the doo-rag and brush, and decided to hang up the clippers altogether and became part of the crew, too. Then Earl came home from the service and decided that being out at sea was a little too much for him, so he never went back. With that, the crew was official, and their headquarters seemed to be my living room as they always met up there.

Things really got uncomfortable when a few guys from Detroit started hanging around my house. There was a man named Larry who was always dressed up like a movie star. He spoke really smoothly with a low pitch, and something about him demanded respect. There were a lot of missing pieces to this puzzle that I didn't fully understand, but my young eyes were soaking it all in.

Mom would be around, but she would never complain about them being there. It was still a mystery whether God had completed His work on her, or if she did not have to leave anymore since there was so much activity around our house. I looked at these men and was able to see how much they had changed in warp speed. I could see all the glamour, but could not help but wonder how this affected my mother. I also noticed that my Uncle Mee-Mee began to drink, which I had never seen him do previously. The guys would sit around drinking, and my cousin Andre would always end up wanting to fight. Earl was built like a bodybuilder from his time in the service, so he would put Andre in a bear hug until he calmed down.

I remember one night when they were all at my house and started early on the drinks. Usually when this happened, my mother would send me to my grandmother's to spend the night, and my aunt would get my sisters and me. On the way out the door, I could see that Andre was already feeling the effect of the alcohol. He kept pointing his finger at my uncle as if he really had a problem with him. Earl did his bear hug on Andre, and Uncle Corn-Waves stood in front of Uncle Mee-Mee as my aunt rushed us out the door. Shortly thereafter we arrived at my grandmother's. Within minutes, Uncle Mee-Mee burst through the door yelling, "Andre is crazy, and he's got a…" *Boom, boom boom!*

My grandmother warned everyone to get down on the floor. The Independence Day-like noises were actually gunshots fired by Andre through my grandmother's front door. I looked over and saw Grandma on her knees praying. We heard a couple of yells outside that sounded like Earl and Corn-Waves. Then the gunshots ceased. Grams told us to stay down for a while, but my Uncle Mee-Mee jumped up in a rage and announced that he was going to kill Andre. As he was running toward the door, my grandmother stood in front of him and dared him to go past her. Right then I was able to see the strength in this woman's eyes. She told him to calm down. He was not to leave her house. Uncle Mee-Mee looked furious, but his stare did not frighten my grandmother. She would not back down.

There was a knock at the front door and a voice called out that it was Earl and he wanted to come in. He announced that everything was okay, and my grandmother slowly opened the door to let him in. He began to explain that Andre was really drunk and didn't know what he was doing. My grandmother snapped and asked if he could see the bullet holes in her door. What did he mean that Andre didn't know what he was doing? She asked if he could see all the people in the house—including the kids—who could have caught a bullet. A little while later, Aunt Gussie arrived and talked with Grams. The police showed up, and she and Grams told them that they did not know who fired the shots.

The next morning, Uncle Mee-Mee and Andre were sitting at the kitchen table with my grandmother. Whatever she said to them seemed to have defused the incident from the night before. Andre apologized a thousand times, hugged Uncle Mee-Mee, and told him that he loved him. Then he was on his way out the door. My grams suddenly yelled, "Not so fast there." She looked at Andre and said that she better have a new front door within the hour. Andre just nodded. He quickly came back with a man with tools. Just as Grams had ordered, the new door was hanging on its hinges within forty-five minutes.

Grandma had been complaining a lot lately about how bad it was getting in the Heights. When my cousin Andre went into his drunken rage, it just added to her already growing concerns. She had been spending more and more time at church, and had even started traveling with the pastors. When the church moved to Clairton, Grandma's mind was already made up. She had wanted to get away from the Heights and the church gave her the perfect excuse. She was very close to the Mitchells, who had been pastoring the church in Duquesne for quite some time. When they told her they were moving, Grams immediately started looking for a place to live in Clairton. She called my mother over and had a long talk with her about her plans.

I sat on the couch in the living room as they talked at the kitchen table. I had not been paying that much attention to their conversation until I heard the word move. I immediately tuned out the TV and gave them my full attention. Grams looked across at my mother and told her that she was tired of the Heights and felt that God was prompting her to get away from there. She said things were getting so bad that she didn't feel it was safe anymore. She went on to say that she had total faith that God was protecting her family through her prayers, but did not like how the children were exposed to so many negative things. A member of the church knew someone in Clairton who was willing to rent her a house, and her plan was to move at the beginning of the following month.

My mother sat there quietly with her head down and did not say a word. As I sat on the couch, my heart dropped. I could not believe my grandmother was leaving me. What was I going to do? Whenever things were going bad or I had a problem, I would always go to her. She was my safe haven. I really could not believe what I was hearing.

Suddenly their conversation shifted. My grandmother told my mother that she had not just called her over to share her plans, but also to let Mom know that her mind was made up. Grandma wanted to talk about my mother's future plans as well. She told my mother how much she had been praying for her. She said that she had noticed some progress and believed that God was going to totally set Mom free from drugs. She told my mother how much God loved her, and all she had to do was surrender to Him. He would help her get her life together.

Grandma said that she was worried about my sisters and me, and that if Mom didn't want to change for herself, then at least do it for the kids.

My mother had still not spoken a word, but I could see all the way from the living room couch the tears running down her face. Grams scooted her chair next to Mom and put an arm around her shoulder. She told my mother that she loved her very much and all she wanted was the best for us. Grandma then got up and walked over to her old-fashioned teapot. While pouring her cup, she revealed the real reason she wanted to talk to my mother: The house she was about to rent was pretty big and she wanted to know if my mother was interested in moving away from the Heights to Clairton with her. I immediately jumped out of my seat on the couch and yelled, "Please, Mom!"

Grandma began to laugh and said, "Boy, who was talking to you?" She instructed me to go outside and play while they finished talking.

I said, "Yes, ma'am," and slowly walked toward the door. Before leaving, I looked at Mom and said, "Please, Mom." But this time I said it with a very soft voice and pouty face, which always seemed to work when I really wanted something badly.

I was out the door and started praying that Mom would agree to Grandma's offer. Yes, I would really miss all of my friends from the Heights, but I could not imagine not being close to my grandmother. Plus, I had already made some friends in Clairton—not even counting the kids I knew from church. I was also excited about the idea of actually living in a house.

Although I wasn't privy to this part of their conversation, Grandma had given my mother a condition upon moving in with her. Mom had to start attending church with her on a regular basis. Grams also offered to take me with her if my mother didn't take the initial offer—something Mom would never have agreed to since I was so close to my sisters and was at times their primary caregiver. I was left in the dark for weeks, and not knowing my fate was killing me. I had bitten my fingernails down to the nub thinking about the possibility of Grandma leaving us there in the Heights.

My Uncle Mee-Mee had moved out of our apartment as his girlfriend Lolita had gotten them a place in the Heights. I was curious about how they would work out because they seemed to be doing a lot of arguing as of late. When he was working his old job, it seemed like they were the perfect couple, but when he took on his new destructive career, things started to go badly. They now had a daughter named Erie. My uncle also had an older daughter with a different girl in the projects, whom it seemed he just donated sperm for. I had never seen them together and he had never referred to her as his girlfriend. He also claimed that he wasn't even sure if he was the father. Too bad Maury's show was not around during that time. So Uncle Mee-Mee had two girls, Erie and Erica, and Lolita was now pregnant with his third child, which was a boy who would be named after him.

Lolita used to be the sweetest girl, but her pretty eyes turned the color of anger. My uncle's new lifestyle may have given her more financial stability, but she had to accept seeing less of him. They were always fighting, and she would accuse him of cheating with other women. Although I had never seen him with anyone other than her, the rest of his crew seemed to be sporting a new chick almost as often as they were wearing a new outfit. My grandmother always tried to talk some sense into Uncle Mee-Mee, but he would just say, "Yes, ma'am," and keep walking out the door. He would physically hear her, but paid her advice no attention.

Within the next week, we got a surprise visitor. It was my grandmother's oldest son Geno. I remember him walking through the door with his army suit on. He was still physically fit, but he had this look in his eyes that I would never forget. Grams was the first one to almost tackle him before he could even get through the door. She asked what he was doing home as she thought he wasn't coming until the holidays. He spoke with his head down as he informed my grandmother that he was home for good and not returning to the army. He said he would explain everything to her when they had time to talk. She didn't pressure him right then, but I could see that look of worry that comes over a mother's eyes when they just know something is not right with their child. Geno put his suitcase down and said he was going to see his baby. He was referring to his only child, my cousin Neak. No matter how long he was gone and what was going on in his life, he made it a point to show how much he loved her.

I wasn't sure if he had given Grandma the full explanation of his return yet, but the next day when I saw him by the tree, I knew something was wrong. The fact that he had brought his suitcase to Grandma's house was a sign that he and Neak's mother were no longer together for whatever reason. He continued to hang around the Yum Yum Tree. I also noticed that he had started to drink a lot. I was not really sure what the service life had done to him, but he did not come home the same.

Mom had been pretty quiet for a couple of weeks. I also noticed that she had not left the house at all —for anything. I even checked her room a few times in the middle of the night and she was always sound asleep. It didn't really seem as if anything was wrong. She was really nice to my sisters and me, but I could tell that she had something on her mind. Was it Grandma's proposal? I was afraid to even bring it up again as I had already asked about it a thousand times. Eventually, she warned me to stop asking her about it, but she said she would let me know.

That night I lay on my tear-stained pillow and decided to have another talk with God. "Lord, I thank you for everything you have done for me, and I thank you for working on my mother. And, Lord…let me just cut to the chase. Can you please make my mother accept my grandma's offer? Pleeease, God! I promise that I will start taking church more seriously and reading my Bible more. I know you can do it. My question is, Will you? In Jesus' name, I pray. Amen."

I had heard at church that Abraham negotiated with God to try to prevent Him from destroying Sodom and Gomorrah, so I didn't feel I

school? I thought for a second before it registered, and then yelled, "We're moving?"

She said, "Yes."

I instantly yelled, "YES!" as if it was an echo to hers.

She gave me a smile that was priceless, and told me that I could finish out the week to say good-bye to all my friends. We would be moving with Grams that upcoming weekend. She gave me a hug, and I ran toward my class. I made a pit stop at the boys' restroom. I went in and looked under all the stalls, but didn't see any feet, so I went into one of the stalls. Instead of sitting, I closed the lid and I got on my knees and said, "Thank you, God! You are soooo AMAZING!" I then heard someone walk in the restroom, so I flushed the toilet and pretended to wash my hands. It was Dirty-Meech and a kid they called Gadget. Gadget got his name from a TV show called *Inspector Gadget*. On the show, the inspector seemed to be able to fix anything. I wasn't sure this kid had that same power, but the way Dirty was talking to him it seemed that he was headed to fix something. They both gave me a head nod and I was off to class.

The next couple of days were bittersweet as I was really sad to be leaving my friends. We had been together since we were practically babies. I had some new friends in Clairton, but it would be very difficult to replace the bond that the kids from the Heights had made. On the other hand, I was very excited to be getting away from all of the drama in the Heights, and I never wanted to see the Yum Yum Tree again. I also took comfort in knowing that I still had a lot of family in Duquesne, so I would always be going back to visit.

Just like that, we were loaded up and headed down River Road. It was a road that most people traveled between Duquesne and Clairton. It was alongside the Monongahela River, which was one of the three major rivers that joined together in the city of Pittsburgh, and could be one of the scariest to drive on. Its snake-like roadway forced you to keep both hands on the steering wheel at all times. It was the only two-lane traffic road that was sandwiched between the river and the train tracks, and it reminded me of a roller coaster. No matter how many times you drove it, you still held your breath.

Shortly after leaving Duquesne, we passed through a town called Wilson. We knew immediately we were close to Clairton because of the smell. If I were to describe the stench as rotten eggs, I believe that description would be rather generous. Instead of bright lights and fancy buildings, Clairton looked more gothic than anything. It had one of the longest running steel mill operations, and production was still going on of some sort. The mill's massive and tall structures commanded your attention, and the smoke seemed to overpower the clouds. After a brief history lesson from the person hired to drive our moving truck, it finally dawned on me where the projects that Omar lived in had gotten its name, "Millvue." The projects sat on the top of the hill and the only building that you could see from there on the skyline was the steel mill. I had been holding my breath. I could not see how people got used to this smell. After letting out the air that I was holding in, we made a right up a hill and then another right onto the second street on the hill. Soon after, the driver made an abrupt stop and announced that we had arrived at our destination. We all jumped out of the truck. My grandmother had been following in a car behind us.

So there it was! It was the first house that I would be living in. I had lived in the projects since the day I was born, so this was a really big deal to me. It was a huge white house with a ton of windows, and it even had a big yard. My grandmother unlocked the door, gave us a tour, and told us where everyone would be sleeping. I could not believe this was happening. I hugged my grams and told her, "Thanks!" and she looked at me and said she didn't deserve credit as God had made a way for us.

We unloaded all the furniture. Grandma asked that everyone stick around the house for the next couple of days and help put everything in its place. By Sunday morning we were almost done, but Grams put everything on hold as she was not going to miss church. Mom had gotten up early and was getting herself ready for the service. She and Grams had gone shopping the previous week and she was looking really nice. I hadn't seen her in dress clothes since DAR-DAR's funeral, but today was a different occasion. DAR-DAR's funeral was a representation of death, and today Mom was clearly representing life.

"Glory, glory hallelujah. Since I've laid my burdens down, I feel better, so much better, since I've laid my burdens down." That was my grandmother, rocking side to side, banging her tambourine, and singing as if she was in the shower and no one could hear her. She didn't really care if she was off-key. And the fact of the matter was, when she got inside the church, she would tune everything out. It was just God and her at the service alone.

The Mitchells' church had a certain feel that made it very difficult to sit in your seat during the service. The band was orchestrated by all of their kids. It was Derek on the organ, Andre on the drums, George on the bass guitar, and the youngest son Teddy sitting next to Andre on the drums. He was clearly the next protégé. When the service really got going, Pastor Mitchell would grab the bass guitar from George, and his wife, Thelma, would scoot Derek off the organ. They would show us where all of their kids' talent really came from. Mom sat and bobbed her head, but she never got out of her seat. My aunts, Ron and Bam, and I were on our feet trying our best to stay on beat to the music, but Grams kept throwing us out of sync with her off-beat tambourine.

After a few more up-tempo songs, Pastor Mitchell grabbed the mic. The band seemed to be in sync as they slowed the music down to a soft worship melody, and Pastor Mitchell began to speak. He closed his eyes for a few seconds. When he opened them, he pointed his finger directly at me. My reaction was to look behind me. He had to be pointing at someone else. He then said, "No, you, young man," and then asked me to come to the front.

I slowly got out of the hard wooden seat and cautiously walked to the front of the church. I had no idea what to expect. He stood quietly for a few seconds with his eyes closed as if he were calculating what he was about to say. Pastor Mitchell spoke in a very calm tone and said that I was a special young man. He went on to say that I had a "calling" on my life, and that God was going to use me to bring many people to the Kingdom. He said that I would go through a wilderness stage just like the children of Israel had, but if I obeyed God, I would actually see the promise land. I stood there as if he were speaking a different language. I did not understand all that he was saying to me. One thing I was able to recognize was that he was saying almost the exact same thing that Pastor Carter had said a few years back down on the Heights basketball court during the outside service.

Pastor Mitchell told me to lift up my hands. He put some oil on his hands, palmed my forehead, and began to pray. I could hear my grandma's voice saying, "Thank you! Thank you! Thank you!" I couldn't comprehend what all of this meant, but I was sure of one thing. Whatever God had for me, I wanted. I was a little bothered by the wilderness stage Pastor Mitchell said I would go through since I was not a big fan of wildlife. I wondered if the wilderness that he was describing had nothing to do with wild animals and the jungle, but instead with the environment and the very people who I lived around. I had already promised God that I would do better if He answered my prayer, so at that moment I made up my mind that I would really try to follow Him.

At the next week's service, I came fully prepared. I had asked my mom to buy me my own Bible, and I also brought a pen and some paper to take notes like Grandma always did. If Pastor Mitchell called me up again, I would be prepared for whatever he had to tell me. So when the music went soft, I had butterflies in my stomach. But I discovered I was not his target this week. Regardless, his message had a definite effect on me. He looked at my mother and asked her to come to the front of the church. She had a shocked look in her eyes. She was hesitant but followed his directions. I heard my grandma yell "Hallelujah!" as my mother walked toward the front of the church.

Again, Pastor Mitchell was quiet for a few seconds as he calculated his words. He squinted his eyes and the words that he spoke seemed to have the power of a tidal wave. He told my mother that the fervent prayers of the righteous availeth much, and it was the prayers of her mother and her son that had her standing there right now.

"Wait a minute. How in the world did he know that I had been praying for my mother every day?" I thought.

He continued to speak to her and said he had named the church "Free Holiness Church of Deliverance" because he believed that it would be a place where people are delivered. He looked into my mother's eyes and asked if she was truly ready to be set free. She slowly nodded her head as he continued to speak. Pastor Mitchell asked her to repeat the Sinner's Prayer after him. Afterward, he said there was a condition to her deliverance, which was faith. He told her that if she had faith as small as a mustard seed, God could move mountains, and right there today she could be delivered from the addiction of drugs.

Before he prompted her to do it, Mom immediately raised her hands and began to repeat the words "thank you" over and over again. Pastor Mitchell first put oil on his hands, and then took the bottle and poured it over the top of my mother's head. Her whole body went limp so fast that the man standing behind her didn't have time to catch her. Pastor Mitchell went on with the service as if nothing had happened, and Mom stayed on the floor the entire time. As he was giving the benediction, my mother got up. She had a smile on her face and a look in her eyes that I hadn't seen before. Everyone rushed to the front of the church and gave her a hug as if she had done the greatest thing in her life. And in fact, she really had. From that moment on, Mom would never touch drugs again. No rehab, no AA meetings, no 12-step, no incarcerations, and no detox. This life change happened through the power of God. I had read about many miracles in the Bible, but this was the first I had seen in person.

Things became so great! Mom landed a job at a nursing home and never missed a day of church. She seemed to be more involved in everything that I did. I finally put the pads on again and signed up for middle school football. I was happy to be putting the equipment back on, but it was a little strange to wear any other uniform but that of the Dukes. Now I was a Clairton Bear. On the first day of practice, I was greeted by two kids named Terrill and Jay Jay who gave me a stern warning that I had better not give the playbook to the Dukes. I was still adjusting to a new group of friends. As much as I used to stay in Clairton over at Omar's house, it seemed like we didn't hang out that much once I moved there.

One thing that I really did enjoy was that Clairton had a large community pool. We would go there every day during the summer to swim. I'll always remember one particular day. I had been swimming for weeks and swam like an Olympic champion in the shallow water. I had not tried to swim in the twelve-foot deep section of the pool yet. But that day, I spotted a girl standing by the deep end. She was light-skinned with long pretty hair. Although I thought I could swim like an Olympic champion, she was actually built like one. I stood there and stared at her, hoping that she would look in my direction. Guess what? This time it actually worked. She looked at me and smiled, but then jumped off the diving board into the deep end. I looked at her with envy as I watched her swim to the ladder. Seconds later, she jumped into the shallow water where I was. I immediately splashed her with water and she just started laughing. She then asked me the million-dollar question: "Why are you swimming in the kiddie pool?"

I tried to think fast. I could not say that I was a chicken who was afraid to swim in deeper water. My hesitation gave her an opportunity to fill in the blank. She said, "Oh, you're scared," and started laughing at me.

I poked out my chest and quickly said, "No, I'm not."

She decided to call my bluff, jumping out of the shallow water and saying, "Come on then."

Mareese Comer

I remembered riding around West Mifflin on my bike, trying to find that other girl without an address to go to. I had been riding my bike singing a love song even though I barely knew the words. I still could not believe the power that girls had over us guys, but the girl in the pool was really, really cute. I took a deep breath and decided to follow her to the deep end. She went to the diving board and bounced on it a couple of times, then did a perfect dive into the water. It was bad enough that I was trying to prove my manhood by going in the water in the first place, but I was definitely not jumping off the diving board. After she climbed up the ladder, I took a deep breath and whispered, "God, help me." I did a light sprint and cannonballed into the deep.

I had practiced opening my eyes under water, so that would not be a problem, but I immediately sank toward the bottom. I paddled my way up to the top. As my head popped out of the water like a seal, it happened. I was so used to my feet touching the pool floor in the shallow end that even though my head was out of the water, I suddenly began to panic. I paddled as hard as I could but my body would not stay above the water. I started to choke on the water in my mouth and my nose was starting to burn. Then suddenly, I was able to breath and my head was above water again. Maybe God had saved me, or maybe I had figured it out—I wasn't sure which. But then I heard a lifeguard talking to me, telling me that I was going to be okay. She had her arm around me and gave me a floater to hold on to. After she pulled me out of the water, she took me inside the locker room and went through all the standard medical procedures to make sure I was okay. The pool staff then asked if I wanted a ride home. I begged them to let me stay and promised them I was fine. They made me sit in the locker room for a while and called my mother. After talking to her, they reluctantly agreed to let me stay.

I walked out of the locker room wondering, "Why had I failed?" I always swam in the shallow water without my feet touching the bottom for a long time. Just then the girl came up to me and apologized. She said she hadn't realized that I didn't know how to swim. I told her I was

116

okay and that I would talk to her later. I had something I had to do. I jumped in the shallow end and swam underwater for about twenty seconds without my feet touching. I got out of the pool and ran over to the steps on the diving board. I could see the lifeguard stand up on her post, waving her hands. I ignored her signals, ran, and bounced one time on the board and jumped as high as I could. I kept my body vertical and let my feet hit the water first. After almost touching the bottom of the deep end, I began to swim under water just as I had done in the shallow end. By the time I poked my head out of the water, I was already at the ladder ready to get out of the pool. The lifeguard was already in the water, prepared to save me. She quickly noticed what I had done and smiled. You see, I actually did know how to swim, but I had to get over the fear of deep water. That day I realized that fear can hold people back from a lot of things in life, but if a person believes that he or she can do it, it can be done.

I got out of the pool. The girl was standing there with a smile on her face. I looked at her, smiled back, and asked her if I could walk her home.

Chapter Ten

Game Related

MY GRANDMOTHER, MOM, SISTERS, AND aunts had moved away from Burns Heights to a city where we actually had our own street address instead of a unit number. And living in a house gave us a lot more privacy. I could even play hide-and-seek with my sisters and they would not be able to find me until I came out of hiding. Yes, we were very happy to be out of the projects, but I never anticipated when we were moving that we would actually live right across from another one.

Blair Heights was one of two housing developments in the city of Clairton. Although I had stayed weekends at the other one, this one was quite different. Its red brick buildings were situated on the left side as you went up a hill. On the right side was my street. Unlike Burns Heights, Blair Heights seemed to be more open to the public since there was really no entrance or exit. If you simply drove up that street, then you were actually in this project. At this point, I had never crossed the street and entered. I had been warned that I was not allowed to go over there. Although it may have been off limits for me, that did not prevent the project kids from coming to play on our street. Instead of playing tackle down at the field on grass, we now resorted to touch football on the cemented street. One of the things I quickly noticed that these kids had in common with the kids from Burns Heights was that nobody ever wanted to be at home.

The first kids who I met from Blair Heights were Flav, Hutch, and Biz. They accepted me right away and we would play touch football almost every day. We would also sit around and talk about the prettiest girls at school. Flav seemed to have all the inside information as to which girls were more advanced than others, and he would also promise me that he would hook me up with the prettiest girl in Blair Heights. He said her name was Pretty P. When I finally met her, I could understand why that was her name. She was beautiful! Flav never kept his promise, though. He said that Pretty P liked bad kids from the projects and I was just a church boy. He also told me that she was a little too much for me. I figured I just had to take his advice.

One thing that stuck out like a sore thumb was taking place right in the front of this project. Although there was no Yum Yum Tree, they did have a drive-thru, and it seemed to be busier than any drive-thru I'd ever seen—including McDonald's, Burger King, and Wendy's. You could combine the traffic at all three restaurants and it would still not compare to the traffic that drove past the front of Blair Heights. As I sat on our porch with a bird's eye view of this high-traffic operation, I figured out that this project was serving forbidden fruit even though there wasn't a Yum Yum Tree. And although Burns Heights was bigger in size, it was no comparison to Blair Heights when it came to volume. I wondered if the forbidden fruit was the same drug as the one sold at the Yum Yum Tree. Regardless, the supply and demand in this neighborhood seemed to be at an all-time "high." I would later learn that the drug was different. While in Burns Heights they used a glass pipe for their forbidden fruit, in Blair Heights people needed a syringe or a needle to partake. When cars approached these projects, guys would literally get in fights trying to take a customer's order. It could be the middle of the day or the top of the morning, it did not matter, and all this business was in plain sight. I sat there on my porch in amazement as I watched this chaotic scene.

I had escaped Burns Heights but now I was facing Blair Heights. Yes, it was good that I didn't live in the projects anymore, but I just couldn't seem to shake the atmosphere. Luckily, I found peace in knowing that I was more involved in church, which kept me busy and away from the streets. The biggest positive life change was that my mother had been totally delivered from drugs. And at this point, my life consisted mostly of school and football. There wasn't much time for anything else. Oh, except girls. I had to start making time for them, or better yet, they started making time for me.

One day I was in the lunch line waiting to get my tray and was getting teased by a girl from our church. She was doing an imitation of me from the previous night at church. She began by explaining how Pastor Mitchell had put his hands on my chest and I started to dance around the church like I had ants in my pants. She said it was so funny because she couldn't tell if I was being serious or pretending to be filled with the spirit. I didn't really respond aside from giving her a slight smile as if to say, "Please, shut up." I wasn't really bothered until I saw the girl right behind her with her hands over her mouth laughing at me. I looked at her and asked what was so funny, and she just looked back and laughed louder. I was a bit embarrassed, but what was actually comical was that I had seen this girl around school several times and wanted to talk to her. Now, just because I had been feeling the spirit at church the night before, she was standing in front of me starting a conversation. Look how God worked.

Our school's mascot was a bear, and she was one of the Honey Bears—also known as majorette cheerleaders. What made majorettes better than regular cheerleaders was that they wore bathing suits instead of cute pleated skirts with matching tops. She continued to tease me, and I quickly recognized that she was not shy at all. Her eyes were so beautiful up close, and she had a smile that was already making me melt. After the teasing went on for a few minutes, I jumped past the small talk and asked her name. Her smart response was, "Why?"

My smart remark back was, "Because I want to know."

She chuckled and then said her name was Amber. I quickly came back and said that was a beautiful name. I had heard the name a million times and hadn't paid it much attention, but I referred back to an earlier life lesson when I thought about how a name was only what you made it, and this girl made the name really beautiful. From that point on, we became friends. We never made vows as boyfriend and girlfriend, but there was an unspoken understanding that we really liked each other. I previously had crushes on girls but this was different. I wasn't sure if it was because I was getting older, or because this girl brought out something different in me. It was probably both.

When we weren't in class, she would be chasing me down the hall as if we were playing tag. Every time we were around each other it was an adventure. She made going to school fun for me. After school I would walk her home past the community pool, as close to her house as I could get without her family seeing me. Her family was actually our problem, in addition to the fact that we were too young to really know about dating and had cultural differences. Amber was Italian and came from a working family. Although at the time I had moved to a house, I was still a black kid from the projects. What was so special about our relationship was that Amber and I were blind to our differences. It was obvious, however, that her family would not accept it. Whenever there was a school function or dance, we would find our way to each other, but our bond always seemed to be a secret despite lasting for quite some time. We were never exposed to each other's family. Eventually, we both gravitated toward dating within our own cultures, but I still wasn't quite sure if that bond was really broken.

Mom started to give me a little more rope and gave me money to shop at Century 3 Mall. One weekend I was catching the bus with both of my aunts and a couple of friends from church. We weren't going shopping for any particular reason aside from hanging out with each other, but I would still sneak away at some point and try to collect a few phone numbers. We also enjoyed just going to eat together at the food court. This particular Saturday went pretty well until the bus ride home. When we got on, the comedy show immediately began. We were making fun of each other and how our parents would sing and dance at church. It was all fun and games until I decided to pull out a marker and draw something cool on the poster on the back of the bus. No one was paying attention until the bus came to a sudden stop. The marker flew out of my hand and my Aunt Bam fell off her seat and onto the floor. We looked out the bus window and realized that the driver had stopped. He wasn't even at a bus stop. In a deep, commanding voice he said, "Hey, wimp rag! Get off my bus!" We all looked around in confusion until he said, "You, in the blue shirt! Get off my bus now!"

I looked around and realized I was the only one on the bus with a blue shirt. Then I began to panic. He explained that I should not have been writing on his bus. I realized we had a serious problem. We were in the middle of Route 51 and this was the last bus running. I had no idea what we were going to do, as I knew they wouldn't let me get off the bus by myself. That's when my Aunt Ron walked to the front of the bus and I first recognized the power of intercessory prayer. I saw her put her hands in front of her body in a praying position and begged the bus driver not to kick me off. She told him that we did not have another ride and this was the last bus to Clairton. She said that I was sorry, and then looked back at me and quickly motioned for me to come to the front to say it myself. I looked at the driver and said, "I'm sorry, sir." He gave me a mean look and told me to never let it happen again. Then he pulled away. The comedy show was over after that, and we did not speak a word until the bus arrived in Clairton.

Grandma believed that making the choice to move to Clairton was a brilliant idea, but she was starting to realize that moving to this street might have been a big mistake. The more we saw how bad Blair Heights was, the more we understood that it wasn't much different from Burns Heights. In fact, it may have even been worse. People were always fighting to get to the cars that came through the drive-thru, and we could also hear gunshots from time to time. The good news was that my mom was working a lot and this new environment didn't seem to affect her at all. I believed that it wasn't the new address that changed her, but a change of mindset, and more importantly, a miracle from God.

I was in the dining room trying to finish my homework when Grams came in the house livid. She was complaining about how tired she was of how people acted in front of the projects. She said she had a talk with the landlord and decided to move to a different area in Clairton that was closer to the school. She said she had moved out of Burns Heights to get away from all the drama and didn't want to deal with it in Clairton. She said she would let us know when, but we were definitely moving.

Grams had dropped a bomb, but in the next couple of weeks Mom would launch a nuclear weapon. She gathered my sisters and me and told us that she had been talking to my stepfather over the phone for the last couple of months. He finally seemed like he had his head together. She said that now that God helped her get herself together, she could help him get back on track. She said she was very hesitant, but she really wanted to help him because he sounded like he wanted to help himself. She went on to say that he would be getting out of prison in a couple weeks. She was going to look for a place for us to live, so we wouldn't be living with Grams anymore.

My sisters just sat there in silence. They were too young to really comprehend what she was saying. Although I believed that Mom wanted them to know what was going on, the conversation was really for me. To be honest, I had no problem with what she was telling me. I liked my stepdad Ricky. When he was around, Mom seemed happy, and he always paid me lots of attention. I really thought he was a good man who was just bound by drug addiction, which led to a life of crime. The things he taught me as a youngster were all positive, because when he went on a drug binge, he would go away from us. My only real concern was whether Mom could withstand the temptation if he came back only to relapse. Would he drag her back into that destructive lifestyle? I knew that she was a very strong woman—and even stronger now that she had given her life to God. But was she strong enough to fight off drugs, the most powerful demon I had ever seen?

Mom informed us that she had told him that she was not going to live in sin. She gave him the same condition that Grandma had given to her: He had to give his life to God. She even added some extra spice by telling him that it was time to take their vows. One thing that I was certain of was that my mother really loved this man. If you took away his addiction, he was an excellent example of how a man should treat a woman. The question was, was he really ready this time?

Grams found a house a couple of blocks from school and was prepared to make the move from Blair Heights. She let us know that the move would be taking place within weeks. She found a smaller house because my mother had decided that we would try to mend our family. My Uncle Mee-Mee and his girlfriend, Lolita, had called it quits after trying their best to stay together. His life had become a life of partying and infidelity and she just couldn't take it any longer. So when he found out that Grams was moving again and that we were looking for our own place, he decided that he would move to Clairton with my grandmother. For some reason, Grams didn't give him the same ultimatum that she had given to my mother upon moving in. Uncle Mee-Mee ended up changing cities, but his lifestyle remained the same. It actually was enhanced, as he was then working out of two cities.

My Uncle Cornell made the move as well. He had connected with a girl named Bridgette and had two daughters with her. Therefore, the entire operation had moved to the Steel Mill City. Things got even crazier when they began to party every night. I would see them with a different woman almost every day. There were times when I would be at Gram's and they would be in the basement counting money. I would find a way to go down there to be nosy, but they would not make me leave. I would watch piles of money being counted on the bed. I had never seen so much money in my life, and I started thinking how I could do what they were doing when I got a little older. The thought of my mother's struggles had somehow escaped me.

The good news was that Mom had finally found a place for us to live, but the bad news was that she chose somewhere she felt she could afford until things got a little better. It was kind of hard to believe, but yup, we were moving back to the projects. This time it was the same project that I had visited many times before, Millvue Acres. It was where my friend Omar lived. I couldn't help but wonder why it was so important for us to get away from Burns Heights if we were just going to go right back to the projects. I had so many fears about this decision. I found a little peace in knowing that God was a serious part of our lives, but just as Pastor Mitchell had preached, "When you will to do good, evil will always be present." I was worried that, as good as we had been doing, the evil of the projects would affect us. Mom didn't seem to be worried at all as she was really focused on work. She had also developed a deep love for God. She was actually a brand new person.

We moved in a couple of weeks before my stepfather got out of prison. By the time he got there, Mom had already furnished the small project apartment. She had also scheduled a small wedding at the church on a weeknight—she was dead serious about not living in sin. My stepfather arrived and seemed to be really on his game. He immediately got a job and was attending church with Mom on a regular basis. As much as they had been through, it was amazing that everything was going so well. It wasn't too long before Mom was announcing that she was having another baby girl. Now, this was truly a surprise, and it would only add another bundle of joy to an already happy household.

My stepdad spent a lot of time talking to me about girls. He taught me how to iron clothes and even how to cut hair. I was learning so much from him. He always had us laughing around the house. He would also urge mom to cut me some slack as I was going to high school now and needed to be treated like a young man.

Mareese Comer

Brittany was born about seven months later and she was the prettiest little baby that I had ever seen. She instantly adjusted to our household and became the center of attention. She was my little Boo Boo, and I made sure I played with her every day after school.

My stepdad would come home from work and clean the whole house. There were times when he would even cook dinner for us. Yes, I was worried about this move, but it wasn't nearly as bad as I thought it would be. My family was intact and these projects were actually not as bad as the previous two to which I had been exposed.

Millvue Acres seemed to be full of life. Although I was certain that there were some of the same activities taking place, they seem to be hidden more than in the other two projects—or maybe I was just not paying attention. I did notice that it became a hangout for my uncles, and Andre and Earl would also come over from time to time.

I finally reunited with Omar, Joe Joe, and Kenny Man. They also introduced me to Phil and Carlos. These guys were already cool, but when I moved up there, I became part of the family. Even the troublemakers Terrill and Jay Jay lived up there. We spent countless hours playing touch football in the middle of the projects. And after we were done, we would go get a quarter Freezy cup from Ms. Honey. This place seemed like a cookout every single day.

Mom continued to make me go to church regularly, but I didn't mind as I had established my own relationship with God. So, besides football practice and church, the rest of my time was spent hanging out in the projects with the fellas. This is also where I finally realized that I could have girl friends without liking them in a certain way. I would later learn the term was platonic.

I hung out at the house of the project beautician, Ms. Geraldine, with her daughter Tia, her niece Kelly, and their best friend Rashida. This was our regular hangout. I also became good friends with this girl named Rae-Rae. She was a really cool girl and we always walked back from school to the projects together. I wondered why she liked walking

126

with me even though we didn't like each other in that way. I eventually figured out that I was just a designated book carrier and she would always hand me her books right after school. Despite the many negative things that went on in the projects, the positive was that it was really a community of people that treated each other like family. It was like living in a huge mansion where everyone was related.

High school was pretty fun, and I was finally getting back to the sport I loved. Football practice was like an after-school club. And the one thing that both towns where I lived had in common was that they were always competitive in sports. They were the two closest African American communities, so naturally they would become rivals. No matter what week Duquesne and Clairton played, it was like a high school Super Bowl. Both schools may have excelled in sports, but academics were a whole other story. Some of the best athletes on the team would be biting their nails toward the end of the season, hoping they were eligible for the last couple of games.

There was one particular teacher who would never be forgotten at Clairton High. Her name was Ms. Perry. She was a teacher not to be played with at all. She didn't care how good you were at sports. If you failed her class, then you were failing it. She wouldn't cut anyone any slack. She was one of the few African American teachers who was very serious about our education. She would give someone detention one day, and be nice to them the next day as if nothing ever happened. I guess she balanced out the newer teachers who really didn't care if we excelled in school or not.

I remember having a crush on a girl in her class named Tara. Tara was brown-skinned and tall with long, straight hair. She was probably the smartest girl in the class. I don't know if my crush came from the hope of getting some help with homework or the fact that she was cute. Whatever my excuse was, I worked up the courage to get her phone number. My stepfather would smile when he saw me talking on the phone about nothing. Tara and I talked a few times until I realized that her intellectual conversations were a little too heavy for me. The topic would shift to schoolwork when I just wanted to know her favorite color. I knew that I was really starting to like girls, but I was still trying to figure out what I liked about them—or more importantly, what they actually liked about me. I wondered if this was just an adolescent thing or an enigma that would last a lifetime.

I had been away from Duquesne for quite some time now. I really didn't stay in touch with my childhood friends, but I did occasionally stay on weekends with family members. Mo-Joe and Lump were also playing high school football. Lump, of course, was still playing the quarterback position. He had grown to be a giant, literally, at six foot six. He was also becoming a basketball superstar. Mo-Joe also stayed in the same position that he had played on the field in the Heights. His running back skills had gotten even better, and coaches were saying that he had the potential to break a lot of high school records. None of these things were a surprise to me. What did surprise me, however, was Bear. He never wanted to play football when we were growing up in the Heights, but somehow he had developed an interest as he approached high school. Coaches were saying that as a freshman, he had the best hands on the team, and his speed was blazing. He also joined Lump on the basketball team, so they were headed for great careers in sports.

Damien was still the same. He did not play sports at all. However, instead of being a tour guide for kiddie excursions, he directed his focus on becoming a ladies' man. He said high school girls were too slow for him and he had gotten the attention of a few adults. He was the smoothest talker I had ever heard. While I was having trouble learning how to communicate with a smart high school girl, he was drawing attention from grown women.

Ju-Ju was the only friend I hadn't seen at all. He had moved away from Duquesne to a nearby town. Bear told me he had seen Ju-Ju a few months back and he was still looking like a million bucks—except now he had all the jewelry to go with the fly gear. Bear also said that when he saw him, he was in a line at McDonald's. When he pulled out his money to pay for his food, his knot was the size of Mount Rushmore. All of my friends seemed to be doing okay—except for Rodney.

I saw it all on the news a few weeks earlier. My mother had to call me to the living room. She couldn't believe what she was seeing. Duquesne High School was surrounded by police cars and Channel 4 News was doing the broadcast. My mother hadn't said a word, but when they showed a picture of Rodney, all I could do was stand there with my mouth open, looking at our nineteen-inch tube television with aluminum foil on the antenna. The news anchor announced that he was named as a suspect in the shooting of another high school kid. They said he was already in custody and may be tried as an adult. I still could not believe what I was hearing. I knew as a kid that Rodney would pick fights, but I would've never imagined him shooting somebody. I thought back to the time on my porch when he had prayed for his mother. I thought about all the times we played together and how silly he was. I also thought about how determined he was to become a rapper. This did not make sense at all!

Rodney was sent off to prison for a very long time. I wondered if I would ever get the chance to see him again. Because guess what? I wanted to. No matter what had forced him to make that terrible mistake, I still knew the real Rodney. The real Rodney was a good kid who shared some of the same pain that I had in my eyes growing up. If I ever did get the opportunity to see him again, would he be a different Rodney?

Every time I went to Duquesne for the weekend, I would also hear about or see some sort of bad situation. About a month earlier, I had watched the police shove a head into the back of their car. That head belonged to the record-breaking scorer in high school basketball. Yup, it was Dirty. He had finally broken the record of all-time highest scorer at Duquesne High School. Unfortunately, shortly thereafter he obtained a record in the judicial system. There were so many stories like this of kids who were so talented but would fall victim to their surroundings.

That alone put an end to their dreams to be something really special. Were those loose wires and the gun in the glove box a sign when Dirty had given me a ride to school in the stolen IROC years ago? I did not understand why they were arresting him. I also couldn't understand what kind of temptation was so strong that he would abort the mission of having a very promising career. Sports were fun to play, but as Jay Z would later say, there was always "the allure of the game." And he was not talking about the game of basketball. If Dirty had had discipline, he eventually could have had his number printed on the back of an NBA jersey. But because he didn't, he instead had his number printed on the front of his shirt. Would this be a one-time thing or a cycle he would go through for many years to come?

I really did like staying in touch with my old friends and family, but the real reason I had a sudden interest to stay in Duquesne was girls. I had started talking to a girl named Kristy who lived in a development that was closer to the Kennywood amusement park. They called it Duquesne Place, and for some reason it wasn't looked upon as a project. But it operated the exact same way. I had to do a little research on our family tree so that I could find a family who lived up there to accommodate my stay. Through my digging, I was able to find that my cousins Duke-Don and Lance lived there with their mother, Pam. I had to take advantage of it. To show how good my research was, not only did Pam live in the same development as Kristy, she actually lived right next door.

I would beg Mom to let me go over there almost every weekend. Pam treated me like I was one of her kids. Kristy was a half and half girl who had a very outgoing attitude. At this stage attitude was kind of important, but what had me even more was that she really knew how to kiss. This girl really had my attention. Unfortunately, she was also getting attention from other guys. I remember being over at Duquesne Place one weekend and saw Kristy standing in the hall with this kid named Tony from the Cochran Dale projects. She had an awkward look on her face. Tony just smiled at me as if I wasn't a threat. As I approached them, I said, "What's up?" and gave her a hug. She gave me an after church hug, and then things went silent. Tony then spoke to her as if I wasn't even standing there. He reached in his pocket and pulled out a wad of money, asking Kristy when she was going to let him take her shopping. Kristy didn't respond, but I could see the smile on her face that said she was ready to go.

That whole weekend was pretty strange. She tried to convince me that they were just friends. I couldn't say that I was afraid of too many things, but I was definitely intimidated by this Tony. And it wasn't fair at all. I could barely scrape up enough money for lunch at school let alone compete with someone who was apparently selling drugs.

All that week this situation seemed to be on my mind. When my mother gave me money to go to the mall to buy Easter clothes, I had already figured out the plan. Mom's instructions were to take the $150 and find something nice to wear to church. I was okay following her directions, but I had to make a few adjustments. I took the $150 that Friday morning to our local bank and went inside to the counter. With a nervous look on my face, I politely asked if I could get some change. The lady smiled and said, "Sure, no problem." I placed the crispy hundred-dollar bill on the counter. The teller then asked how I would like the change. "Twenties, tens, and fives?"

I looked at her and said, "All ones."

She looked at me with a puzzled expression, making sure she had heard me correctly. She asked, "So you want one hundred one-dollar bills?"

I said, "Yes, ma'am."

She told me it would take a moment, and then relayed my request to another teller. Within minutes, she was back with my change. I took the paper bands off the ones and put the crisp fifty-dollar bill around them. I could barely fit the wad in my front right pocket, but to be honest, I really liked the feel of it. My plan was to go to the mall the following day to get my Easter clothes. But before that, I had to pay Kristy a visit.

I arrived at her house. She was a bit surprised and said that she thought that I had told her the week before that I was not coming over there anymore. I smiled at her and said, "How in the world could I stay away from your pretty face?"

She made a weird face, said "whatever," and walked to her room. I followed her in. We small talked a little bit, and then it was time to show her what was up. I reached into my pocket and pulled out the knot, asking if she wanted to go shopping. She immediately froze and looked worried. "Wait a minute," I thought. "Where is that smile that she had on her face when Tony pulled out his knot?" This was really weird.

Then she began to speak. She wanted to know where I got the money. I told her to not worry about it, but that's when she went off on me. She told me that the reason she liked me was because I was different than Tony and the rest of the guys. She said she was not impressed with drug dealers because they were eventually going to go to jail. I stood there in her room speechless. I had read this girl all wrong. I had embarrassed myself enough, so instead of staying the weekend I decided to just go back home.

As soon as I got in the door, Mom asked where my new clothes were. I quickly responded that I was going shopping the next day and had just gone to visit Kristy. Then Mom totally caught me off guard. She told me to give her the $150 so that I wouldn't lose it. I instantly fired back, saying that I wouldn't lose it and I would be okay. But Mom's eyes looked skeptical. She demanded that I give her the money to hold. I slowly reached into my front pocket and handed her the money. When my stepdad saw me hand it to her, he immediately busted out laughing so hard that he fell on his knees holding his stomach. Mom, on the other hand, did not think anything was funny at all. In fact, I saw a look in her eyes that said I was dead meat.

It did not take an explanation for Mom to figure out what I had done. She knew she had given me a one hundred-dollar bill and a fifty-dollar bill. She was also wise enough to know that the only guys who carried around wads of money were drug dealers. She slapped me across the face and asked me if that was what I wanted to be. I played stupid. Tears filled my eyes and I said, "What are you talking about?" She then raised her voice and asked me again. I stood there speechless, tears rolling down my face. My stepfather put his arm around my mother's shoulder to prevent her from committing murder and to calm her down. She went on to say that I was not leaving the house for weeks. Since I had to pretend to be someone else to impress a girl, I was not allowed to be around one for a while. She told me that she would get me what she felt like getting me to wear to church on Easter.

Was I really trying to impress Kristy, or was I actually becoming a monster?

Chapter Eleven

ROCKY MOUNTAINS

MOM WAS REALLY BEGINNING TO worry about me. The Bible stated that once a demon came to a house and found that house clean and all swept out, it would bring back more powerful demons with him. Mom's house was clean and swept, and she had totally been delivered from drugs, but her fear was that these demons had come back with more power and were targeting her son now. She had been completely oblivious to the things I was exposed to at an early age. But once her eyes had been opened, she made it a point to try to protect me from this deadly lifestyle.

She started to see a lot of little signs that I was headed in the wrong direction. She had even warned my uncles and cousins to stop giving me money all the time because I would only want more of it. More importantly, she didn't want me to think that it came easy. They didn't listen to her. I was their favorite. Not only was I good in sports, but also a tough little kid. Plus, I had a strong love for God, as there had been many seeds planted in my life. Would these seeds grow, or would they be choked out by the thorns or wilted by the blazing hot sun?

I had resisted the temptation of hustling for such a long time. Was it now becoming too hard to fight it off? Mom did everything she could to keep me from falling into the trap. She made me go to every service. She drove me to every football practice. She would even find things to do like skating, the movies, or any other event that would keep me busy, and then finally she played her trump card. She told me that she had gotten in touch with Danny Mangrum, the man who had started the Boys Club in Duquesne years ago. He was now living in Denver, Colorado. She told me that they had agreed that I would go to Denver for the summer. We all thought that traveling across the country by myself would be pretty frightening, but thinking back about how much this man had helped me as a kid gave me comfort. I thought about Mr. Mangrum taking me to visit my real dad in jail. And then I thought about how much this man had taught me about God. Yeah, I was starting to fit in a little better in the projects, but I didn't feel like I was doing so badly that Mom had to put me in a box and ship me off to the Rocky Mountains.

The school year was ending. I came home after class one day and asked Mom if we could talk about this trip to Colorado. She just looked at me with her nose turned up and said that there was nothing to discuss. My ticket was already purchased. "Wow!" I thought. "So now I don't even have a say in where I'm going." The teenager in me wanted to protest so badly, but the man in me realized that this might not be such a bad idea. And the kid in me recognized that it didn't matter what I thought when my mother's mind was made up.

Within the next couple of weeks I was dropped off at the Greyhound bus station. Mom had gone over a list of instructions about a thousand times. Based on the way I had been acting lately, she felt I was grown up enough to take the trip alone. She gave me a Bible, a couple of books, and a Sony Walkman radio. She had gathered up a nice chunk of money for me and I was on my way. As I walked through the Pittsburgh Greyhound station, I observed all kinds of people. There were people who had bags lying next to them on the floor but didn't look like they were going anywhere. I guess you couldn't consider them homeless if they slept at the bus station. You would think that traveling alone would have bothered me, but coming from where I was from, there would probably be nothing on this trip that would surprise me. Add in the fact that I thought I was pretty tough anyway, and this trip would be no problem at all.

Mom went to the counter and picked up my ticket. She walked me to the gate where my bus was taking off. She gave me one last pep talk and a hug. She teased me, asking if she could have a kiss. I turned up my nose while smiling at the same time. I wanted to say, "Silly rabbit, kisses are for kids." At least kisses from their mother anyway. I got on the bus and never looked back at Mom. I had been on several road trips, but this would be the first one on my own. I put on my Walkman and leaned back against the seat. "Colorado, here I come," I thought. I had no idea what to expect when I got there, but I was sure of a two things: I would definitely be attending church, and I would be in good hands. Mr. Mangrum was not someone who pretended to be a church member. He really had a strong relationship with God.

My first stop during the bus ride was in Chi-Town. I could already see how people were starting to look different. Mom's instructions were not to get off the bus unless I had to change buses. She went over the itinerary again and again, so I knew I would have to change in Chicago. I had an hour to waste, so I decided to go to a hot dog stand to try one of the city's famous dogs. I wore a look of confidence on my face so no one would see me as prey. I also felt secure because Grams had grabbed my hands in the car on the way to the bus station in Pittsburgh and prayed that God would keep me safe. I knew people felt that sometimes God didn't answer their prayers, but when my grandmother prayed, you could take it to the bank.

After Chicago we rode through Iowa and the cornfields of Nebraska, which seemed to last forever. During the ride, I read the book of Mark. It was about a man with a legion of demonic spirits, and the woman with the issue of blood. I also read parts of the book of Job where he lost everything, yet refused to curse God. I knew this trip was going to help me in many ways. For one, it definitely got me closer to God. And Mom was right. I did feel myself slowly but surely getting away from the things that seemed to be pulling me away from Him. I had heard a message at church a few weeks earlier out of the book of Galatians. The Apostle Paul was explaining how the flesh and the spirit warred against each other so that you could not do the things that you wished. This war was definitely going on inside of me right now. I hadn't even seen a view of the mountains yet, but I had already thought about how my life was going. It wasn't as if I wasn't trying, and I did consider myself to be a child of God, but the temptations in my hometown were getting really strong.

I arrived at the Denver Greyhound station and was instantly able to tell that I was in a way different place than the 'Burgh. I saw only a few black people that I could count on one hand. Instead of Timberland boots and fitted caps, I was now looking at cowboy hats and alligator boots. I grabbed my suitcase from under the bus and went inside the station to look for my ride. Within seconds, Mr. Mangrum appeared out of nowhere. He shook my hand as he greeted me and said, "Welcome to the Rocky Mountains."

I said, "Thanks," as he reached for my suitcase. I yanked it toward me and said I had it covered. I wanted him to know that I was not the little kid from the Boys Club anymore.

We headed toward his house and I began to finally take notice of the view. I could definitely understand why they called this place the Rocky Mountains. There seemed to be mountains everywhere. The view looked like a portrait. It was so beautiful! And unlike Pittsburgh, where you had hills and trees almost everywhere you looked, this place was wide open and flat. We got on the highway and I spotted Mile High Stadium to my right. I saw the big white horse on the front. Wow! I thought of the great John Elway. I didn't say much on the way, as I was still dealing with reality setting in. Mom had really sent me way across the world.

We pulled onto a street called Federal, and every single person that I saw looked like they were from another country. I had never really seen what a Mexican person looked like, but now they were everywhere. We stopped at a store to grab a few things, and when I heard a couple of people speak, I really started to feel out of place. Where in the world did Mom send me? And how in the world was I supposed to understand Spanish when I cheated on every single test that I had taken at school? We drove into Mr. Mangrum's neighborhood. Not only had I not seen any black people, but I also hadn't seen any white people, either. It was really weird. I quickly realized that he lived in a Mexican neighborhood. We pulled up to his duplex house. He occupied the front part and his mother occupied the back part with his brother Mark. I dropped my suitcase off inside his house, and then he took me next door to meet his mother.

Jannie Mangrum was a sweetheart. She welcomed me into her home as if she had known me since birth. I looked in the kitchen and she had already prepared a huge meal for my arrival. I also quickly took note of all the pictures and signs that made it clear that she was a child of God. Her husband had died years ago, but there was no sign that she was alone.

Feeling out of place would have been an understatement for me. Not only did I feel like I was in another part of the world, but I was also staying with people from a culture other than my own. Yes, I was used to Mr. Mangrum—he had really helped me in my younger years. However, staying with him for the summer was on a whole other level. When he lived in Duquesne, I remember him taking me to restaurants to eat, but there was no way these people's food would be even close to as good as Grandma's.

I sat at the table and Mr. Mangrum said grace. I put only teaspoons of each item on my plate, as I did not know how this food would taste. To my surprise, the potatoes had really, really good flavor. That gave me the courage to try the other items. By the time I was done, I had filled my plate up twice. Mrs. Mangrum was a real chef! What was even better was that she didn't just prepare my arrival meal, but actually cooked for me the whole summer.

The next morning as Mr. Mangrum was getting ready for work, he woke me up and said the table was set. "Table was set?" I thought. "It's seven o'clock in the morning. Had his mother gotten up that early to cook breakfast for me? Man, that was really sweet, but I will let her know that where I'm from, our breakfast during the summer was usually served around lunch time." I said, "Okay, thanks," but did not get right up. I heard the door shut, and he was off to work. After tossing and turning for a bit, I decided to get up since I could not get back to sleep. I had called Mom the night before and let her know that I made it safely, so today I would just relax and take some time to myself.

I got out of bed and went to the kitchen to see what was on the table for breakfast. To my surprise there was no food at all. Instead there was a note from Mr. Mangrum along with a whole bunch of newspapers with highlighting everywhere. There was also a twenty-dollar bill on the table. The note said, *"Good morning. I am glad you came to visit. I had a long talk with your mother and she felt that coming here might do you some good. I have highlighted several places in the newspaper where you could go and fill out applications for a summer job. I have also left money and a bus schedule. Keep in mind that you will be attending church on Wednesday nights and Sundays, so if you get hired, leave open these days. Hope this is a great summer for you as God continues to work in your life."*

I read the note three times, but the only words I could catch were "summer job." Summer job! Why had my vacations always translated to work? Last time it was in the blazing hot fields of the South, and now it was in the blizzardly mountains of Colorado. Mom had never mentioned this, but now I realized it was part of her plan. She stressed the importance of taking two forms of ID with me even though the bus station only required one. Oh well, I guess my day of relaxation was replaced by searching for a job.

So I got myself together and stopped over at Mrs. Mangrum's to tell her good-bye. She asked me if I had eaten, and I told her I grabbed a bowl of cereal. She told me to be careful and wished me luck. I walked out of her house embarking on a search for something that I'd never had before. In fact, I had never filled out an application. I realized that my mother was trying to send me a message, and trying to create a positive pattern for me to follow. Up to this point, almost every dollar that I had gotten had been given to me. My uncles and cousins would just hand me money for no reason. And from the looks of their lives, they never had to work hard for any of it, which is probably why they gave it away so freely. I was old enough to understand that there were pros and cons to everything. A pro to their lifestyle was that they were making a lot of money, but they were actually becoming the cons.

I had no idea how this would work, but I knew one thing about myself: If a challenge were set before me, I would do everything in my power to meet it. My first stop was at the Villa Italia Mall. I went around the food court and grabbed a few applications. I then noticed how pretty the Mexican girls were, so I figured I would fill out some apps and see if I could meet a few senoritas in the process. I walked around for a while and then I saw her. She had beautiful dark hair that went all the way down to her lower back. Her skin was as smooth as a baby's, and she had the prettiest eyes. And guess what? She was walking right toward me. I cut off her path and said, "Excuse me."

She looked at me with confusion. I then started talking but she cut me off and said, "Lo siento. No speak English."

"Oh my God!" I thought. I am really in trouble down here.

She smiled, stepped around me, and said, "Adios, amigo."

After that I was scared to approach anyone else in the mall, but my mission to get a job continued. I filled out a few apps the best that I could, but all I could put as previous employment was a summer job program when I worked at the fire station. I wondered if picking peas in the fields down south would look good on my application. After a few hours at the mall, I decided to walk down the main street toward the house before I jumped on the bus. Then I realized that I had been so busy looking at girls, I had not gotten anything to eat. I noticed a Wendy's about a block up on the left, so I decided I would go there to eat.

I went in and ordered my food. I sat by myself thinking about where I was and what I was doing. I wondered if anyone would actually hire me. Just as I was throwing out the trash on my tray, the lady behind the counter asked if I was from around there. I wasn't sure if she picked up on my East Coast swag or if there were just not a lot of African Americans in that area, which was probably the case. I told her I was from Pittsburgh, but I was here for the summer and looking for a job. She looked at me and said, "Today might be your lucky day." She handed me an application and I filled it out as neatly as I could. She called me the very next day.

You see, Mr. Mangrum and my mom didn't know whom they were messing with. Getting a job was easy for me. Reality was, God probably directed me to the right place at the right time. So here I was starting my very first job. Mr. Mangrum congratulated me, and I called Mom right away to tell her the good news. She told me that she was not surprised at all as she knew that I could do anything that I put my mind to.

I went to orientation that week and got my uniforms. Mr. Mangrum had to help me fill out a W-2 as I had absolutely no idea what that was. They started me out on the grill, and the first thing I recognized was that there was a real system to getting these burgers out the window. I would line up a row of raw square patties, and then rotate that row to the right until I ended up with about five rows of patties. The first row to my left being raw meat and the last row to my right being the meat that was ready to go on a bun.

I was given a schedule of what days and times I had to be there. I was told to be in my uniform of tucked-in shirt, belt, and work shoes. In order for me to be employed there, I had to follow their rules and adjust to the way things were done. I thought about my uncle and cousins back home, and how they seemed to have an abundance of cash flow despite the fact that they woke up when they felt like it, wore what they wanted to wear, and didn't seem to follow any particular kind of system. No one was telling them what to do—well, at least for the time being. I picked up on things pretty fast at work. The manager said that I had the greatest personality and the most respect that she had seen in a teenager in a long time. Things went well, and I continued to work there during the summer.

I also found a gym close to Mr. Mangrum's house and started working out for football season. I would be getting home right before camp. This was the year that I planned to really make a name for myself. None of the Clairton kids knew who Church Socks really was, so it was time to show them. I was confident in my skills, but I had to get my body in shape since high school football was at another level. I stayed pretty busy in Colorado. I worked most of the week, and on my days off I was at the gym. And oh, there was church on Wednesdays and Sundays.

On our first trip to Mr. Mangrum's church, I was really caught by surprise. We pulled up to what looked like a mall but was actually the church he attended. It was called Marilyn Hickey Ministries. This place was humungous. And it wasn't like there was a specific space in the building that was occupied by the church. No, the entire thing was the actual church. The sanctuary looked like a concert venue and every seat seemed to be filled. There were thousands of people standing and singing praises to the Lord. If you didn't know the words (which I didn't), you could look at their gigantic TV monitors on either side of the stage. The music was more contemporary and way different than I was used to, but it was very catchy. This place had a really soothing feel to it. When Marilyn spoke, she seemed to be teaching the word of God instead of whooping and hollering like they did at the churches I was used to back home, but by the time she was finished, she had the exact same effect on the congregation. People were rushing to the stage with their hands up and there were a lot of tears shed.

I always went to the main service on Sunday, but on Wednesday night I went to their youth ministry, which was about the size of the church I was used to. I did feel a little awkward, as I was one of the few minorities there. This was a predominantly white church. It was rather difficult to get used to the rock-style gospel band, but what I got used to very quickly was how they treated me. In their eyes, I was no different than them. Every time I showed up on a Wednesday night, several kids greeted me. And during the service, it was a sight to see teenagers really crying out to God.

I started to get more involved, and I really liked the feeling of peace when I was there. It was like everything that I had been through had been forgotten. I began to talk to God more during these services. They would also have some fun activities group discussions about what it meant to be a Christian, and what our responsibilities were to God. These were things that I had never thought about and just felt that my main responsibility was to simply show up for church service. I was learning that although going to service was necessary, I had to have a relationship with God every day of the week. I was soaking all this in and taking mental notes. I already had a strong faith in God as He had clearly answered a lot of my prayers. I considered myself to be saved since I had said the Sinners Prayer a few times at my church. But what I was now learning was how to have a real relationship with God—a relationship where we communicated regularly, a relationship where I took the time to learn and know Him through His word. Yes, I did read my Bible from time to time, but I knew that I didn't study enough to really learn what I needed to help fight off some of my strong temptations.

This church was way different, but I was actually starting to like it. I was learning so much that I had not paid attention to previously. It also made me realize that the reason I was starting to get out of hand was because I was slowly but surely slipping away from the church. I would make up excuses not to go. Although Mom used to make me go at times, she would always remind me that I was accountable for my own decisions and my walk with God. This trip seemed to be really paying off. I had a real job, I was getting bulked up at the gym, and I was really enjoying church.

Mr. Mangrum also took me to the mountains so I could see them up close. Man, was this a sight to see. If a person did not believe in God, they would change their mind after seeing His beautiful mountainous creations. We also went to the Royal Gorge, which had one of the longest suspension bridges in the world. This bridge was connected to two mountains. It was very scary to look down, but it was the prettiest sight I had ever seen. It was the middle of summer, yet there was snow on the peaks of the mountains.

That was the biggest misconception of Colorado. Many people thought it was the coldest state in the country. And while it was true that it often had snowstorms that would force people to stay in their homes for days, outside of the mountains, Denver seemed to have way better weather than where I was from. Back east it was humid in the summer, even at night. But in Colorado it cooled down so much at night that you didn't even need air conditioning. I had to say that I was really enjoying my vacation.

However, again as the Apostle Paul stated, "When I will do good, evil is always present." I had noticed the basketball court by the school a few times as I was walking to the bus stop, and usually no one was there. But one day I was on my way home from working a day shift and the court was full of people. Now, football was my passion, but where I'm from, you learned to play pickup everything: pickup basketball, pickup football, pickup Wiffle ball, and (of course) pick up girls. And that's what caught my attention. The court was full of guys playing, but there seemed to be cheerleaders on the sidelines in their regular clothes. I decided that instead of going straight home, I would meet some new friends. I stood there watching them play but had not said a word. Back home, I would be lucky to get on the court since we had phenomenal athletes who lived in the projects. But watching these Mexican kids play basketball made me feel like I was the next Michael Jordan. And that's what they began to call me after one of their friends twisted his ankle and they asked me if I wanted to play. Despite work boots and a Wendy's shirt, I decided to take the offer. After carrying my team to three straight victories, they accepted me as part of their crew. I even saw the cheerleaders whispering about me. It was amazing what being athletic could do.

After a couple of games, we exchanged names and I told them where I was from. Not only did they invite me to play ball, but they also invited me to hang out with them. At first, I just stuck with the basketball. But the more we played together, the more I wanted to hang out. I eventually gave in, and boy, was I in for a surprise. I don't know why I thought drinking and partying only happened in the projects and in black neighborhoods. I realized then that the same things happened way across the country within a whole different culture.

I walked into the house of one of my new friends and it was full of people. The music was blasting. I was surprised to hear they were playing the same rap music that they played in Millvue Acres. A couple of kids were sitting on the couch with beers in their hand and girls on their laps. I didn't really agree with the beer, but the girl on the lap looked like a pretty good idea. I then saw the crew in the kitchen that was clouded with smoke. "Boy, oh, boy," I thought, "what have I gotten myself into?" I kept thinking that I had seen these things at home and had never participated, so why should I do it when I was way across the country? I did end up taking a small sip of beer as I did not want to seem like a party pooper, but I knew in my mind that I was way out of place. It made me realize that Mom sending me to Colorado for the summer wouldn't necessarily keep me out of trouble since there would be trouble everywhere. I just had to make the choice. I still played ball with them, but limited my interaction to the hoop court. I did think one of my friend's sisters was beautiful, but she was only fifteen and already had a kid. Wow! I thought that only happened in my "hood." I was very proud of myself. I had faced strong temptation and was able to fight it off. I also felt like I had an obligation to God to at least try to do the right thing.

The summer was coming to a close and I had worked my last week at Wendy's. I stayed around the house and was starting to prepare my mind for the trip home. I remember lying on Mr. Mangrum's couch and all of a sudden hearing a bang on the door. What made me jump up was that I recognized that this was not a normal knock simply asking if someone was home. It was a knock that said something was wrong. I jumped off the couch and looked out the peephole. It was Mrs. Mangrum. She had a terrified look in her eyes. I quickly opened the door. She was waving me to hurry and come over to her house. She was talking really fast and I couldn't tell what was wrong.

Before she got to her door, she looked at me and said that I had to get a lady out of her house. *A lady in her house?* She then explained that when she went downstairs in her house, there was a lady on the floor. She said it seemed like she was really drunk and could barely talk. I wasn't sure how Mrs. Mangrum might have known this, but I was used to seeing people in the projects like that all the time. If Mr. Mangrum's mother was in danger, there was no way I was going to let something happen to her. She had cooked all summer for me. So I walked down the stairs in my project-mode and was prepared to defend myself if I had to. By the time I got down there, the lady was standing up. Mrs. Mangrum was right, she did seem like she had had something to drink. However, what Mrs. Mangrum couldn't recognize that I clearly saw was that this lady was under the influence of more than just alcohol. I had seen it way too many times. I guess she had apparently wandered into the wrong house. I asked if she was okay and then politely escorted her out of the house. Mrs. Mangrum thanked me a thousand times, and I relayed the story to Mr. Mangrum when he got home.

The one thing that I learned during this trip was that no matter where you went in this world, the same kinds of things were happening. This lady was clearly dabbling in the same forbidden fruit that they had back where I was from. Yes, your environment has a direct effect on your life, but those same temptations would be everywhere.

My time had run out and it was finally time to go back to the 'Burgh. I thanked Mr. Mangrum for giving me an opportunity to see another part of the country. I told him how much I had enjoyed myself and that I would probably be back next summer. He dropped me off at the Greyhound station with the same instructions that Mom had given me on the way there. Yup, I was on my way home. Return to sender.

Chapter Twelve

GAME TIME

I MADE IT BACK TO the 'Burgh without incident. I was very anxious to see my family. I hadn't really talked to anybody while I was in Colorado except for Mom, and Rashida, my friend from the projects, had written me a few times. We had become really good friends. We liked each other briefly in middle school, but we ended up developing a platonic friendship. Plus, she was into the older high school kids during that time. I was happy to receive her letters and quickly responded back. Besides them, I had no other contact with people from home, so I couldn't wait to see everyone. My mom told me that she was bringing my little sisters with her to pick me up. I was so excited to see Ash, Quel, and Boo Boo, as I called them.

Mom must have missed me, too, as she was there when the bus pulled up. I got off the bus and squared my shoulders as if I had been away in the service for a couple of years. I was bum-rushed with kisses and hugs. Grandma always knew how to make me feel good—she told me I had gotten so big. "Look at those muscles," she said. All I could do was smile. I knew what she was doing, but I actually did believe her this time.

We left the Greyhound station and stopped over in Duquesne at my Aunt Debbie's house. Aunt Deb was my favorite aunt. She was my grandmother's third child and was born after my mother. Aunt Deb always had a huge smile on her face. When you entered her house, instead of hearing gospel music, you heard Luther Vandross or Fred Jackson. I don't know if it was the music or what, but she was in a good mood the majority of the time. And if she was upset, you did not want to be at her house. In fact, you probably didn't even want to be in the city of Duquesne.

She was my grandmother's only child who had not migrated to Clairton. She liked Duquesne better. She had also chosen not to follow Grams to church, because she lived the life of the party. She had four kids: Maud, Corey, Little Greg, and Courtney. They stayed in Duquesne, but we all remained close because Grams would gather up all the kids from everywhere for church on Sundays. My aunt was also a very smart woman. She had furthered her education after high school and always seemed to land an excellent job. She never had a problem with drugs—or at least I wasn't aware of it. Alcohol, however, was the poison that she picked. We got to her house and, as always, it seemed like a birthday or holiday. She was always happy to see us. She knew I had been gone all summer so she ran to me with the biggest hug. We stayed at Aunt Deb's for a little while, and then we were on our way home to Clairton.

We pulled in to the projects and it seemed as if the place was on pause. Everything appeared to be in the same place as when I left. Some guys were playing touch football, same ladies were sitting outside of our building talking, and the same people were hanging out of their windows watching the action. As I was pulling my suitcase out of the car, I was attacked by a couple of my friends. They started to ask questions, but I told them to give me a minute and I would be back out to tell them about the whole trip. I got inside of our apartment and I was greeted by a very high-pitched scream. My stepfather said, "What's up, baby boy?" and the tone of his voice showed how happy he was to see me.

Honestly, I was happy to see him as well. When I was in Colorado, I was hoping that he and Mom were doing okay. I made it a point to pray for them every morning, along with making a few silent requests at church. From the looks of things, everything seemed to be intact. I told my family a little about the trip, and then said I was going outside for a bit. Before leaving, I asked Mom if I could go to the mall the next day so I could go school shopping. I told her that I had saved up almost a thousand dollars from working. My stepfather teased me and said, "Look at you, champ. Now you don't have to go to the bank and get no one dollar bills." I smiled and just shook my head as I realized that they would never let me forget that.

I went outside and all my friends were waiting on me. Rashida was the first one to yell, "Hey, friend!"

I responded by saying, "What's up, everybody?"

They asked me a million questions. I told them all the details of the trip. While I was talking, Carlos came out of nowhere and said, "Man, I have to talk to you, and it's very important." I looked at him with my squinty eyes, wondering what he was up to. I told him to give me a minute while I continued to talk to the rest of my friends. I could see the funny look on Rashida's face as if to say, "Don't even bother." But Los was my boy. We played football together and always seemed to be in the same classes. Plus, we always hung out together in the projects. I had to see what was up with him.

Before I walked off, Tia screamed, "Ohhhh!" as if she remembered something that she just had to tell me. She asked me if I had heard about Robb Brody.

I looked at Tia with a smirk and said, "How in the world would I hear about Robb Brody way over in Denver, Colorado?" I thought she was going to tell me that he made it big. He and two other kids named Easton and Neil had formed a rap group and had already recorded an album. They were a replica of Kid 'n Play as they wore high-top fades and always dressed alike. I looked at the faces of each of my friends and everyone looked sad. I broke the silence and said, "Well, are you going to tell me or what?" She then said he was murdered. "Murdered?" I thought. I immediately became sad because Robb was a really good kid.

150

He didn't live in the projects, but we went to the same school. He was definitely not the kind of kid who you would think something like that would happen to.

They gave me a few details about how he had been shot, and I could not believe what I was hearing. We automatically think that bad things always happen to bad people, but this was clearly not the case at all. I kept thinking, "God, why?" and then I remembered my grandmother saying to never question the hand of God.

Carlos was standing across the street, looking at me as if he were waiting for me to finish. I told the crew that I would be back after I found out what was bugging him so badly. I went over to him and he immediately started talking. He said that I had to talk to my uncle for him. Now I was really confused. Why in the world would he want me to talk to my uncle for him? He then explained that he had learned to hustle, and he needed to be connected. I looked at him like he was crazy and said, "You must be out of your mind."

He said, "No, I'm not at all."

He reached into his pocket and pulled out a knot that looked identical to what that kid Tony had pulled out when I was visiting over in Duquesne. He said if I hooked him up with my uncle, then he would show me everything he knew and I would make a ton of money. I looked at him and said that I didn't need to know what he knew. I had made almost one thousand dollars working all summer. He immediately busted out laughing and said, "All summer? Well, I made almost $1,000 for working just this week, and it wasn't even full-time." I was still resistant but his comment did trigger some thought. How did he make what I made all summer in just one week? I thought about all the rows of meat I had to flip to make that money, and here he was telling me that he did it while twiddling his thumbs.

I quickly changed the subject and asked if he was ready for football camp. He told me that he was going, but if things kept going the way they were, he might not even play. Wow! This was crazy. Then I explained to him that my uncle would kill me if I ever mentioned drugs to him. He had made it clear to me that he would give me money and buy my clothes, but I had to stay away from the street game of hustling and continue with the game of football. Los wouldn't give up. He still begged me to try.

As Grams always said, the devil was always busy. I hadn't been in the projects for an hour, hadn't even unpacked my suitcase, and he was already after me. I had to be honest with myself in admitting that I really did like the way that $950 felt in my pocket. The thought of earning that—well, I don't know if I could calling it earning—but making that much money in almost a week was pretty enticing. I thought about when I was a kid in the Heights and E.T., Boojie, and Ken Hicks were playing that song by KRS-One out of a new Saab. "Love Gonna Getcha" was the love of money finally catching up to me. The book of Timothy stated that the love of money was the root of all evil. I had been fighting off this demon for quite some time. Was it becoming too strong for me?

Football camp was the following week and I was really ready. I had been working out the whole summer. Some of the fellas teased me and asked if I was on steroids because "them guns were looking so right." Carlos kept his word and showed up for camp, but all he talked about was hustling. He bragged about how many pairs of Jordans he bought for school, and he had already gotten about a month's worth of brand new clothes. I had worked all summer and my uncle had even given me money for school clothes, yet my closet wouldn't be anywhere close to what he was describing. Camp went pretty well otherwise, and the coaches were starting to notice that I had a new pep in my step. I felt faster and stronger, and was prepared to have a great year.

But as I was feeling faster and stronger with the football pads on, I was starting to feel slower and weaker when I was in the projects. I spent all the money that I had worked all summer for, and I was trying to figure out what I wanted to do. Mom suggested that I get a part-time job, but it would have been impossible to play football if I worked. Why was it so important for me to have money all of a sudden? Was it having $950 of my own, or was it the cash that I had seen in the hands of guys who didn't seem to have to work hard for it? I had everything I needed. I had a project roof over my head and there was always food in the refrigerator. The truth was that I didn't need anything, but it was the things that I wanted that were becoming the problem.

Needless to say, I finally gave in. And once I did, things changed instantly. It reminded me of a Bible verse: "No temptation has overtaken you but such that is common to man. God is faithful, and he won't allow you to be tempted above which you are able. But with the temptation, always make a way of escape." Yes, the temptation was strong. I was not the only kid in this project who had this temptation, but I had many opportunities to escape. Why hadn't I taken them? I also knew that there were a couple of other friends who had also crossed over to hustling, so it was becoming the thing to do.

There was one exception, my friend Omar, who refused to have any part of this life. He would say with confidence that he would never, ever sell drugs. How did he have that strength? He didn't even go to church regularly. I later found out that when he was a young kid, his mother had gotten into trouble for selling reefer. The experience of the police coming to his house and arresting his mother was enough to scare him away from that lifestyle for good. So while I was making the vow to never use drugs, he was actually making the vow that he wouldn't allow drugs to use him. I really admired this kid. Here he was in the same projects as us with many opportunities to cross over, yet he had a strong enough mind to refuse it. I wish I could've said the same for myself, but I was standing in quicksand and sinking very fast.

I finally had the talk with Carlos that he had been urging me to have. I first made it clear to him that I could not talk to my uncle right now. He would kill me if he found out that I was doing it. I told Carlos that I would work with him on a small scale so that I could learn how things operated. I also told him that I could only do it late at night. I would lock my bedroom door and climb out of my window. My uncle would kill me if he found out, but my mother would… Well, if there was anything worse than death, that was what would happen to me. Carlos agreed, but only under the condition that I would eventually hook him up with my uncles and cousins. He said he was making good money, but he needed a stronger connection because he was paying too much and wasn't getting enough product to sell. I agreed, but was hoping that we would figure out something different, as I knew I could not approach my uncle about this.

The first night seemed to be pretty simple. I took a butter knife from the kitchen so I could lock my bedroom door the old-fashioned way since there was no lock on the doorknob. I lay on my waterbed waiting for my mom and my stepfather to go to sleep. They stayed in the living room watching TV pretty late. My other problem was that Mom's room was right next to mine. If she happened to look out her window, she could actually see me climbing out of mine. One thing I had going for me was that we lived on the first floor of our building. I was tempted to make my escape while they were in the living room, but thought it might be too risky, so I lay patiently on my back while floating on a balloon filled with water. It felt like I was getting seasick, but I was probably nervous about the mission I was about to go on. Should I abort the mission and just go to sleep? Before I could finish the thought, there was a light tap on my window. I pulled back the curtains and could see Los with his palms up to the sky as if he were asking if I was still coming. I whispered that I had to wait until my parents went to sleep before I went out, but I was coming for sure. He gave me the thumbs up.

I heard the television go off as if he had turned it off with his thumbs up signal. Okay, that was good. But I still had to wait a while until they fell asleep, or at the very least got comfortable. After about twenty minutes, I felt it was time to make a move. I slowly rolled off the waterbed without making a splash. I had already put on my clothes, but had the covers over me in case Mom peeked in to say goodnight. I grabbed the butter knife off the dresser and slid it in the crack of the door frame. I walked toward the window on my tiptoes and slid it open inch by inch until I had enough room to climb out. The funniest thing about being in stealth mode was that our apartment was right in the center of the projects, so anyone who was awake would clearly see me. That was the thing about doing wrong. Somehow you thought you were invisible, but that was only a perception of yourself. Everyone else could clearly see you. Working out over the summer really paid off as I climbed out my window in slow motion. I closed it behind me and was out. I then did a drill that we did at practice. I crawled on all fours so I could get past Mom's window. As soon as I stood up, I heard, "Boo!" It scared the heck out of me. I jumped like I had seen a ghost, but it was Los being the clown that he was. I bumped into his chest with my shoulder as if I was making a block for a teammate. It didn't affect him at all. He was still laughing about scaring me.

To my surprise, I saw a couple of other high school kids standing around like they were waiting for someone. Phil had on his hoodie with his hand inside it, twisting his so-called dreads. He looked at me and jokingly said, "Ewwww. I'm telling your mommy on you." I turned up my nose at him and followed behind Carlos.

We went into one of the project hallways at Millvue Acres, and I guess that was where my orientation would start. Carlos pulled out a plastic baggie filled with a ton of little pebbles that looked like Ivory soap. Each of these tiny pebbles was individually wrapped in plastic. He said the smaller ones were worth $10 and the bigger ones were worth $20. I was doing the math in my head. From the looks of the bag, I could see now how he was able to make so much money. He told me to follow him. He gave me about $200 worth of pebbles and said we would split whatever I got rid of. I held up one of the pebbles in front of me and thought for the first time about the light bulb-looking object that I had found in Mom's drawer many years ago. I just froze. Los looked at me and said, "What's wrong?"

I shook it off and said, "Nothing." Oh well, too late to turn back now. Within the first hour, I had gotten rid of everything he gave me and I was back for more. I could not believe how badly these people wanted these pebbles. Los had given me the spill on how to approach people. He would point out someone who was looking for forbidden fruit because he couldn't be in two different hallways at one time. It did not take me long to get comfortable, especially since I had seen a lot of these people around the projects.

There was one lady who I was not surprised to see. They called her Tub. I always saw her standing around the projects and walking with both hands on the collar of her shirt like she was closing it tightly so that no cold air would get to her. She always looked like she was cold no matter what the temperature was. And it very well may have been that the temperature had nothing to do with it. It could have been the condition of her heart. This lady had the biggest smile that I had ever seen. She was always so nice to us kids. We could tell something was wrong and knew she was bound by drugs, but somehow you were able to look past this and see that there was something more to her than what she was bound by. Tub was walking right past me when she suddenly stopped and asked what I was doing out so late. I thought about my words because I knew she knew my mother very well. She got impatient with my stalled response and started to walk off, but I quickly spoke up and said, "I'm holdin'." She immediately stopped and turned toward me. She gave me a disappointed look, but what I was holding seemed to have more power over her conscience. She pulled out a twenty-dollar bill and handed it to me. From that point on, she came looking for me at night.

By the time I climbed back in my window, it was five o'clock in the morning. I had given Los his split, and I was $300 richer than when I had climbed out of my window. I took off my clothes and pulled the knife out of the door, and then literally dove on my waterbed. I was so excited! I was making a lot of noise, but now I was home free if my parents woke up. Carlos was right. This was easier than I thought.

What was very difficult was the next day at school. My alarm clock still went off at six thirty in the morning, so I had to get up and get ready as if I had slept the whole night. And Mom would always check to see if I was gone in the morning. I could not show any signs of mischief, so I was off to school on time. I was doing my best to stay awake, but I kept nodding off. By the time I got to football practice, I might as well have been one of the blue dummy pads that we held up for drills. I went to one of the kids that worked as a trainer. His name was Jeff Wade. He was the coolest kid in the locker room. His older brother was our quarterback, so Jeff did whatever he wanted. He was a very hardworking kid who did a good job taping our ankles, and he did the store runs for us on his bike. He was also infatuated with cars. He was the only middle school kid who would shine your car like it was just freshly painted. I handed Jeff a twenty-dollar bill and told him to go get me something from the store to keep me awake. I told him to keep the change and he peeled off on his bike. He brought back an energy drink and it seemed to help a little, but I could tell I wasn't my normal self. I looked over at Phil and could see his dreads hanging out of his helmet. For some reason, he was his normal self. Maybe he was used to the night shift and my body just hadn't adjusted yet.

The next couple of weeks seemed to be the same routine. I was still climbing out of my window, and I was making a lot more money. I was becoming a regular face of the night shift. Somehow I adjusted to school. I had not missed a day, and I seemed to be able to maintain a good grade point average. Football, on the other hand, became a struggle. Staying up all night just didn't seem to fit with the physical workload that we had at practice. I still stayed on the team because I couldn't let too much change or Mom may have figured things out.

I still hadn't had the conversation with my uncles. I was too afraid. And I could tell by his cars and the way he dressed that Uncle Mee-Mee was making more and more money. He and Uncle Cornell started hanging out with this guy named Krafty. From the sound of his name, you knew he was someone who understood the streets. Krafty used to come over to my house with my uncles. He was really respectful to my mother. He would also give me money. My Uncle Mee-Mee started to trust me more, and gave me bags of money to put up for him if he didn't want to drive with it. I would never open the bags. I would just hide them in the house. He usually came back to get them the same day, but there were occasions when it would take a couple of days. He was completely unaware of my new job, so when he would give me money, I continued to take it or else he would think something was wrong.

I remember the day Uncle Mee-Mee pulled up in his Caddy in the projects and told me, "Come here." I jumped in the passenger seat. As he drove around the block, he handed me a bag and asked me to put it up for him. He would be back for it the next day. He said he was going out and didn't have time to put it up. I had no problem with it as I had done it many times before. So he dropped me off, and I put it up without a thought. Later that night as I was preparing for my shift, curiosity got the better of me. I wanted to know how much money my uncle had made that day, or probably minutes before he handed to me. I was only planning on staying out for about an hour or so that night because Los had already told me that we were low on product. I had no problem with getting home early. I really needed the extra sleep or I was going to be riding the bench on the football team. I opened the brown paper bag and could not believe what I saw. There were two bundles of money, but it was the white, golf ball-sized nugget in a plastic bag that grabbed my attention. I knew my uncle was well aware of what was in his bag, and I had no intention of being a thief, but I did have something else in mind. I couldn't help but think of why my uncle would even ask me to hold a bag that had drugs in it. I mean, I was okay with the money, but why would he give me this when I knew he didn't know about my late night job? My other question was, was this the first time the bag had drugs in it? Probably not! I sat there for a minute floating on my waterbed and decided I would do something that my uncle would either love me for or hate me for. Either way, I had to give this a shot.

I took the golf ball out with me. When I showed it to Los, his eyes just lit up. He asked where I got it. I told him to not worry about it. I just wanted to know if he thought we could get rid of it that night. He immediately said, "Yes," but explained that we would have to sell a little bit to the fellas so that we could get the money fast. He said it was about an ounce and looked like it was solid. I grabbed his arm, looked him in the eye, and told him that this had to work because if the plan backfired, I was dead meat. I also told him that if it worked, then he may get the wish that he had been begging me for. Then his eyes really lit up.

Before we got the chance to break it down into pebbles, we had already gotten $600 from fellow hustlers. It hadn't even been thirty minutes. Once people got samples of what we had, it spread like wildfire, and we had was cash to show for it. I asked Los how much he normally paid for an ounce and he said $1,000. We had almost $2,000 in our hands. I gave Los $500, took the rest, and climbed back in my window.

I knew I was taking a risk, but I had to prove to my uncle that I was ready. Instead of taking the other $500 and putting in the thousand that it would normally cost, I just took $200 and put the rest in his bag. I grabbed a piece of paper and wrapped it around the $1,300. I wrote on it, "Unc, I'm ready, put me on." When I gave him the bag, he would see that I got rid of his golf ball and would know I was ready.

Saturday morning after film at football practice, I was walking toward the projects when Uncle Mee-Mee's car pulled up next to me. He told me to jump in because he needed that bag he let me hold. I jumped in. He asked me about practice and I said it was cool, but had nothing else to say. His friend Krafty was sitting in the passenger seat and I was in the back. My stomach was starting to ache, and it felt like I had to go to the restroom. Before I jumped out, both of them handed me a twenty. This time I looked at them and said I was cool. Both of them had a look on their face like something had to be wrong with me. I jumped out, ran into the house, and grabbed the bag. I went to the driver's side and handed it to my uncle. He asked me again if I was cool. They started to pull off, but by the time they hit the second speed bump, I saw my uncle's brake lights. Then he put the car in reverse. I was about to run, but I thought if I was man enough to do what I did, then I had to be man enough to see what he had to say.

I knew he was coming for me so I walked slowly toward his car. Krafty opened the passenger door and they ordered me to get in. My uncle didn't speak for a while, so I thought I was either dead or he was putting me on. I quickly found out that neither of those would happen. My uncle didn't kill me, but he snapped out on me like never before. He told me that he would never put me on. He said that I was a talented young man and that I could go far in football. He told me that I was crazy, and that someone could have robbed or killed me. He said that he would never let me hold anything again, and I shouldn't have even looked in his bag. He told me if I needed anything, he had my back, but I was trying to play the wrong game. His friend Krafty just listened and didn't say a word. They drove me back around to the projects and my uncle said he was going to get me the next day.

Uncle Mee-Mee had a conscience and I knew he really cared about me. He also knew how hard my mother was trying to keep me off the streets. What he didn't understand was that, although I knew he didn't want me in that life, I was so influenced by his. And even though he may not have wanted to put me on, I was turned on by the way he lived. He and my Uncle Cornell had the nicest cars and the prettiest women, and always dressed to impress. How could a poverty-stricken kid not be impressed with that? They were clearly role models whether they wanted to be or not.

I thought about my other two uncles, Geno and John, who were older than my Uncle Mee-Mee. He seemed to have so much more than them. Uncle John couldn't stay out of prison, and Uncle Geno had come home from the service and fallen victim to alcohol and the forbidden fruit. One thing all of them had in common was that Grandma had instilled impeccable qualities that couldn't be ignored. All of them had a big heart like hers. It was just life choices that had spun out of control.

Although my plan may not have gone the way I wanted, and Uncle Mee-Mee refused to put me on, it did seem to grab the attention of his friend Krafty. When he was sitting in the passenger seat not saying a word, I thought it was just out of respect for my uncle. But he was just taking notes.

The following week Krafty approached me in the projects. He called me into one of the hallways and I thought he wanted to reinforce everything my uncle had told me. I was totally wrong. He told me that he really liked me and that I had a lot of heart. He said he admired what I did. He looked at me and asked me if I was really ready. I thought for a second. I figured he was trapping me, but I looked him in his eye and said, "I've been ready." I told him that I had already been hustling at night, but didn't want my uncle to know. He told me that he already knew. He saw me climbing out of my window one night and was tempted to tell my uncle, but it was none of his business. He thought I was climbing out to see a girl, but when he saw me talking with Chick, he knew what I was up to.

Chick Green was one of the favorite guys in Millvue Acres. People liked him because he was a really great person who had an incredible sense of humor. People would hang around him just to get a couple of laughs. Everyone knew he was bound by drugs, but everyone treated him as the person he really was. After my first couple of nights out, I recruited Chick to help me get rid of the pebbles. Every two pebbles he would get rid of, I would give him one for free. It also prevented me from having to deal with everyone directly. If Krafty had seen me climbing out of my window, I wondered how many other people had seen me, too. I was hoping that it never got to my mother.

Krafty reached into his pocket, pulled out two golf balls in a plastic bag, and handed them to me. He told me that he was only charging me $900 apiece, so I would owe him $1,800. My eyes lit up. I told him that I got him and I wouldn't let him down. That night I climbed out of my window, met up with Carlos, looked him in his face, and said, "Game time."

Chapter Thirteen

Mom Tried

Big said it best, "Because the streets is a short stop/Either you're slingin' crack rock or ya got a wicked jump shot." I had slowly been losing interest in the game I loved—football. And my jump shot was definitely not wicked. I held my own in pickup games, and looked like a superstar down in Colorado with the Mexican kids, but I had to be realistic. My jump shot was flat, so I guess I'd have to stick to the crack rock.

The night shift crew was even starting to hang out together during the day. Phil, Kenny Man, and Joe Joe lived the same life as me. Omar never indulged, but he still hung around us regularly. We all still went to football practice and hung around the projects in the evening. We never clocked in until late night when our shift began. There was also a kid who lived right outside the projects, who we called Big Amp. He was a guy who everyone envied because of the way he dressed. He had the latest everything and always had on a fresh pair of sneakers.

I had been hustling for months and had no problems at all. I wasn't sure if I had quickly gained respect, or if I was just the beneficiary of the respect that my uncles had already earned. That all changed as I was standing outside of building three and a very old man approached me. I had seen him around and remembered that they called him Mr. Malachi. He wore big, brown cargo pants with suspenders attached to them. He had a long, gray beard that reached all the way down to his stomach. His walk suggested that he had had some rough years. I was a little thrown off seeing him out late at night in the projects. I guess he must have known if I was out this late, then I must have been up to something. He walked up to me and whispered, "Are you holding anything?"

I furrowed my brow and couldn't believe that this old man was actually trying to shop. I was always taught to respect my elders, so I couldn't disrespect this man, but I really felt bad about serving him. He must have sensed my hesitation. He pulled out a balled up bill from his pocket. I couldn't tell what amount the bill was, but I could see that it was green. I finally spoke up and asked him what he needed. He responded with a strong tone and said, "Well, son, that just depends on what you have." He asked me if I wanted the money or not. He suggested that we step into the hallway so he could see what I had. Something was telling me to follow my instincts and run away, but I had gotten used to following the scent of money.

We entered the hallway, which I didn't really have a problem with as I preferred to do private transactions. He asked again what I had. I had gotten into the practice of wearing shorts under my pants. I would put a few pebbles in my pants pocket and leave the rest in the pockets of my shorts, along with most of my money. When I pulled out a few pebbles, Mr. Malachi immediately whipped out a long machete from his cargo pants. I moved my focus away from his weapon. I wanted to see if his eyes were cold enough to commit murder. He quickly looked away, so that told me he didn't really want to hurt me. He told me to give him everything. I had to think quickly. I wanted so badly to take a swing. It would not have been disrespecting an elder. It would have been defending myself. I reached into my pockets and emptied out the remaining pebbles. I handed them to him but didn't say a word. I was thinking, "If this man leaves this hallway, then there was no way he was making it out of the projects."

He must have read my mind. He reached into his other cargo pocket and said that if I made any fuss when he walked out, he would shoot someone. He showed me a shiny .32 revolver. I wondered why he used the knife in the first place if he had a gun. I guess he wanted to add a shock factor to the robbery. He walked out of the hallway. I still wanted to yell out to the fellas, but then I thought that if something happened in the projects that night, my secret life would probably be exposed. So I let him go without incident. When I told the fellas about it, they said I still should have said something when he left the hallway. I told them that I wasn't worried. He did not get the real stash, which was in my shorts pockets.

Carlos spoke up and said, "See, I told you that we need to buy some heat. If we had guns, we could prevent things like this." Part of me agreed. I did not like what had happened to me, but I did not like the idea of carrying a gun. I already had a guilty conscience about my job in the first place. Carlos didn't care what I thought. The incident scared him a little. He had already been talking about buying a gun because we were out late at night. He said anything could happen.

Within the next couple of nights, Los showed me his new toy. I had just climbed out of my window and was getting ready for my shift. Los had the hallway door open to Building Four. He was standing in the doorway and yelled for me to come over. I walked into the hallway and he closed the door. He then pulled out his new toy and pointed it at me. "Give me everything you got, including what's in your shorts pockets," he said. I initially jumped, but then knew he was not serious. The gun, on the other hand, was very serious and very real—even though it wasn't loaded. Plus, I knew my friend wouldn't hurt me—or anyone else for that matter—unless his life was in danger. But it still gave me chills when he pointed it at me. I pushed the gun away from my face. Los just laughed. I said to myself, "This guy is way too silly to be carrying a weapon." Los then told me that what had happened to me the other night would never happen again. He said we would pay more attention to each other whenever one of us went into a hallway. I couldn't argue with him as he had already purchased the gun. I was also a little bothered being robbed by a senior citizen with a machete.

Everything else seemed to be running smoothly. I had saved up a nice chunk of money, and I hid my new shoes and clothes in my locker at school so Mom wouldn't ask questions. I also told her that my uncles still gave me money, but that would only be believable for so long before she questioned them—especially since she didn't like them giving me money.

One night I was getting ready for my night shift and had to wait until my little cousin Derek, who my grandmother had been taking care of, fell asleep. He was spending the night at my house and Mom had sent him to sleep in my bed. It didn't take long for him to fall asleep, so I went ahead with my normal plans. I slid the butter knife in the door frame to lock my door shut. Now I had to be extra quiet so I wouldn't wake up Derek. I had gotten used to climbing out like I was a ghost and didn't make much noise. But for some reason, tonight I seemed to be making more noise than usual. I knocked over a paper cup full of change that was sitting on my window ledge. Derek rolled over. I thought I had woken him up, but he just changed positions. I finally made it out and peeked back through the window to make sure he wasn't awake. He was sleeping like a baby, so I continued with my mission. The night went pretty well. I got rid of everything except for one golf ball, which was about an ounce. Around three o'clock in the morning I was starting to feel pretty tired so I decided to turn in early. I climbed in my window and noticed that Derek was now sleeping at the opposite end of the bed. "Boy, he's a wild sleeper," I thought.

I took off my clothes and put the money in my secret compartment under the dresser. I lifted the top right corner of the water-filled mattress and hid the golf ball under it. I was so exhausted that I just jumped in bed and was out until my alarm clock went off. I slept past a couple of snoozes and then finally jumped up. I got myself ready for school. As I was leaving my bedroom, I noticed the butter knife on the floor by my stereo. I picked up the knife and couldn't remember if I had pulled it out of the door, or if I had forgotten to put it in the door frame to lock it in the first place.

I was almost out of the projects when I saw the craziest thing. It was a man named Denny who was outside Building Seven. As cold as it was, he had on only his underwear. I knew that just a few hours earlier I had met him in the hallway and sold him a few pebbles. I remember giving him a super deal since I was about to go in for the night. It was now seven o'clock in the morning. It also happened to be the time that most of the children left for school. I thought about my little sisters walking past and I decided to see what Denny was up to.

When I got to him, I noticed that he was smacking and scratching himself as if he were getting eaten alive by bumblebees. He started running around in circles, and then he picked his pants up off of the ground and started slamming them into the cement. I realized Denny was not planning to hurt anyone. He thought he was the one who was being attacked. I called his name a few times to try to help snap him out of it. He looked at me as if he had just noticed me for the first time. I picked up his pants, shirt, shoes, and socks and escorted him to the closest hallway. I assured him that there was nothing on his clothes and he would be okay. He sat for a few seconds, seemed to be gathering himself, and finally put on his clothes. After he got back to his senses, he looked at me and said, "Boy, whatever that is that you gave me is fire."

"Fire" was the term we used to describe something that was really good. I hadn't witnessed all the effects of drugs and how they affected people differently, so this was new to me. Apparently, when Denny got high, he felt as if bugs were eating him. I honestly had never given much thought to the effects. I was only worried about how fat my pocket was.

School was normal that day. I was anxious for it to be over because I had a few things to get done. I wanted to finish selling the last golf ball so that I could pay Krafty his money, and then buy my own product. Yup, it was time to start purchasing so I could get a better deal. I could also sell my own product at my own pace. I decided to go straight home and check in so I could spend the evening meeting up with a few friends.

When I got inside our apartment, all hell broke loose. Mom was waiting for me with a look on her face that said my life was over. She had her mouth poked out and both of her eyebrows were slanted in the middle of her forehead. Mom was light-skinned and had beauty marks on her face, but when she was mad, her face turned red. I looked at her and was really tempted to make an escape—I still had my hand on the doorknob. But she killed that thought by rushing toward me like a freight train that had lost its brakes and was picking up speed. She grabbed both of my shoulders and began to shake me hysterically. Then she slapped my face harder than I had ever been slapped before.

I really didn't know what to do. I figured since I had gotten a little bigger and stronger, I would just bear hug her so that she wouldn't hit me again. She started yelling at the top of her lungs and told me that I was the biggest fool she had ever known. I held her as tight as I could until my stepfather came running over and grabbed her, trying to calm her down. I looked at her and saw tears rolling down her cheeks. I was so in shock that I hadn't had the time to really think about what was happening. My stepfather told me to have a seat while he held my mother as she broke down crying in his arms.

My mouth poked out and I furrowed my brow. And when I saw Mom break down, my frown turned into an even sadder face. I thought about the last time she had broken down like that. It was when my sister Dar-Dar died—the event that had forced her into a wild excursion filled with drug and alcohol abuse. What had I done that had hurt her so bad? "Ohhh!" I thought, "she must know about my night job."

After she gathered herself, Mom told me that she wanted me out of her house. My stepfather chimed in and told her that she shouldn't say that because I would just get even worse. She went on to say that Derek had to use the bathroom last night, but he couldn't get out of the bedroom, so he started kicking the door really hard. She and my stepfather had to break the door open, only to find out that I was gone. "Ohhh," I thought. It was coming back to me. That's why I had seen the butter knife on the floor by my stereo. It had probably flown out when they broke the door open.

Mom said that one of the ladies from the projects had already told her weeks ago that she saw me late at night hanging with the drug dealers. But Mom did not want to believe it. So after learning I was gone that night, she said she waited until I went to school and searched my room. She found a bag of crack cocaine under my water bed mattress. She immediately flushed it down the toilet. Now that grabbed my attention! For the first time, I spoke up. I said hysterically, "Mom, why did you do that? You're going to get me killed because I owe someone for that." She raised her voice again, telling me that it didn't matter because I was going to die anyway, or end up in prison if I kept selling drugs. I had no response for her comment. Luckily, I did have the money to pay off Krafty in my secret dresser compartment. I would still have some cash for myself, too. But still, losing a whole ounce was a big deal.

What was even a bigger deal was something that I hadn't given a lot of thought to. My mother had been delivered from drugs for several years. I thought about how many tears I had cried while she was bound, and about how many times I had begged God to deliver her. I thought about all the times I had to take care of my baby sisters so they would be safe and have something to eat. I sat and thought about how angry Mom was. I could tell that the anger was no comparison to the hurt that she felt. She was sobbing like a baby in the same way she was when Grandma was holding her in her arms after my sister's funeral. The demon had tormented her for years. One of the main reasons she wanted to be free from drugs was because she realized all the hurt and pain she had put her kids through. She realized the weight she had put on my shoulders at a very young age. Those regrets would seep into her mind and she would feel sorry about what I went through. God had delivered her totally from this demon. She saw all the drug addicts and dealers regularly in the projects, and yet she wasn't even tempted to turn back to that addiction. It didn't even bother her, and that's why she was so sure of her deliverance. She had not abstained from drugs because she went away to rehab or prison. She had not attended regular meetings to stay clean. She did none of that. She was living in the projects with the demons but had the strength to put it out of her mind. I thought about how God had taken the drug out of my mother's hands, and after all these years, I was the one who put it back in her hands. What if she had gone into the bathroom after she found the crack, and instead of flushing it down the toilet, she decided to get high again and relapsed? There was no way that I would be able to live with that on my conscience.

My thoughts were interrupted by my uncles barging through the door like they were the police looking for someone. I knew these guys were far from the police, but I also knew the suspect was me. I wasn't sure how much my mother had told them over the phone, but they seemed furious when they entered the apartment. Before they got a chance to say one word to me, my mother turned her rage toward them. She told them that she couldn't believe they would ruin my life by putting me in the streets. I was so confused, but I was scared to interrupt Mom. Uncle Mee-Mee put his hand up and said, "Wait, wait, wait. I don't know what you are talking about, but whatever he is doing, it is not because of me. Yes, I was giving him stuff to hold for me, but I stopped doing that a while ago. I made it clear to him that I didn't want him to hustle. So let me make this clear to you. I did not give him anything to sell."

Mom suddenly went silent, trying to figure out whether she believed him or not. Uncle Cornell confirmed what Uncle Mee-Mee said. All of a sudden, all eyes in the room turned toward me. I wanted to imitate Scooby Doo and put my hands up and say, "I didn't know," in a barking dog voice. But I decided it wasn't time for games. I put my head down and looked at our worn-out black and gray linoleum tile while I spoke. I told my mother that they were telling the truth, and I had never gotten anything from them. I told her that they had tried their best to discourage me from the streets. They even made sure I had money in my pocket so that I didn't feel the need to hustle. I said they had not put me on, but in my mind I knew I had been watching them for so long that I was put on by their lifestyle. I told my mother and uncles that I had been put on by one of my friends. I did not want to expose my real connection, which was my uncle's friend Krafty. Mom didn't know what to say to my uncles, but she was still looking at me like she wanted to grab my neck. My uncles stayed for a bit and had a long talk with me about why I shouldn't be hustling. At the end of their pep talk, all I wondered about was why it was so bad for me to do it, but okay for them.

For the next few weeks, Mom watched me like a hawk. She even kept her bedroom window open so she could hear if I was climbing out of mine. After that day, I was really planning to stop. I met up with Krafty and paid what I owed him. I told him about everything that happened with my mom and uncles. I let him know that I didn't tell them I was getting stuff from him. He said, "Good." I figured that since I paid him off that would be the end of it. But Krafty looked at me and said, "I know you want to quit, but do you want to help me get rid of this last load before you quit?" He reached into the pocket of his quarter-length leather jacket and pulled out a baggie with the biggest rock yet. It was the size of a softball. I took a deep breath while eyeing the baggie, and then closed my eyes for a second to think. By the time I opened them, I had already grabbed the bag out of his hand.

I said, "Guess it's time to change my game."

I put it in my pocket and was about to walk out of the hallway. He grabbed my arm and said, "That's four and a half. Thirty-five hundred is what you owe me."

I slapped him a low five with a thousand in my hand, then looked at him and said, "Twenty-five hundred is what I owe now."

He smiled with the largest grin and said, "That's what I like about you, kiddo."

I was very serious about changing my game. Mom had me under surveillance, so I couldn't climb out my window. I had moved on to another level. Most of my customers were people I hung out with, so I could now take care of them during the day. I still made more money breaking it down into pebbles. I would stay at Grandma's on the weekends, and when she fell asleep, I had a whole house to sneak out of. I would then make my way to the projects late at night and hang out with the crew while making extra money.

One particular day would stick with me for the rest of my life. We had recently purchased pagers so that hustling would be more convenient. Los had paged me a few times after school to let me know he had a couple of things set up that night. I knew exactly what to bring. I arrived around two thirty in the morning and was equipped to fill the orders. I met with Los in one of the hallways and we got ourselves organized. Things were pretty calm for the next couple of hours—until Los went into the hallway with his cousin.

His cousin was a much older man who was also a partaker of the forbidden fruit. His habit didn't seem to affect his NFL-player build, and his thick mustache and beard prevented you from seeing his lips when he spoke. He and Los were in the building directly behind the one I lived in, so I tried to stay clear of the windows. But we had learned to always watch each other's back when one of us was in a hallway after what had happened with me and the old man with the machete.

I was standing out front waiting for the next customer to arrive when all of a sudden I heard a loud bang. Within seconds, Carlos busted out of the hallway and took off running toward the woods behind the projects. I couldn't figure out what was going on. Shortly after, I heard another bang echo from far away. I again thought, "Why does this guy have a gun? He is way too silly." I hoped Los was just goofing around as he had done so many times before. But not long after, we found his cousin in the hallway, shot. This was a total surprise to me. He and Los had been pretending to box each other outside the building before they walked

172

into the project hallway together. I knew Carlos well enough to know he would never intentionally harm someone—although he was always prepared to defend himself. He had the biggest heart and would never do that to someone, especially someone he was very cool with. This had to be an accident. Los had pulled the gun on me a few times, but it was all fun and games to him.

His cousin was pronounced dead. I never saw my friend Los after that. I paged him a million times but he would not respond. I wanted to tell him that everyone knew it was an accident and that he could come out from hiding so we could figure things out. I had heard he had a baby on the way, so I knew he would probably contact his baby's mother. Yet no one seemed to hear from him. This really bothered me, because he was my boy. We spent every night together, every day at school together, and every football practice together. We were practically around each other 24/7. I began to hope that maybe after some time had passed and things cooled down, Los would get in touch with me.

But all that hope was gone in one day as I was standing outside. The task force showed up at the projects and jumped out of their vans on everyone. It was a routine sting. They let out the dogs and were in pursuit of any drug dealer. I was lucky that I was sitting still with nothing but one hundred dollars in my pocket. Thankfully, I wasn't holding any drugs. It was broad daylight, and it wasn't my shift. Plus, I had taken some time off and had not been out at night for a long, long time since my boy disappeared. The police and the dogs headed toward the woods behind the projects. They apparently did track down a drug dealer, but unfortunately he was not alive. I was told that a dog found a body part down in the woods and it was later identified as Los. Now this really bothered me. I thought back to the night of the incident. Was that second shot I heard echoing in the distance the bullet that ended my friend's life? The way I saw him run toward the woods I knew something was wrong. Maybe if I had run after him, I could have stopped him from ending his life. This was something that would stay with me forever.

I had been taking it easy but had not totally quit hustling yet. Every time I paid Krafty his money, he seemed to have more product for me. And each time he handed it to me, I did not have the strength to say "No." I had already grown accustomed to buying what I wanted, so it was very difficult to turn back. I had so many negative things happen right in front of me, but I continued to have the "not me" attitude.

They say good girls like bad guys. I was standing in the center of the projects when a car pulled up. It was full of white girls. A guy from my school named Talley was in the passenger seat, and a kid named Tywon was in the back. It must have been my lucky day. Talley rolled down the window and asked if I wanted to come with them. I wasn't regularly hanging out with these guys at the time, but if you were from the projects, then you were cool with everyone who lived there or hung out there. And that was how I met Wendy. If I were judging from the first night we met, there was no way I would have been able to guess her background. She had two of her friends with her, Sara and Rachel. I couldn't really tell who was with whom, but my invitation only stemmed from there being an extra girl.

My first thought was, "What in the world were these three girls, who looked like they were straight out of prep school, doing in one of the worst projects in the Pittsburgh area?" My second thought was that they had picked two of the most unpredictable guys in the projects to hang out with. I was outside trying to make some money, but I figured I could take a lunch break.

Tywon ran into the apartment of the projects' beer distributor. It was a lady who sold 40-ounce bottles out of her refrigerator. He grabbed an arm full of beers and headed to Talley's cousin's house in the building across the street. Within an hour, the prep girls were wasted. Talley and Tywon disappeared into back rooms with two of them, and I was in the living room with Wendy. Yes, I had sipped a little beer, but I had never been a fan of losing control of myself, so I kept it to a minimum, about three or four sips.

I looked over at Wendy and something about this girl told me that she was just trying to fit in. She was so drunk that I couldn't understand what she was saying. She stumbled over to where I was seated and literally fell into my lap. At that moment, I had to make a choice. She was giving me every sign that she wanted something from me, but I couldn't tell if it was the alcohol or her personality. I had heard that alcohol brings out the real person, but the way she looked, and the fact that I wasn't even drunk, made me feel like I was taking advantage of her. I decided that this was a little out of place. Don't get me wrong, my flesh definitely wanted to react, but something inside me said I'd better not. I looked on the table and grabbed a pen. I tore a corner off the phonebook and wrote my pager number down. I stuck it in her front pants pocket and I was out.

In the next couple of days, I got a page from her. I called her back and she thanked me for being such a gentleman and not taking advantage of her. From that moment on, we started hanging out with each other regularly. My instincts a few days earlier were totally right. This girl was the daughter of a pastor in a church in South Park. She was very, very smart and had a voice like a songbird. I still wondered what the attraction was to a couple of project kids from some girls who clearly came from a totally opposite background. Were we their chance to live on the wild side? Were we their chance to act out against their parents and do something that they totally might have disapproved of? I did not have the answers to these questions, but I found out Wendy was a real sweetheart.

She was one of the nicest girls that I had met up to that point. I was around her family a few times, and she was totally attached to mine. My grandmother loved her and did not see color at all. She was also pretty close to my mother. I guess her feelings for me were stronger than the fear of the projects. This girl would drive to the projects, get out of her car, and walk to my apartment as if she belonged there. We dated for quite some time until I finally pushed her away from me. She didn't take that too well. I just knew in my heart that my lifestyle and the direction

I was headed would not be good for this amazing girl. She used to tell me that she was able to see the real me, and I admired her for that, because that was something I couldn't see myself.

Mom had been a little distant from me. She tried her best to continue warning me of the destruction I was headed toward. I wanted to listen, but it was so hard to break this cycle. I always thought that people were addicted to the use of drugs, but I was bound, too. No doubt I was an addict. Another reason Mom was really distant was that she had not only lost the battle with me, she had also lost the battle with my stepfather. He had been going to work regularly and going to church with Mom, and then all of a sudden he disappeared on one of his paydays and stayed away for a few days. When he came back, Mom gave him his final warning. She told him that she had worked way too hard to have to deal with him relapsing. She said that she had given him enough chances, and if he chose that life again, she refused to let him drag her down with him.

Mom was a very strong woman. She had made up her mind that she wasn't going to let anything make her turn back—not my stepfather or me. He disappeared a couple of weeks later. This time Mom was completely done. I'm sure there were times when she couldn't find the words for my stepfather or me, but one thing she could say was that she really tried.

Chapter Fourteen

Ballin'

"Up early in the morning, first to hit the block/Lil bad muthaf***a/ With a pocket full of rocks."

I was in my room blasting the stereo Mom had gotten me last Christmas. I didn't know all the words to 2Pac, but my favorite part was coming up.

"And they say how do you survive weighin' 165/In a city where the skinny n****s die?"

"I'm straight ballin'."

I took another break after everything that had happened with Los. I was trying to tell myself I was done, but my money was getting low. When all else failed, I went back to the scale, which was really needed now that I was selling weight. There was no more playing around with the pebbles. My clientele were no longer users. I was strictly messing with the hustlers now. Either way, I was still serving addicts no matter how I looked at it and how much better I felt.

I had been involved with a few girls around town, but I was so serious about making money that I avoided getting into a serious relationship. I was, however, involved in one that kind of formed unconsciously. Her name was Erica, and we had gone to the prom together the previous year. We never dated before the prom. In fact, I didn't even remember talking to her that much. Our prom date was excellent though, and we were matched to a T. I remember how much fun we had, but I was a bit distracted. Erica looked very pretty and her hair was done perfectly, but the fact that she wasn't my girlfriend at the time made it acceptable for my eyes to roam. And they were only roaming toward one place. It was Amber. She looked like a beautiful mermaid in her sequined gown. Her makeup was flawless and her body was…well, let's just say that she was the perfect majorette. We hadn't talked too much the past couple of years, but I still felt my stomach flutter every time I saw her. And I could not keep my eyes off her that night.

Then it happened. It was like I became a zombie and she had just cast a spell on me. I marched toward her with my arms straight out and my palms down. I got in front of her and I said, "Would you like to dance?" She didn't answer me, but the biggest smile came over her face as if she knew that moment would happen. So here we were at the prom with other people while holding each other like we were supposed to be on the date together. And the truth was that we probably could have been, barring our cultural difference. Erica may have been a little bothered, but she understood that we were not even a couple. We went to the after-prom picnic the next day. After that, Erica and I could not be separated. There was no note that said, "Circle yes or no if you want to be my girlfriend." We never even had the conversation about commitment. But we somehow knew that we suddenly belonged to each other.

Erica lived right outside the projects, so I would walk her home almost every night after she came to my apartment to visit. She came from a really close family who automatically accepted me. She lived with her grandparents, and her grandmother was a very sweet lady who did not play any games. In fact, I was kind of scared of her. Her grandfather was my favorite. He swept in front of their house every morning when I went to school. He teased me during the summer because I worked for the city painting sidewalks. He was retired, but he would always ask me if they were doing any hiring. He continued to ask me this well after I had worked that summer job. As wise as he was, he probably knew that I had taken on a new career in the streets.

Erica and I were pretty close as we spent a lot of time together when I wasn't on the clock. And she respected that as I showered her with gifts. Eventually, her cousin and I even became really cool. They called him D-Wee. The "D" came from his first name, and also because he was the opposite of a street baller or hustler. He actually had a wicked jump shot. And he was the best defender on our high school basketball team. Erica and I may have been together, but D and I were inseparable. We became more than best friends. We were more like brothers. We hung out with each other all the time. Although his main sport was basketball, he also played my kind of game: hardball. I wasn't talking about America's favorite pastime. D became a hustler. And since we both started having extra money, we became shopping partners. We would hit the mall or go downtown together to get the flyest gear.

I was well into my senior year and I was really "ballin'." And while I had finally let the street game win me over, my childhood friends were actually making a lot of noise. Lump, Bear, and Mo-Joe were the superstars of the Duquesne Dukes. People were saying that they had one of the best teams in the city of Pittsburgh. Lump was a six foot seven quarterback who had a rifle gun, and guess who his target was? Bear. This was the kid who never wanted to play football down at the field, but he was becoming one of the best high school wide receivers. Mo-Joe could finally say he was better than me. I used to score more touchdowns down at the field, but now he was scoring almost every time he touched the ball in a high school game. He would entertain the crowd with Heisman poses, and he would fall backward into the end zone like the Nestle Plunge commercial. The Dukes had not lost a game that year and were predicted to break the single-season record with a perfect season. I couldn't help but think what I would be doing had I dedicated myself to the right game. Yeah, I was making a lot of money, but did I really enjoy what I was doing? I was happy for my friends because they were having a ball doing what they had loved since we were too small to even hold the football with one hand. I was also proud of them for not falling victim to the strong temptation that I was bound by.

Rodney was still in jail. The way my mom put it, I would be following him if I were lucky enough not to have something worse happen. Damien was still a womanizer, and I heard he was also switching over to the game I was playing. I hadn't seen Ju-Ju in years, but I heard he was living a life full of fast cars and beautiful women—as he predicted he would as a young child. But Bear, Lump, and Mo-Joe were holding strong to their childhood dream of playing the game of football.

Mom had finally had enough of the project life. Things had gotten better, and she was moving away from Millvue Acres. She couldn't blame the place for her two fallen soldiers, as she was proof that you can overcome temptation. Were we just not as strong as her, or was it that we hadn't totally surrendered to God as she had? Part of her probably felt that had she not moved back to the projects then things might have been different. Oh well, one thing she had learned to do was trust God, and she still believed the Lord was going to prevail in the end.

Grandma and Mom teamed up and bought property right across the street from the high school. The one thing that I knew about my grandmother was that God continued to bless her, and she continued to be a blessing to everyone. I was not surprised at all by this new living situation. The property was two big houses that were fenced into one yard. Gram's house had five bedrooms and was situated in the front. Mom's was the three-bedroom in the back. You could go out Grandma's back door and after a short walk across the dirt yard, you would be at my mom's back door and the kitchen. I joked with my mom, telling her that now when she put me out, I wouldn't have far to run. She just gave me a look and shook her head. Then she said, "Oh, don't worry. In a few months when you graduate, you are definitely getting out for good." What she didn't know was that was my plan anyway.

After we moved into the house, Mom gave me the whole basement, which was like my own apartment. I could have company and she would never know they were there as I had my own door. After the first couple of days there, she called me up to the kitchen table. She said she had a few things she really needed to discuss with me. She said she had given her all to prevent me from becoming what I was at that point. And although she would never ever totally give up on me, she was turning me over to the hands of God. She went on to say that what was done in the dark would always come to the light. Selling drugs on the graveyard shift did not mean that I wouldn't be exposed. She put her head down, looking at the table, and said, "Son, I know you are worried about hiding things from me, but you are living a life that is so transparent, I can clearly see what you are doing. And guess what? The police are going to be able to see what you are doing if they haven't already. But most of all, God sees everything." She then quoted Hebrews 4:13 where it said, "There is no creature hidden from His sight but all things are naked and open to the eyes of Him who we must give account."

I sat there speechless, as I knew Mom always had the best advice for me. I knew very well that God's plans were not for me to become a drug dealer. She then shifted gears as if she were driving a '69 Chevy Chevelle with a 454 big block engine.

She picked up her head and said that she had contacted a Navy recruiter. He would be coming to the house in a couple of weeks to talk to me, and I had to make some decisions as my graduation was quickly approaching. She said that she didn't know how I was able to maintain my grades while living this life, but that showed her that at least I really did want something more. She said that if I didn't make a choice, then she would make it for me, but it would be college or service to our country. I told her to give me a little time to think, but I would definitely choose one of those. She then stood up, hugged me, and told me that she loved me and wanted the best for me.

I walked out the front door and all I could hear was the loud bass coming from the sound system of the best looking pickup truck that I had ever seen in my life. It was something that should have been on TV or in a lowrider magazine. Every thing that Mom had just said to me was zapped out by the music and flashy truck. The pickup was candy apple red with metallic speckles throughout the paint. It must have had twenty layers of clear coat on top of the paint as well because it was shining brighter than the sun. There was a custom black ragtop with a matching cab covering, too. On the back of its tailgate it simply read, "Parental Discretion is Advised," and on the front it read, "Butt Naked." It even had a name that any man would envy. The chromed-out wheels made me think about what the Apostle Paul experienced on the road to Damascus. I was blinded. However, my inability to see came from a different source. The Bible states, "The god-of-this-world 'Satan' has blinded the minds of those who believe not." Yup, I was blinded, but what I could see was the glamour that came with being a hustler.

I stood there with my mouth wide open. All I could think about right then was how I needed a car! I had driven many times before, and I was old enough to have a driver's license. Mom had taught me how to drive at an early age, but I never felt the need to get my license since I didn't have a vehicle. License or not, it was time to move on to the next level. I had money saved, but I needed to hustle a little harder in order to get a car that had the same attitude as the truck I had just seen. It belonged to a guy named Monty. He was the brother of a kid named Lance on my football team. Lance and I had been competing for a running back position, but when I started missing practice because I was playing the other game, he was the first one to tell me that I was getting demoted. Lance was a pretty talented kid. He had size and speed. He was tough—maybe because his hobbies included karate and martial arts. When he announced that he'd taken my position, it really didn't bother me. I knew I had a fat knot in the pocket of my shorts right under my football pants. Besides football, Lance and I had a lot in common.

Both of us were strongly influenced by the men in our families who were real hustlers, drove nice cars, had fine women, and earned a lot of money. His brother was known to always have the best lookin' cars or trucks in our town.

Lance also had an older cousin who had a Benz that I would never forget. It was midnight black with gold trim and wheels. The cousin was sent off to prison, but had left an impression on Lance's brother. I had never really talked with Monty, but I was planning to meet him now that we lived in the same neighborhood. He was obviously playing this game a lot better than I was and I was determined to figure out what he was doing differently. Monty was also pretty smart and was becoming a businessman. He bought a building and was remodeling it to become a local pool hall. He named it the Side Pocket.

The difference between Lance and me was that I had fallen knee deep in the game. Meanwhile, Lance held his ground and took the path of an honest living despite the strong influence to do otherwise. I decided to step up my game. I told Krafty that I needed more work so I could save up to buy a car. My stepfather was out of the picture so I had quickly become the man of the house again. My mother wouldn't take a dime from me if I tried to give it to her, but she couldn't stop me from spoiling my little sisters. I started buying them everything, and I would always take the time to do stuff with them and talk with them. They were getting older so I put the fear about boys in them very early. My sisters really loved me and I realized that they had a great respect for me, as well. I started to buy them gifts as if they were my little girlfriends, and the truth was that they were. I even encouraged Mom to sign them up for dance school to keep them busy. Brittany was still the baby so I was spending countless hours just playing with her. When I came into the room, she would just light up.

I graduated from high school. My mother said she didn't know how I did it. She thought it was a miracle from God to see me standing at the Bears stadium, throwing my hat into the air and holding a diploma in my hand. What Mom didn't realize was that I never disliked school. I just grew to love money. It didn't matter how late I stayed out at night, I knew that going to school was mandatory. And yes, I wanted to make Mom proud. I was a very determined person. If I set my mind on doing something, there was nothing that could get in my way. So my mother and grandmother stood proudly next to me after the ceremony for a picture. I was holding balloons. I looked at a couple of kids who had their mother and father standing with them. I thought about my real dad and my fake dad. Neither of them would be in my picture.

Erica and I hugged, congratulating each other for graduating. We gave each other a quick kiss that said we're allowed to be a couple, but not allowed to do the wedding kiss. She had moved in with her mother, who I really liked—particularly because every time I saw her she seemed happy to see me. She made me feel like she was happy that her daughter had chosen me for her boyfriend. I did have some concerns as to if we were really going to make it. One, she had gotten accepted to college and was going away soon. And two, my lifestyle was becoming way too hard to manage with a girlfriend—especially since I began to get way too much attention from the ladies. So we did our best as teenagers who really didn't understand the actual meaning of a relationship. We also never had consistent examples to follow in terms of what a relationship or marriage should look like. Yeah, we had grandparents, but they lived in a different era when relationships meant something different.

I honored Mom's ultimatum by deciding to further my education and go to school for business. I enrolled at a community college for a semester, and then transferred to Duff's Business Institute. I figured I was already running my own business, so I might as well learn how to operate a legit one. I already had the principles down pat. It was easy. You buy product at a wholesale price and sell it at retail. You had to factor in your overhead to be able to figure out your profit margin. In my case, my overhead included Timberland boots, gold chains, and new outfits. Oh, and really, really good food. I felt that I had this business thing figured out. What I needed from Duff's was unlike the business I was currently in. When you went legit, you had to follow rules. There were tax ID numbers, state licensing, and Uncle Sam to answer to. No matter what your product cost, you had to pay taxes, which was probably the major difference from the business that I was in.

Although we had moved away from the projects, I still hung out there regularly. I mean, why wouldn't I? That was my hood, and that was where my main source of income came from. Plus, I loved the people there. They were my family. And it wasn't just about the dope fiends, as we all knew each other. I took a liking to this kid named Frankie. He was a very respectable guy who was admired by all the kids around his age. He was very tough, but I was drawn to his personality. I started letting him hang around me and I started giving him money. I wondered if I was repeating the same pattern that I had gone through with my uncles. I did have the same intentions. I was just trying to keep this kid off the street. But was I actually feeding his appetite for money just as my uncles had done to me? Would he get to a point where he felt he had to hustle to feed it?

Just as I had planned, my pockets kept getting fatter and fatter. I was spending almost $10,000 of my own money on product, which was pretty good for a kid who spent a fortune on looking good. I had to wear a new outfit almost every day. And forget about wiping shoes off. I'd just go get another pair. People then began to look at me differently. I had no idea how money automatically equaled respect, how with respect came power, and how power allowed you to live freely to do whatever you felt like. That was one perspective at least, and what I felt like at this point was driving a new set of wheels.

There was a guy from a nearby city who used to come to our town to shop. I had what he wanted, and he had what I was looking for. I had something that was going to temporarily make all his problems go away, and he had something that was going to help me stop taking the bus and live up to this new image that I had. I wanted a 1986 luxury sport

Chevy Monte Carlo and he had one with only 30,000 miles on it. It was in excellent shape except that the right fender was gray and the rest of the car was white. I guess he had had a fender bender and had not had it repainted. I told him no worries at all. This boy was getting brand new candy paint immediately.

I worked out a deal where there was little cash involved. He walked away extremely happy, and I walked away feeling like it was a start. What I really felt good about was the way I negotiated the deal. I had control over the whole situation. I even walked away from him when I felt he wanted too much, but he called me back. That's when I figured out that the art of negotiating was simply patience. After completing the purchase and transferring the paperwork, the next place I drove the car was the paint shop. My boy Shawn was by far the best body man in the city. I told him that before I drove this car around, it needed a makeover. And, boy, did he do the job. He painted it cocaine white with a tan custom ragtop. I took it downtown to get the seats totally redone so that it matched the ragtop. Within weeks, the car had a whole new arrogant attitude. Then I took it to Voltaire's to get the sound system done. After the beats were bangin', I went to the mall and got some new kicks. I figured I couldn't just look out for me, so I went and bought the car a new pair of shoes as well. They were chromed out Dayton's with gold spinners and white caps to match the paint job.

Most people started with a small, cheap, get-around car that had issues starting up. It was something that just got them from point A to point B until they saved up for something better. But this was me. My motto was "If I was going to do anything, then it had to be done right." I couldn't ride anywhere without someone putting their fist up to their mouths as if to say that my car was the greatest thing they had ever seen. And that was the problem with us drug dealers. We failed to realize that although we got the attention of all the people who seemed to admire us, we also got the attention of people who really despised us, particularly the boys in blue.

Although we did private transactions, our lifestyles were heavily put on display. I had no problem spending so much money on the car as I had just had a long talk with Krafty. He told me that when he got back from his trip to Detroit, he was going to double what I had been getting. I was ready for it, too. I could hardly hold on to anything that I got from him. He said he would be back in a week or two and would hit me up when he got in. Before he left, I got the last of his supply, so it held me over for a little while. When I ran out, I would just take some time off until he got back.

Monty finally opened up the Side Pocket pool hall and it instantly became a hangout for us. This guy was really smart. The place was state of the art. He had all new pool tables and a huge jukebox in the back corner that never stopped playing music. It was always making money. He also served finger foods like nachos, wings, and fries. It became my favorite spot. I also became a pool shark in a short period of time. As opposed to betting, I was pretty much donating a $100 per game gambling fee to the guys who really knew how to play. So after losing probably a couple of thousand in a few weeks, my game improved drastically. I also liked the Side Pocket because it had become the place where the girls liked to hang out, too.

When I was away from the projects, unless I was on my way to meet someone, I never carried anything with me. However, since this became a regular hangout, I began to take a little something with me. I did this because I had gotten a couple of requests while I was there. I remember being up there one night shooting pool. I was playing against Monty and I was finally holding my own. Prior to this, he had probably taken enough money from me to start up another pool hall. A guy walked up to me named Juicy. He was not that much older than me and I had heard that he was partaking of the forbidden fruit. He leaned toward my ear and whispered, asking if I was holding anything. I found it a little strange, as the pool hall was flooded with ballers. I wondered why he chose me. I took my next pool shot and missed an easy nine ball in the corner pocket. I told Monty to keep shooting, and I motioned Juicy to the back of the pool hall.

The moment I pulled out my sack, he immediately grabbed it before I had time to react. Man, this guy was quick! My delayed reaction allowed him to get a couple of steps on me as he ran toward the door with my product in his hand. I chased after him while weaving through the maze of people who were standing in the pool hall. I felt like I was in pads again and cutting through the linemen trying to find daylight. By the time I got outside, I realized that I did not have a football in my hand. I was, however, still carrying the pool stick I had been using. When he was about three steps ahead of me, I saw him reach into his pocket. I thought he was trying to put something away that clearly did not belong to him. I had already put the pool stick on my right shoulder and had the look of Barry Bonds in my eyes. He suddenly stopped. As he turned around, he pulled his hand out of his pocket. I figured this was not the time to see if this was a ball or a strike, so I had to take a swing at it. By the time he was facing me, my wrist had already crossed the plate. I made contact and the ball was probably out of the park. The heavy end of the pool stick landed right across his forehead and he was down for the count.

I quickly searched for my product, but what grabbed my attention was his right hand. He was still holding on to an old .22 revolver. Part of the handle was missing. I snatched it out of his hand, dug in his pocket, and found my bag. I had lost so much money with this pool stick, but this night I seemed to recover every penny. The pool stick saved my life. Had I not had it in my hand, he would have had the opportunity to turn around and fire at me. From that moment on, I decided that I would only go to the Side Pocket for leisure, and would never try to hustle there unless it was on the pool table.

I finished up selling everything I had left and decided to take a break until my connection made it back from the D (as they called Detroit). Plus, I really needed to focus as business school was starting to get a little intense. To my surprise, I found out that what I actually knew about business was very little—especially when it came to operating a real business. In my line of business, there were no profit and loss statements, and there wasn't a budget sheet or a timeline. I went where I wanted whenever I felt like it. And when I wanted to purchase something, I did it without a second thought. In class, I was learning that there were two very critical things to manage if you wanted to have a successful business. They were time and money, which were the very two areas that a hustler easily lost track of. I was learning how to make spreadsheets and graphs manually. Most importantly, I was learning how to create an effective business plan.

Yes, I was very addicted to the life I was living, but going to school gave me some fulfillment, because deep in my heart I knew that hustling was not a very wise career. And although I felt it was my first choice, I knew that I needed a backup plan. My Uncle Mee-Mee had also gone in the direction of business. He opened up a convenience store in Duquesne called G-Service. They also performed a jitney, or taxi, service. I would go over there and tell him a few things that I had learned in school, but what I learned from him was that he wasn't trying to get rich off his store. Of course he wanted to make money, but this store was just a way for him to validate himself or exorcise his demons.

I had gotten into the habit of getting up early and going to sit with Grandma before I headed to class. By the time I got there, she would already have her Maxwell House brewed and her gospel music blaring. She would open up every single window in the house and go around watering all the plants that she had. She had names for all of them, and would talk to them as she pulled the dead leaves off. Then she would go to the fish tank filled with different kinds of species and drop a handful of food on top of the water. I watched how this woman functioned, and I admired the system that she had in place to take care of her home. To her, everything that God created was important, even the fish and the plants. She always told me that it was important to keep living things around her. She took care of the plants and fish just as well as she took care of the people around her.

I sat at her table, waiting for her to finish setting up her house for the day. Finally, she sat down across from me. She put a plate of breakfast in front of me as if I had been to the restaurant so many times that I no longer had to tell the waiter what I wanted. She knew exactly how I liked my eggs, and how much cream and sugar I wanted in my coffee. She started with a smile and said, "Good morning, baby!" She asked me how school was going and told me that she was really proud of me. She was well aware of what I was doing for a living, but she never condemned me. She told me many times that God's will was going to be done in my life, and continued to pray for me regularly. She believed that in the end He would get the glory out of my life. I did tell her about the incident that happened at the pool hall. She just sat and listened to the story. And that's what I really loved about her. I could be totally honest and still know that she would not judge me or love me any less. She was my homegirl, and our secret little breakfast meetings always made me feel good. After I finished my plate and stood up to go, she would grab my hand and drag me into the dining room to end our meeting with prayer. To be honest, I probably went there for that more than the food. I knew that the lifestyle I had chosen was not the smartest one, but I was wise enough to know that my grandmother's prayers were protecting me. It had absolutely nothing to do with having a pool stick in my hand. I jumped in my car, turned on my Def Sef CD, and was on my way to school. Def Sef was one of the best DJs in the city. He sold more music than I sold crack. And I was a fiend, as I bought everything he made.

After class I was trying to figure out what to do. I was totally out of product, so hustling wasn't an option. I decided to stop over at my uncle's store to see what he was up to. Business seemed to be normal as his cashier was busy checking people out. She told me that my uncle was upstairs, so I headed up the steps.

My uncle had purchased the whole building and occupied the apartment that was above his store. When I walked into his living room, all conversation immediately ceased. My Uncle Cornell, my cousins Andre and Earl, and he were all huddled up, sitting around his table with looks on their faces that said something horrific had taken place. They knew I was heavy in the game, but they still refused to deal with me. And I had no problem with that as I was getting as much as I needed. What they didn't know was that I had the same source as them. They were quiet for several seconds then Andre could no longer hold his peace as he said, "Man, I still can't believe that this happened."

My Uncle Mee-Mee chimed in and said, "Why would he try to drive back to Detroit by himself?"

Then it was Earl's turn. "And why did he decide to go so late at night?"

I heard all the questions that were without answers. I had absolutely no idea what they were talking about until Uncle Cornell said, "Yeah, and I heard he had a lot of money on him."

Then I started punching the buttons on the calculator in my head, trying to add things up. Detroit + late night + a lot of money = Krafty. Oh, wow! I had to confirm my thinking so I asked what happened. My Uncle Mee-Mee looked at me with his nose turned up like he couldn't believe I was in their business, but he answered me. He said that his friend Krafty was driving back to Detroit, fell asleep at the wheel, and was in a really bad accident. They said he had a lot of money on him, but that wasn't as important as the doctors saying that he could be paralyzed for the rest of his life. "Ohhhh, noooo!" I blurted out with way too much emotion in my voice.

All eyes were on me once again. Had I just blown my cover? My Uncle Mee-Mee was a very intelligent man who didn't miss anything, so he looked me right in the eye and asked me if I was getting my product from Krafty. It was too late to lie, so with my head high like I was a grown man, I looked in his eyes and said, "Yes, I was getting it from him." My uncle just shook his head. I wasn't sure if I would ever see Krafty again, but one thing that I had to do for sure was find a new connection.

Chapter Fifteen

GRADE SCHOOL REUNION

PASTOR MITCHELL PASSED AWAY. HE had been ordained a bishop some time ago. I had not been a part of his congregation for a while, but this man had instilled so much word in me as a young child. He had warned me many times that the streets would only lead to prison, addiction, or even worse, death. His wife and kids would carry on the church, along with his legacy, as his wife Thelma was a real anointed woman of God. Grandma continued to be faithful, but I was still on a detour and it was becoming really difficult to find my way back. No doubt about it, I was lost.

Just as I had feared, Erica and I began to drift apart. With her away at school, I had the freedom to do whatever I wanted, which came with the game I was playing and the life I was living. I visited her a few times as her school was only a couple of hours away. In spite of this, we had unconsciously grown apart. Maybe it was just the distance, or maybe it was just our age, or maybe it was just my lifestyle. Whatever the case, we never had a breakup argument or a long talk about making things work. It just naturally dissolved. She was a really nice girl who I liked a whole lot, but maybe I did not like her as much as I liked the person I was becoming.

Lump, Bear, and Mo-Joe ended up breaking the single-season football record of becoming one of the first teams to go undefeated throughout the city and state championships. They won at Three Rivers Stadium and went on to cruise in the state championship in Hershey, Pennsylvania, home of the famous chocolate. Lump would go on to accept a scholarship at Duquesne University, and it was no surprise that he would choose the sport that he became better at, basketball. He could have played either sport, but with his height and hoop skills, basketball became the logical choice. Bear got accepted to a school in Virginia, where he hoped his hands and speed would get him to the next level. Mo-Joe was wanted by a ton of schools, but he had to work on the academic part of gaining a scholarship. His skills were not in question at all, as he could have probably walked on as a starter at Alabama, Louisiana State, Ohio State, or any other school stacked with great running backs. He had size and deceptive speed, but most of all he had something that couldn't be taught: field vision. He had the patience to allow the play to develop, and when the hole opened up, it was a wrap. He was gone. His issue was making sure he had that same vision when he was looking at his textbooks.

Nevertheless, I was proud of my guys. We had been friends since we learned how to walk, and they were headed for greatness. Me, on the other hand, I was striving for greatness but my lifestyle was everything opposite of theirs. Damien was living the same life as me, but we hadn't crossed paths, as he seemed to stay to himself. I had taken some time off from hustling as I had planned, but I did not plan for my leave of absence to be extended a few extra weeks. After what had happened to Krafty, it was becoming very difficult for me to score. D-Wee knew a few people, so we were able to come up with a couple of things to keep us afloat. However, things were nowhere close to the way they had been just a short time before.

I started hanging out more at the Side Pocket as I was always searching for a new source. I considered switching over to a different game because I was running low on money. I had been talking to the first kids I met when I moved to Clairton, Flav, Biz, and Hutch. We had all started out playing touch football together and had all grown up to be a product of our environment. These guys seemed to stick to the product that was popular in their projects, which was the kind that people shoot up in their veins. I never understood their game. They always had some funny name for the drug they were selling. It came in so many different flavors, whereas my product was simply cocaine. Whether it was raw or cooked, it was still cocaine.

While I was searching for a source, these guys were not missing a beat. I was a bit skeptical, though. In their game, they seemed to have to deal with a lot of white people who they may have never seen, thus making themselves more vulnerable to sell to an undercover cop. Plus, the people who sold heroine seemed to go to prison way faster. What I needed to understand was that, fast or slow, if you were in the game—unless you retired—you were eventually going to prison. And even when some guys did retire, that ghost still came back to haunt them. So I stayed patient, hoping that I would get a new connection soon or convince my uncles to help me out since I was now grown. I felt like I was on the sideline warming the bench and yelling, "Put me in the game, coach!" I may not have been on my regular game, but my pool stick was supplementing my income really nicely. The more I played Monty, the better my game got.

One night I was really enjoying myself as I was up about $500 on a guy who thought he was Minnesota Fats. But the only thing that was getting fat was my pocket. The thing I noticed about gambling was that when someone was down, it began to show in their game. This guy was sweating and taking extra time on every shot, only to choke. I finally took his last hundred and was leaving the place $900 richer. I figured I would treat myself to some fine dining out by Century III Mall. My only question was, who was the lucky young lady who I wanted to join me? I had a couple of options to choose from. Ever since I bought a car and was able to get around, it seemed like dates were a dime a dozen. I slapped Monty five with a $100 bill in my hand so I could pay homage to the house, and I left the pool hall.

I headed to my car, walking a little fast because it was raining lightly and messing up my Timberland boots. Then I noticed that there was a car slowly driving to the left of me. I was on the sidewalk, but this car was driving at a snail's pace and the wheels seemed to be mimicking each of my footsteps. After the close call with the pool stick weeks earlier, I purchased a gun to defend myself if my life was on the line. You see, I knew I wasn't a guy who wanted to hurt someone. The way I operated was to be peaceable with all men when possible, but I had to be smart enough to understand that the life I lived and the cash I made automatically made me a target. That night I was prepared. No, I didn't want to hurt anyone, but I was not going to get caught slipping. I quickly reached inside the front of my jeans where I had the 9mm tucked. In one motion, I put my hand with the loaded gun in the front pouch of my oversized Karl Kani hoodie.

The car continued to follow me. What bothered me was that the driver had on a black hoodie that covered his head so I couldn't recognize him. The car he drove did not say he was someone who wanted to rob me, but maybe that was why he drove it. I kept my calm and looked straight ahead, and was only about ten steps from the driver's side door of my car. As soon as I put my hand on the door handle, the driver pulled up next to me and pointed an empty hand at me while pulling the hoodie off at the same time. I gripped the handle of the Glock and turned quickly, ready to fire. But as I was pulling it out, I saw the guy laughing.

I tucked the gun back into my hoodie, and from that moment on the game was really on. It was a friend, and he had a big smile on his face. I had seen all my other childhood friends pretty recently, and had heard so much about him, but hadn't seen him since grade school.

His car confirmed that he was doing every bit of what they said he was. It was a brand new black drop-top IROC-Z with peanut butter leather seats and chromed-out Daytons that had way too many spokes to count.

But yes, it was he in the flesh. Mr. Ju-Ju. I put the alarm back on for my car and jumped in the passenger seat of his. We hugged each other like there was no traffic behind us urging us to drive off. I was so happy to see him. I noticed that he was a little chubby compared to the little Ju-Ju I knew, but that must have been from eating so well. He pulled off and we talked. My first question was, "What in the world are you doing in Clairton?" I figured it could only be one of two reasons with him: money or women. He quickly and proudly said that he was dating a girl named Von. "Von?" I thought, but then said, "Ohhhhh, Voooon!"

He said, "Ohhhhh yeeaah, Voooon."

Von was a girl who I went to high school with and was arguably the prettiest girl in school. She belonged to the best athlete in school and that was hands down a guy we called Bo (because he really knew everything—especially when it came to sports). Usually there was a guy in each sport who claimed the title of "the best," but Bo claimed all three sports at our school. If it was football, then he was reversing the field only to run a seventy-yard touchdown. If it was baseball, then he was hitting a home run. And if it was basketball, then he was doing a reverse double-pump, backward dunk. It really didn't matter because he was probably one of the best overall athletes that we would ever see. The biggest question for all of us from poverty-stricken neighborhoods was, were we strong enough not to fall victim to a life that was destined to destroy us, thus making talent a nonissue? So Von was dating the best baller at our school, and from what Ju-Ju was telling me, she was still dating a very good baller—it was just in a different kind of sport.

As we drove off, I began to think back to the last time I was picked up by an IROC. I was on my way to school and it was Dirty driving the car. This time I saw no loose wires and the keys were in the ignition. The difference was that one was stolen and this one was clearly paid for, but would both drivers share the same fate? Ju-Ju had just dropped Von off, so we decided to get something to eat and catch up since it had been a lot of years. After we finished dinner, I got dropped off at my car to go get all the money I had put up so I could go shopping. Yup, my friend had exactly what I had been looking for. It was back on and in a major way.

My motto was "Stack rocks like Colorado." We were childhood buddies, but now we had a symbiotic relationship—it was mutually beneficial. I needed him for a consistent supply of product. He needed me for a consistent supply of that almighty dollar. And what made this reunion so special was that, in this game, you had to form trust with someone you were dealing with to calm the fear of getting robbed or even set up by the police. Since Ju-Ju and I went way back, there was automatic trust. We knew that our love for each other would not be based on our business transactions, but instead on the fact that we really did love one another. That same night after our first transaction that is what we told each other. "I love you, bro." And we really meant it. I had already made a name for myself in my city, so getting rid of the work was no problem. My only problem was trying to figure out what to do with all the money that came so quickly. Ju-Ju not only had A-1, or the best product, but I also received the best prices because we were friends. And to top it all off, he had an unlimited supply, which made me by far one of the most popular guys in town.

D-Wee and I were close. I needed someone who I could trust around me at all times, and he was definitely that guy. We had a lot in common. He had a really big heart and was a bona fide hustler. He loved to dress fly, he was a chick magnet, and most of all he was smart. Both of us were knee-deep in the game, but were smart enough to further our education simultaneously. We both understood that the game we were playing was only temporary. I was in business school and D-Wee was commuting to Penn State College. We were around each other so much that we figured it would be okay to live together, so we teamed up and got an apartment way out in a white neighborhood away from where we worked. It was perfect. We got along very well and developed a real love for each other.

I told Mom I would be moving out. She did not protest, but told me that I needed to be careful and really start thinking about changing my life. The truth was that I actually was thinking about changing, especially now that I was making enough money to start a legit business.

We furnished the apartment with band new everything—in other words, made it very comfortable. While buying furniture, I suddenly had a thought. I had tried to give Mom money several times, but she would not take anything from me. She called it "blood money." So I decided that I would take matters into my own hands. I arranged for my sisters to have a mall day with my mother within the next couple of weeks. I set everything up for that day and went to her house and threw out all of her furniture—couches, TVs, kitchen table, appliances, even pictures on the walls that weren't portraits. Then I had everything new delivered. I figured I had put her in a position where she had to take something from me. I loved this woman, and I wanted to show her my appreciation.

When she got home, I got the expected phone call that ordered me to the house immediately. When I got there, she fussed at me for a while, but she could see in my face that my kind gesture was from my heart, no matter how I was able to do it. She told me that it was so slick the way I did everything. She let down her guard, reluctantly hugged me, and said thanks. So, although she wouldn't take money from me, I continued to do nice things for her regularly. I even pulled the same trick with her car. I asked to use it, traded it in for something better, and just dropped off the keys. She warned me that I had better stop doing those things, because what made her happy was to see that I was safe. My sisters had no complaints as I was spoiling them to death.

I had totally lost touch with Amber after I graduated from high school. I often thought about her, though, especially since I had to drive past the house she grew up in almost every time I entered Clairton. She was a really good girl who grew up with a solid family structure and in a pretty safe environment. Wilson was like the suburban area of Clairton. Most of the white folks lived there. Their grass was cut and watered. They had political flags stuck in their yards. We drove through there once, but knew that it was not our area to live in. It was their little world. But it was a false expectation that the kids wouldn't interact with us project kids. We all went to the same school, but we were different. Eventually, some of those middle-class white girls started to like some of us low-class black kids. Although the parents may have looked at it a certain way, all us kids just saw each other as people, and color wasn't important. The white and black kids at my school were all friends, and that's what I really liked. You would always have your bad apples, but for the most part, everyone got along really well.

Despite that, we seemed to stay in our own neighborhoods. And that's why it bothered me when I heard that Amber was at an apartment that was a known hangout for drug dealers. I mean, not to turn my nose up at drug dealers, because I was in the field, but I considered myself more of a broker than a dealer. It just sounded more professional. I knew exactly what went on in this place because I had dropped off a delivery a time or two. Every time I went there, it was like a party was going on. It didn't matter if it was the middle of the day. Knowing this sweet, smart, beautiful majorette who I went to school with was there seemed way out of place. I couldn't help but wonder if she was doing okay, so I made a few phone calls. Within the hour, I had Amber on the line. I wanted to see how she was, so I arranged to pick her up in the next couple of days. When I was on my way to get her, she suggested that I come later because she had to do laundry. I told her to put all her clothes in a bag and we would take care of it.

When I picked her up, all I saw was the beautiful smile that I remembered. I was really happy to see her and still got the stomach flutters. However, I could see that behind the smile, something was going on with her. I hadn't yet taken anyone to my new apartment as D-Wee and I decided that it would be our little hideaway, but I trusted Amber. I knew she would never do anything to hurt me. Out of respect, I let my boy know that I would be taking her there.

She spent a couple of nights, and I put the game on pause, as I had to make sure she was okay. She told me that she left home and was now living at the house where I picked her up. She told me that she was not using drugs, but she was drinking very heavily. I asked her if there was anything that she needed, but she said no. You see, I had a lot of women after me at that point. Although I didn't think I was a bad looking guy, I was wise enough to know that most of them were impressed by the life I was living or the car I was driving. That definitely wasn't the case with Amber. She liked me when I barely had enough money for lunch at school. And I often wondered if her parents would have given her their blessing about us, and would we have had a good relationship? Oh well, such is life. I sat and listened to everything she had to say. I sat there with her head on my shoulder, rubbing it, and telling her everything was okay. I was trying to figure out if this was my opportunity to see if we were supposed to be together. I mean, she had left home, so her parents were out of the picture. One single thought snapped me back to reality, "the life." I knew that I really cared about this girl but wasn't sure if it would be good for her to be involved with me at this point. She would demand all my attention, and there was no way I was going to stop getting that money. The other thought that seemed to leave a throbbing pain in my chest was, how could I ever be with this woman if her family didn't accept me?

My pager started to blow up, so I told her to stay as long as she wanted but I had to make a few runs. She declined and said she wanted to go back to the apartment where I picked her up as she had a couple of friends there. We were on our way out of the apartment when she grabbed her black plastic garbage bag full of clothes. I had totally forgotten about it. I told her that we could go to the mall and I would buy her new everything, but she declined again. Instead, we went to the closest Laundromat so we could get all her clothes washed. Then I dropped her off.

I tried to reach her a few times after that but didn't have any luck. The next I heard from her, she was having a baby. Half of the baby's ethnic background would be the same as mine. I wasn't sure if she was going to be with the father, or if it was something that just happened. I wondered how her parents felt about this. I had to admit, I was kind of jealous, and I wondered if I should have done everything I could to keep her at my apartment that day. Oh well, I guess I would have to live with the thought of could have, should have, and would have for the rest of my life. And I would always wonder if this was the girl I was supposed to be with. Hmmmm…

D-Wee and I were always together. When we weren't, I seemed to be hanging with Ju-Ju. He still couldn't believe how much money I was bringing to him. He said he had no idea I had turned into the hustler that I was or he would have gotten in touch with me sooner. He explained that he was only dropping Von off when he was riding past the pool hall and noticed a walk that could only be mine. He did hear that I was living in Clairton, but he didn't really know what I was up to. He said that as he looked closer, he knew it was me and decided to try to scare me. I told him that he almost got himself shot. He laughed and said I didn't have a chance, and if he had had a gun in his hand, I would have been shot before I turned around. We laughed for a minute about it, and then it was back to talking business.

He told me that I was coming at him too fast, and I would have to prepare my own stuff—in other words, start turning cocaine into crack. He told me that I would make way more money as there would be "extras," as he called it. He said he knew someone who could teach me. I was with it one hundred percent, and that was the purity of what he gave me. It was wrapped like it was fresh out of Columbia. The look and smell of it said power, and that was exactly what I was chasing. I told D-Wee the good news that I had landed a new connection and he was so excited. This was a whole other level of the game, and I was ready.

When Ju-Ju and I met, we would never just do a transaction. We would get something to eat, buy some clothes, or stop by one of his lady friend's house. I knew he was dating Von, but there were a few things that just came with the game. Beautiful women were just one of them.

We stopped at a house in a town called Wilkinsburg. He told me that he was taking the game to another level and hoped I was ready. What he didn't understand was that I had stood outside for countless nights selling dimes and twenty rocks until I saved enough to buy more product from Krafty. I was happy that we had formed a business relationship, but I wanted him to understand that I was already a certified hustler. Another thing I wanted him to be clear on was that I wanted to buy my own product, and didn't want collateral so I could go at my own pace. Plus, I wanted to be my own man.

We pulled up to the house where we would be having this serious discussion. But when we got inside, the girl behind the door grabbed my attention immediately. She was stunning. She had a short, perfect haircut that complemented her smooth, light skin. Her body filled out every part of her outfit. Ju-Ju grabbed her immediately and kissed her in a way that said he was claiming his territory just in case I was having any thoughts. I was into the beautiful woman thing at this point, and every woman who I saw him with was close to a dime. He asked her to excuse us.

We sat at the kitchen table to talk. He explained to me how things would work, and it was my chance to let him know that I was my own man. As he was talking, I heard someone coming down the steps. I hadn't seen his girl walk upstairs, so I knew it was someone else. When that someone else hit the bottom step, everything around me seemed to freeze. Ju-Ju was still talking and I could see his lips moving, but could not hear any words coming out of his mouth. It was like he was muted. All of a sudden, as if a thought bubble appeared over my head, I had a dream while I was wide awake. In this bubble, I was standing at the altar getting married. I sat at the table, mouth wide open with drool about to drip out of it when Ju-Ju clapped twice in front of my face and yelled, "Earth to Church Socks!" He then looked behind him and saw what had put me under the spell. It was Carmel. Her name was almost like the smooth creamy complement to chocolate, but her complexion was more like French vanilla. Her silky, jet-black hair went halfway down her toned back, and her subtle brown eyes had the look of confidence and humility at the same time. Her lips looked as soft as pink cotton candy. The coats of gloss made them look as though they were made of glass. Her sheer satin, bell-bottom, pinstripe pants seemed to highlight a perfect figure. The stripes went vertically past the back of her legs and formed a half circle at the perfect length. Her biracial skin tone was light enough to highlight the beauty marks on her high cheeks. In other words, this girl was beautiful.

Ju-Ju snapped me out of my trance by giving me an underhanded insult, saying, "Man, don't worry about her. That's my girl Dana's sister, and she is a little too much for you." He said everyone was after that girl, but she was not impressed with the ballers because she was very smart and headed for college.

"Hmmmm," I thought. "Maybe he's right, but at some point, I have got to meet this girl in a different setting."

We finished our talk and seemed to be on the same page—or maybe we weren't, because when I gave him my money, he still handed me way more than I paid for.

The little kid named Jeff who used to be the trainer at football practice had finally grown up. And although he didn't hustle, he still liked to hang around the ballers. Since I used to pay him well to do bike runs to the store, he still had respect for me, or appreciation if you will. He also still had an infatuation with cars, as he seemed to get the keys to everyone's ride, including mine. He continued to detail automobiles and had gotten a whole lot better at it. But even when he wasn't detailing, he started to hang around me a lot. He was my boy. He had just shined up the Monte Carlo. I was ready to take a spin downtown when my mother came out of the house and said she had an emergency. She needed to use my car. "Boy!" I thought. "Right after he had just put the Armor All on the tires." I wanted to protest, but this was something that my mom had never asked me. Of course I couldn't refuse. Plus, it had to be important, because she didn't like driving my car. So I called my main man D-Wee and he pulled around the corner in his custom SS Monte Carlo to get me.

It was painted triple black with chrome and maroon stripes as accents. The seats were all custom and the same color as the car. But what made his car really customized was that he cut the roof off and made it into a convertible—the only one you would see. I jumped in the ride and we were off on a shopping spree. D-Wee and I weren't just business partners, we liked being around each other. After wasting about $1,000 on shoes and clothes, I was headed back to Mom's to pick up my car. All of a sudden, I got about thirty pages from my mom, so I knew something was wrong. It did give me comfort, however, that the pages were coming from her house. I decided not to call back since I was only five minutes away.

When I walked into my mother's house, I saw her sitting on the couch, rocking back and forth. Her eyes were red like she had been crying for hours. My grandma just sat on the opposite couch with her hands folded in front of her face. *What was wrong?* My mother then started to speak. I could see her hand shaking as her nerves were getting the best of her. She said that she would walk before she ever drove my car again. She explained that she was driving through a town called Homewood since it was the quickest way to get to where she was going. She had asked my grandmother to ride with her so she wouldn't be by herself. As she approached a light, she wasn't paying much attention because she was listening to Grandma talk. Then out of nowhere, a guy with a ski mask and a gun ran up to her window and ordered them to get out of the car. Her instincts told her to step on the gas, and she drove through the red light, almost running into a pickup truck. She hoped that no bullets were fired as my grandmother kept calling out "Jesus." She continued to drive until she was far away and had even passed up where she was going. She drove to my Aunt Debbie's so that she could cool down a bit.

I had never given this any thought, but I had just put two women who I loved to death in real danger. My car was so flashy that it was grabbing the attention of carjackers. And if it was grabbing the attention of carjackers, then it probably had the attention of everyone else, including the police. I hugged my mother and grandmother and apologized to them. I made the decision that day to sell the car. I also decided that I wouldn't buy any more fancy rims. Any car that I bought had to be factory, and if I needed to fix it up, then I wasn't purchasing the right car.

My high school sweetheart and I had finally drifted apart. I went to visit her a few times at college, and we finally realized that we were kids when we got together and still had a lot of life to live. There was no bad breakup or hard feelings toward each other. I did, however, continue to visit since my friend Omar was also a student there. The fellas and I would go up and crash parties. It was Phil, Omar, D-Wee, Biz, a couple of others, and me. We would load up a couple of cars and be on our way.

One night we went up for a concert and decided to take a stroll through the ladies' dorms. It actually seemed pretty peaceful. We almost made it all the way through when Phil noticed a door near the end of the hallway was open. There was a large pizza box sitting on the bed in the room, so Phil asked if he could have a slice. The girl inside had an awkward look on her face, but we knew Phil was just being silly as always. With a reluctant look, she said, "Sure." After a little conversation, we found out this girl was from Philly, and she and about six of her girls were going to be at the concert together. We met up with them, went back to their dorm for the after-party, and played spades most of the night.

The girl we originally met was named Tracy, and she was a very pretty girl who was tall but petite. She had the mannerisms of a girl who came from a good family. Her soft, shoulder-length hair hinted that she had come from a tropical island. Her face was just as pretty as Jada Pinkett-Smith's, but with lower and fuller cheekbones. Her smile said that she was very comfortable with who she was, but you could tell there was something behind it. Her body suggested that she was still on a journey to womanhood, which somehow I really wasn't paying attention to. No one looked at her as a candidate for getting to know, as we all just looked at her as a very nice girl. So every time we would go up to party, we would go to her dorm and sit around and talk before we went out. The first couple of times, I realized that Tracy and I had some really good conversations. I couldn't say that there was an attraction there as she was very different than the girls I was used to. Oh, she was very, very pretty and had the face of a princess, but we just formed a good friendship where neither of us was thinking about dating. She was a very smart girl who seemed focused on her schoolwork and was determined to make something out of her life. I was serious about school, too, but my extracurricular activities had me destined for trouble. The more I found out about her, the more interesting she became to me.

We stayed platonic friends for about a year, and before I knew it, we were spending more time together. I would drive up to visit her, and she would come down to my apartment on her free days. This felt a little awkward because I had been avoiding the word commitment. However, I was really starting to like this girl. I was still unsure as to what we really were or where we were headed, but neither of us seemed to stop whatever it was.

She started to ask more questions about what I did. I let her know that I went to school but also worked for my uncle at his convenience store. I would say that was a lie, but I did go over there regularly to apply what I had learned at school to his business. But I was not on his payroll and never clocked in, so it basically was a lie. There was no way I could tell this girl I was a drug dealer. But honestly, how could she not know? I wore very expensive clothes, drove a very nice car, and wore jewelry like Mr. T. If she didn't know in the beginning, it had to have been clear the more we were around each other. Ray Charles would have been able to see it. However, I believe that she started liking me, and just accepted the life I lived and the gifts that came with it. So we were periodically seeing each other, but still hadn't officially become a couple. We were not intimate, either, so I looked at it as a very strong friendship that had potential. Until then, I still had to live my life and see what lay ahead.

Mareese Comer

My uncles saw and heard about the way I was living, and they wanted to meet with me. I was prepared to hear the lecture about what I should and shouldn't be doing. I had heard it a million times. And I understood when I was a kid, but not at this point, because I was a grown man. What made things different for me? They had hustled their whole adulthood. They had the finer things in life, so why couldn't I have the same things? When I got to my Uncle Mee-Mee's house, he was there with my Uncle Cornell and my cousins Earl and Andre. They were sitting around the rectangular living room table that had a mirror in the center of it. It began with small talk about family and things that were happening in our town, and then Andre broke the silence and hit me with a door blow. He picked up his chin, looked at me, and said, "We want in." At first it didn't register, but then I realized that he was talking about the game. After all these years that I begged these men to put me in the game, they were now looking at me like I was the coach. Who would have thought that after all the times my mother accused them of giving me drugs to sell, the first time they would be exchanged would be me giving drugs to them? It was a very awkward moment as I had great respect for these men, and they had done so much for me growing up. They had also tried their best to keep me out of trouble. After I looked at each of them to confirm that they were serious, I squared my shoulders, picked up my head, looked them in the face, and said, "By all means."

Things just seemed to be getting better and better. I was able to buy whatever I felt like and I went wherever I got the urge. The crew and I would still hit the college parties and hang out in the projects. Everyone seemed to be doing just fine until one day the unexpected happened. I got a call from Omar and I could not believe what he was telling me. I felt I was a pretty intelligent guy, but this was something I could not figure out. He told me that our boy Phil was dead. He then told me he died of a gunshot wound to the head. I immediately raised my voice, asking Omar if they knew who did this. In my mind, we were going to take care of them. But Omar kept his cool as if he were playing a game of poker. "We won't have to worry about that," he said.

I furrowed my brow and asked what he was talking about. He then said that Phil killed himself. Now, out of all my friends, Phil would have been the last one I would have expected to do something like this. He was always happy! He would be twisting his dreads while freestyling a rap that only made sense to him. And out of all of us, he was one of the smartest guys. He got good grades without effort. We had spent so many late nights out in the projects hustling together, and we had gone to so many parties together. But now he was gone. I couldn't believe what I was hearing. Was there something hiding behind his smile? Or was this simply an accident and he was being silly? This is something that we would never have the real answer to. All we had to go on was the great person he was, so we had to assume this was not done purposely.

As sad a moment that this was for all of us, this was a time that would never be forgotten. This is when we showed the unity that we had with each other. Every one of us men from the projects went out and bought black suits. We rented a super stretch limo and went to Phil's funeral together. After the funeral, we honored him by spending the whole day together. We rode through the city of Pittsburgh. We went to the top of Mount Washington and looked at the skyline. We were all together. Yeah, it may have taken Phil's death for that to happen, but it was a moment that would never be forgotten. Neither were the hangovers we had the following morning.

Chapter Sixteen

Outta Control

"However, I stay Coogi down to the socks/Rings and watch filled with rocks!"

Life was good! Word began to spread that I was "that guy." I had even gotten the attention of other wholesalers in the area. I was no longer searching for a connection. Now the connections were searching for me. I still kept my loyalty to Ju-Ju, but at this point I was always on deck. If one plug was out, the other outlet was on. And it got to the point where none of the wholesalers really had enough for me. My clientele had skyrocketed. I was getting rid of product while I slept, while I was awake, even while I was out somewhere enjoying a good meal. D-Wee and I were a perfect team. I grew up in Duquesne and he grew up in a nearby town called McKeesport. We both graduated from Clairton so that gave us the keys to three different cities—or better yet, "keys" for three different cities. Because of him, I was able to get money in McKeesport. Because of me, he could get money in Duquesne. And we had Clairton on lock. So we pretty much had our choice about where to do business. While most people bragged about controlling a block or streets, we were controlling area codes. What made us so special was that we did it with charm. There was no gunfire or the threat of violence, because everyone loved us. Although we were living the life, we really were good people. We always took care of our hood and the people around us. We were offering the best product for the lowest price, so who could be mad at that?

I kept my word and got rid of the Monte Carlo. Instead of two friends having matching outfits like when we were kids, D-Wee and I took it to a whole other level and just bought brand new trucks. And since my life was moving so fast, I decided that a new Honda CBR 600RR bike would help me keep up.

People didn't envy us, because we showed so much love to them. A lot of people thought that drug dealers were naturally gun-toting mass murderers, but we were college students who dressed like we were shooting a rap video—every single day. If it was the Super Bowl, we were there. All-Star Weekend? We were there. If it was a Tyson fight, we were there, too. We even made our way over to Honolulu to check out the Pro Bowl. Most people woke up and tried to decide where they would go that day to run errands around town. Us? We would decide what state we wanted to be in.

D-Wee and I formed a bond that could never be broken. And when business was being taken care of on a high level, it was just the two of us. No uncles, no cousins, no friends—just us. We kept it that way because we trusted each other more than ourselves. Loyalty would be an understatement to describe what we had for each other. I couldn't even remember having a disagreement. We just loved each other that much. It got to the point where hustling didn't even take up too much of our time. It seemed like we were either shopping or spending time with the ladies. They began to know us everywhere we went, and you would rarely see one of us without the other. It was amazing how money made you feel. Neither one of us was disrespectful or arrogant, but we understood the power that just came with what we were doing.

I remember we went downtown to the most popular clothing store in Pittsburgh. It was called Mo Gear. I had a good eye for clothes, but D-Wee was the real natural. He could make a Kmart T-shirt and shorts look like Gucci products. He just had a real eye for coordinating. We arrived down at Mo Gear and I decided that if we were going to be spending our money, they needed to know who we were. And if they knew who we were, well…we expected to get a discount. I walked into the store and asked the cashier for the owner. The medium-built lady with the blond Dennis Rodman short haircut brightened up and said, "Is there something I could help you with?"

I smiled back at her and said, "Sweetheart, I was just wanting to meet the owner since we will be bringing some revenue to this business." I don't think she liked my response, but she got on the phone and called a nearby office. Within minutes a guy named Morris walked in. I said to myself, "I should have known Morris was from Israel. He was smart enough to know that African American men didn't save up money for rainy days, made sure our bills were paid on time, or even invested in the stock market, but we would definitely spend our money on clothes." When he walked in, his cologne overpowered the store. He wore tight-fitting jeans with a business shirt—no tie and the top button undone. His salt and pepper hair grew past his shoulders and showed his wisdom and bravado.

The Rodman look-alike pointed to me. I was dressed in my favorite Fruit of the Loom white V-neck T-shirt and plain shorts. My appearance did not translate to someone who wanted to talk business, but he must have noticed a look in my eyes. He walked over to me and reached out his right hand. I grabbed it and pretended like it was one of those exercise grips. An old man told me that a man is judged by the strength of his handshake. He must have been right because I could tell by Morris's slight smile that he understood me before I even spoke a word. I introduced myself, and from that moment on, anytime I walked into his store, his staff knew that I would never pay retail for clothing. No one who was with me, or just mentioned my name, would pay retail—ever! I had to show Morris that talk was cheap, but my taste was expensive. I told him I wanted three Coogi sweaters, two Pelle Pelle jackets, and a few other odds and ends. We left after spending about $3,000 on clothes.

Our next stop was Wood Street to see my man Pablo. He owned the gold shop. I didn't fool with gold so he would always take me to the back, open his safe, and show me the real jewelry, the stuff we called ice. I was always amazed when he would pull out a handkerchief full of diamonds. That day I just wanted a few studs that were as big as my pinky nail.

One thing I did notice was that these kind of shops were owned by people from overseas. We were clearly the consumers, and their money came as easy as ours did. However, they had no fear of anyone taking something from them, and if the police showed up at their place, then it was probably to protect them. I was in business school and I was saving a ton of cash, so I had to start thinking about an exit strategy from the game. I already felt bad because I had not followed through with the game I really loved to play. My dreams of being in the NFL were long gone. But I justified it by saying I would at least make close to an NFL player's salary. There were still some major differences between the two career paths. While some NFL players feared injury, they would always be insured. In my game, I was fearful of things worse than injuries, like death or being thrown behind prison bars. A football mishap might just be season or career ending. A mishap in my game could be life ending.

Ju-Ju and I still did some business, but we didn't have a lot of time to hang out. He invited me to a cookout, so I thought it would be a good opportunity to catch up. D-Wee and I showed up at the park and grabbed our customary donation of beer out of the trunk. There were already a lot of people there, and I noticed a couple of faces that I had seen when I went out to a club with Ju-Ju. He really didn't say who was throwing the cookout, but I figured if he was inviting us, it had to be cool. One thing I knew was that there would be a lot of people there who lived the same life as us, so we would fit in just fine. I also knew there would be lots of food and drink, plus too many women for us to count.

I was sitting on a park bench talking with D-Wee and enjoying the sundresses and miniskirts when all of a sudden D-Wee's lips continued to move but I could no longer hear a word he was saying. My mouth was wide open, and I must have looked liked I'd seen a ghost. D-Wee didn't clap in front of my face, but he read my eyes and looked behind him. It was definitely not a ghost. It was Carmel! It was as if she was walking in slow motion with the wind blowing through her hair, and she was walking right toward me. As soon as she got a few feet away, Ju-Ju stepped in front of me to hug Dana and say what's up to Carmel. And there went that daydream. I tried my best to keep my eyes off of her, but it seemed impossible. Then all of a sudden, she grabbed a plate and sat on the bench across from me. Within seconds, we sparked up a conversation that never seemed to end. I was a regular guy today. No jewelry, no expensive outfit, just a fresh haircut, a Fruit of the Loom T-shirt, and some big-pocket Karl Kani blue jean shorts. She mentioned that she was about to go to Atlanta to check out a hair show, and I told her how my aunt in Tampa was heavily involved with it. We chatted for the rest of the cookout, and when she got up, she gave me her number and I walked her to her car. Ju-Ju gave Dana a hug and gave me a look as if to say that he couldn't believe she gave me her number. Her beauty had already captured me, but what impressed me was her level of intellect. And her personality was addictive. She had a smile on her face the whole time we talked. I couldn't wait to take her out, but I had to wait a few days to call. Plus, she said she was going to Atlanta, so I'd just wait until she got back.

I gave her a call within the week and we set up a date. I was trying to figure out what I should plan, but I thought a nice dinner would be a good start. I showed up at her house and rang the doorbell. She looked out the window and greeted me with her beautiful smile. She opened the door and came out with some ice skates draped over her shoulder. I gave her the weirdest look. I had no idea why she had ice skates. She read my inquisitive expression and said that she wanted me to take her ice skating. I laughed a bit and let out a very drawn out, "Okaaay."

I couldn't help but think back to the time I rode my bike through West Mifflin as a kid, looking for a girl with no address, and the day I dove into a twelve-foot pool and almost drowned. Now I was going to fall on my face on some rock solid frozen ice. The things we do for beautiful women!

As strange as that may have seemed, I was actually impressed. A woman that knew what she wanted. If we hadn't looked the same age, you would have thought she was my mother by the way she was pulling my hand and leading me around the rink. I was taking very cautious steps instead of skating. The whole experience was very different, but I really enjoyed myself. My life was going so fast that I had lost sight of the fun things in life, or the simple things as one might say. We grabbed a bite to eat, and then I dropped her off at home. The date went great. Ju-Ju was right about this girl. She was not at all impressed with my lifestyle when she asked questions about my plans for the future. She was very impressed that I was in school studying business. Most drug dealers where I was from didn't even get their high school diploma, let alone further their education.

Carmel and I continued to see each other. We went on several dates. Then she went off to college. I paid her a couple of visits, but the distance seemed to be too much for us to form something special. With the life I was living, who knew if that would have really been possible. But what I liked was that she brought things out in me that the game seemed to suppress.

From a materialistic standpoint and in the eyes of those from a poverty-stricken neighborhood, drug dealers were viewed as some kind of heroes, but in the eyes of society as a whole, you were invisible—or better yet, a villain. Normal people paid their bills. When they made a purchase, such as buying a car or house, it helped establish them and make it easier for future purchases at a better interest rate. There was a record to show how responsible they had been (or not been).

A drug dealer didn't even exist when it came to the real world. Everything he purchased was done so with cash. If something could not be purchased with cash, then the drug dealer would look to a family member to put that purchase in their name. No matter how much money a dealer made on the street, it wouldn't matter to a bank that was issuing a loan. They needed pay stubs and a track record to show that the person seeking the loan really existed. There was also a fear in the back of a drug dealer's mind that if something bad happened, such as getting arrested, then the police would seize items if they were in the dealer's name, which didn't make sense at all. How could a person be so careful protecting their material items, yet be so careless when protecting their own life, which was far more valuable? Hustlers just simply wanted what they wanted, whenever they wanted it.

At that point, what I wanted was a house. But unfortunately, my only pay stubs were from the summer job at Wendy's in Colorado years ago. I knew I was a good talker, but somehow I didn't think the bank would go for that. And although I was more than willing to put down a sizable down payment, that still wouldn't have been enough unless the payment covered the cost of the house. It would have been ridiculous to try and buy a house with that much cash. It would have been a red flag that could have expedited a trip to the place where dealers were probably already headed: prison. So I got with a family member who allowed me to capitalize on their hard work and good credit to make my life comfortable. Their hope was that my lifestyle would not eventually ruin everything they had worked for. I believed that that would never happen, so I got an assumable mortgage for a very nice three-bedroom house that was far away from the neighborhood where I worked. I liked the apartment with D-Wee, but this would give me more privacy. I was making so much money that I needed to be where no one would drive to see me unless they called to see if I was home. Family and friends were allowed, of course, but you just never knew if the wrong person could find out where you laid your head.

The place I found was a yellow brick house that was newly remodeled, but it still needed new everything inside. I ended up changing the living room walls to all mirrors. Even the vertical blinds, light switches, and power outlets were mirrored. Of course, it still wouldn't have been right without a sixty-inch Sony big-screen TV with surround sound stereo. I never developed a wicked jump shot, but I had to have a basketball half-court in the backyard. Since I didn't have much of a yard growing up in the projects, I made sure that this one was properly manicured. By the time I got finished, the oldest things in the house were a couple of outfits that I had bought a few weeks earlier. Everything else was brand spanking new. Mom tried to talk to me about doing way too much, but in my eyes, I was giving myself a hideaway. In everyone else's, I was in plain sight, or even worse, sticking out like a sore thumb.

Things had slowed up a bit, and we were waiting on our next move. D-Wee had a great suggestion. He said we should take a break and do something different like a road trip. I asked him why we would do that when we could just hop on a plane and get there faster. He said that it would give us some time to really think about everything that was going on in our lives.

The thing about D-Wee was, I always listened to his advice. Even if it seemed as if I wasn't listening, I was. You see, I was a go-getter. I was the one who lived without fear. I was willing to take chances if they seemed like they would pay off. D-Wee had the deductive reasoning in our relationship. He would often bring me back to earth. And although at times a by-any-means-necessary attitude was needed for our lifestyles, there had to be a happy medium. My next question to him was, "Where are we going?"

He looked at me and said, "Does it really matter?"

This little conversation would stick with me for a very long time. He may have been talking about the road trip, but the question was so applicable to our lives.

We rented a car and hired a driver named MarV. We didn't pack one piece of luggage. We stopped at Def Sef's house and grabbed a ton of mixtapes. We stopped by a record store so D-Wee could grab his oldies, and then we were on the road. We told the driver that we decided to tour the East Coast. We went to Philly, New Jersey, New York, DC, Maryland, and anywhere close that had a mall to shop and good food. Out of all the places we had previously traveled, including on a plane, I would have to say that this was by far one of my favorite trips. We killed all communication with everyone except close family, and we really had time to think about where our lives were headed. We had the oldies to relax us, and Def Sef's mixtapes to excite us. There were moments of silent thought, and there were moments of dying laughter. But my best friend and I had the time of our lives, and most of it was spent inside a car.

D-Wee probably could see some things that I wasn't paying attention to, so he wanted to take me on a road trip to clear my head. He also knew it would be beneficial to himself. During the trip, it was the first time in a long time that I started to think about change.

I also thought about Tracy on this trip. We had still been in touch, but we had not yet committed to each other, so it was not forbidden to see other people. I knew I was starting to care about her, but I still wondered if she was the one for me. She was very pretty and very smart. She was also very different. I was attracted to the good girls, but I wondered if I really liked the bad girls. Tracy was well aware of the life I lived. When we did see each other, she reaped some of the benefits. But my greatest fear was that one day I would be hauled off to prison and she would pretend that she never knew who I was. Oh well, I guess I would have to really talk to her and start making some serious decisions.

When we made it back from the road trip, it was as if the world was waiting on us. The relaxation and easy breathing automatically turned back into the pressure of the game. We dropped D-Wee off first. I told him that I would follow our driver to the airport to take back the rental car. MarV was cool. We were aware that he partook of the forbidden fruit, but he was a little different. He was a guy who could keep his priorities straight in spite of his habit, which meant he owned his own car and held a job. He just wanted to take a load off every now and then. We paid him well for driving on the trip. He suggested that we give him something other than cash, but that was against our rules. We did not give drugs to people who used anymore. I didn't know why that made us feel better when we were supplying neighborhoods, but the users were getting it from us anyway.

MarV got out of the rental and into his beat-up, pint-size Chevy hatchback. I followed him to the airport. I returned the car, went out front, and jumped in the passenger seat of his bucket. As he was pulling away, I quickly yelled, "Wait, stop!" He slammed on the brakes and pulled back to the curb. I had to get out. Now, I was not the overly obnoxious kind of guy that rushed up to every woman with some corny line that he had rehearsed a million times. And I could hardly be considered desperate for the attention of women. However, there were times when I saw someone and just had to meet her.

Her name was Mona. She stood curbside, holding onto her purse strap as if she was unsure of the Pittsburgh air. Her pretty brown eyes and long eyelashes seemed extremely focused on each car that rode by. Her light, stonewashed jeans hugged the lower part of her five-foot frame, but she still maintained class. Her black, short leather biker jacket with zippers showed that she had a wild side. I had previously been a fan of long, pretty hair, but she instantly changed my mind with her Halle Berry haircut. Her face was way different than Halle's. She had a light complexion with small, pretty lips, and cheeks you wanted to pinch but that didn't suggest fat at all. To call her beautiful would have been an insult. She paid no attention as I approached her.

As I got closer, I could read her look. *Please, don't bother me. I had a long flight.* I thought about the car that I had just gotten out of and the fact that I had just come off a long road trip — without a haircut or shave—so I had to rely strictly on my personality. I said hello and apologized for disturbing her. I told her that she had gotten my attention and I would risk being slapped in the face to meet her. That immediately brought a smile to her face. I told her it was not a line but how I really felt. That at least got me in the door for a conversation—or she could have just been passing the time while she was waiting for her ride. Nevertheless, I believed strongly in seizing the moment. Her Boston accent did not hide the education in her speech. She told me that she had just graduated from Hampden University and had landed a job in Pittsburgh. "Okay, cool!" I thought. "More information to go on."

Since I knew that she was new to the area, showing her around a little would probably be right up her alley. My suggestion of being a tour guide brought another smile to her face. Then her eyes lit up and I could see her ride was approaching. Before I could say anything, she told me to take her number and we could possibly set something up. I smiled at her and jokingly said, "I thought you'd never ask." She chuckled while getting in the car and saying good-bye. In my mind I said "for now" because I was definitely going to call. I was totally against the notion of love at first sight. I believed that two people had to get together and figure out things about each other first. Does she like eggs scrambled or sunny-side up? Does she leave her cosmetics all over the bathroom? Does he greet her with flowers? Does she greet him with a kiss? And once those things are figured out, depending on the level of interest, either adjustments are made or it's on to the next person.

Of course, the initial attraction was based on appearance, but that was only the bridge to something deeper. What I really liked was that this woman had seen me get out of the worst looking car possible and that my attire did not suggest that I was one of wealth, yet she was eager to give me her phone number. She had no idea that I drove brand new cars and bikes. She had no idea that I wore diamonds and $600 sweaters on regular days. She had no idea that I had purchased my own house before I was over the legal age to drink. Yet she had suggested that I take her number. The fear of dating women from where I was from was that they knew all of these things, so was their attraction really to me or was it the life?

A few days passed and I finally gave her a call. After I dialed the number, a recorded operator came on the line and said that the number I had dialed was disconnected or not in service. Hmm…so she had given me the wrong number? I chuckled to myself as I thought for a minute. I unballed the piece of paper that I was about to throw away and said to myself, "That smile she gave me was way too genuine." I redialed the number and her lively accented voice answered after the second ring. I exhaled a short breath of air and joked with her that I thought she had given me the wrong number. Her response was quick and sure. She said that she would have not given me a number at all rather than giving me the wrong information. I went with small talk and asked how the city of Pittsburgh was going so far. She said that she was still adjusting. I then cut to the chase and suggested that we get together for dinner. She accepted and we set a date and time.

This was the part that got a little tricky for me. Should I ask to borrow MarV's car and play the role of Prince Akeem in *Coming to America*? Should I go to Goodwill and get a donated outfit? I sat and struggled with this dilemma because I really liked the fact that we were connecting without all of the extra stuff. I then realized that I would have been acting if I did all those things, and needed to accept my actual life. Although it may not have been the real me, this was the person that I had become. I decided to drive my own truck but do away with the diamond studs and the jewelry. I decided to dress like I normally did, as dressing like a peasant would be a total turnoff. I picked her up, and from that first date, we continued to spend time with each other.

We did dinners, movies, and nothing at all. And she loved the bike rides that I would take her on. I was even teaching her how to ride my motorcycle until she dropped it and I had to pay $1,000 in repairs. I wasn't really worried about the repairs. I just wanted to make sure she was okay. We bonded and established a true friendship that I hadn't been used to. She was also the only woman besides Tracy that I had brought around my mother. She invited Mom to her apartment, and cooked red beans and rice for her and my baby sister. She was a real sweetheart! She eventually saw that my life was far from the car that I had gotten out of at the airport, and my road trip attire didn't complement my pockets. However, I knew that our friendship was based upon a genuine encounter. I had been able to figure out anything that the game sent my way, but right then I found myself in a real quandary. I was getting really close to this woman, but I also knew that I really cared about Tracy.

Tracy was away at college. No, we hadn't officially committed to each other, but we would still talk a lot and I would also visit her quite often at school. Although these women were very similar when it came to intellect and beauty, they were way different when it came to personality. Tracy wanted me to take care of her; Mona wanted to take care of me. Tracy wanted me to figure out where we would go; Mona made suggestions of where we should go. Tracy wore the fruitful Victoria's Secret lotions; Mona wore the secret scent of a woman who shopped at Macy's. Tracy spoke little about her family; Mona was an open book about hers. Both of them were special and had captured a place in my heart, but I was really confused. I found myself putting up a wall toward both of them in fear that I may make the wrong choice. It was very wrong to be spending time with both of them, but it was hard to let go of either.

Then all of a sudden, I realized that the choice was being made for me. Tracy told me that she was thinking of transferring colleges and moving to Maryland. It was a surprise, but I promised that if she went, I would still visit her. The news may have prompted me to spend more time with her, knowing that things were coming to an end, and it did give me a little relief because I did care about her. And in the back of my mind I feared that my lifestyle would eventually bring pain to whomever I was with, as I might be hauled off to prison, leaving them to fend for themselves after introducing them to a life of luxury.

While I was awaiting confirmation of Tracy's transfer, I was thrown off guard by a sudden announcement from Mona. She had already talked to me about her mother being sick. I wasn't sure if my lack of real commitment had anything to do with it, but she told me that she was moving away from Pittsburgh. I thought, "Wow! What a coincidence that both of them were leaving." I guess that made things really easy. Instead of trying to choose one, both of them were gone. Mona made the move, but we still stayed in touch. I wished her well as I knew she had to do what was best for her.

A little while later, Tracy was visiting her mother and called me. She said that she really needed to talk to me. I was already prepared for her to tell me that she had been accepted to the new college. I told myself that I would congratulate her and respect her decision, as I knew she would be doing what was best for her as well. I told her to give me a few minutes as D-Wee was dropping me off at my house. I opened my front door and called her back at the same time. She answered on the first ring. Instead of saying hello, she said, "I'm pregnant," in a tearful voice.

I told her that I would call her right back and hung up the phone. I stood inside my house behind the door to let the words that she had said sink in. I knew that we had been doing things that grown people did to have a baby, but since the first time as a teenager that I had explored a woman's body, I had been responsible enough that I never heard those words from anyone before. There was never a doubt that I was the father. Not only was I the only one who she was intimate with during that time, but I also was the only one she had ever been intimate with, period. The phone rang and interrupted my thoughts. I could see that it was her calling me back. I answered the phone. In a crying voice she said, "It's two of them!" This time I couldn't hang up because she was way too hysterical, so I sat on the couch and figured I would just say what I had planned to say when she called the first time: "Congratulations."

Twins? I didn't really know what to say. Although I had never heard those words before, I wasn't the least bit upset that they were coming from her. Her news changed everything. Just a couple of short weeks ago, I decided there was no need to try to start thinking about a serious relationship. I figured two of the women who were potential candidates were skipping town on me and I was definitely open to new possibilities. Yeah, I would be cautious—especially after what just happened.

I ran into a girl name Charla. She was a girl who was actually from the town I grew up in. She had moved away some time ago, just as I had. We were at a party that my cousin Earl was having and she mysteriously ended up sitting in my truck with me. If there were any word to describe Charla, I would use the word "woman." She had a darker complexion than I was usually attracted to, but her long, pretty Apache-like hair compensated for that. The way she dressed showed that she had taken some time to prepare herself, and through her clothes you could see a swimsuit-ready figure, but she refused to compromise her self-respect.

We began to talk quite a bit, and laughter would be the bulk of the conversation. She had such a great sense of humor and was so easy to talk to. Although I couldn't say that we never crossed the line, we were somehow able to establish a friendship that was hard to describe. I would go over to her house late at night to sit on her couch and laugh with her. I would stop by in the middle of the day just to chat. We both knew that we had no intentions of marriage, and no expectations of a commitment. This was not a sexual relationship. Somehow, I would get pleasure simply by being around her and not having to even touch her. Now that Tracy had dropped the bomb on me—better yet, twin missiles—I figured I had better reevaluate a few things.

As close as D-Wee and I were, we began to drift away from each other, particularly because of the imminent direction of our serious relationships. I had double trouble on the way, and D-Wee had just informed me that he also had one in the oven. He had been dating a girl from Clairton named Pretty P. It was the same girl who the kid Flav warned was a little too much for me when I had just moved to Clairton. Pretty P remained the beauty that I had noticed when we were kids, but I was now seeing what Flav might have been talking about. She and D-Wee always seemed to be fighting. And these were not the kind of fights where a couple just said a few harsh words over the phone. These were the kind of fights where the only way they would stop is if the police showed up, which was not good for D-Wee (as he wanted no police contact whatsoever).

Ju-Ju and I had not seen each other as much, either. Our business had almost become nonexistent, as something had happened between him and his connection. He never really told me exactly what was going on. Instead, he just started to separate himself from me, but I was so connected that Ju-Ju's absence didn't affect me at all. I would have helped him if there was a struggle, but Ju-Ju's pride wouldn't allow that to happen.

Rodney was still incarcerated, and I was told that he would be released within the next couple of years. I wondered how he would adjust to life after being away from society at such a young age. Lump was continuing to excel at Duquesne University, and may even have had a chance at the NBA draft. At the very least, he would get a sizable contract to play overseas. Mo-Joe had difficulty fulfilling a scholarship offer due to some academic struggles, but he had not given up. He was still trying to get into school, and was playing semi-pro football to keep his body in shape. And my very best friend as kid had gone away to play ball in Virginia. He got a bit distracted, however. We had always stayed in touch, so when he told me he would be home, I told him I would pick him up. When he got in the car, he sat his six two muscular frame in my passenger seat and had a look on his face that I would never forget. I asked if he was okay, but he responded by just saying that we really needed to talk.

Bear was not just a great friend. He was like family to me. I decided that we would go to my house to talk. He had never been there, but I really did trust him so it was not a big deal to me. When we got to my house, he took a few seconds to walk around, uttering a couple of *oohs* and *ahhs* to show how impressed he was with my living situation. He had known for

225

some time that I was making a lot of money, but he had not been around me enough to really see it. I grabbed two bottles of water and pushed the automatic ice button on the refrigerator to fill up our glasses.

Then we sat down at the dining room table for our little talk. Bear began by saying how frustrated he was at school. He said he loved to play ball, but was tired of being broke all the time. He went on to say that he, too, had a baby on the way and wanted to provide for his little girl when she was born. I thought that his frustration might also have been due to being away from his girlfriend at school while she was home pregnant with his child. He asked me how I thought he would feel if he couldn't take his little girl to McDonald's and buy her a Happy Meal. I couldn't respond to the question because I couldn't even imagine not being able to pay for lobster—let alone a value meal. To me, the value of a meal depended only on how good it was. The price really didn't matter.

I remained quiet and let him get everything off his chest before I finally spoke. We sat across from each other and I realized that each of us envied the other. He was so impressed by my life, but what he didn't know was that a part of me would have loved to trade places with him. I knew at some point that the ride of fame and glamour would end, and I wasn't sure if there would be a fatal accident before I got off. I admired that he was doing something he loved to do. And although he may have been having financial struggles, he would eventually be in a position where his finances would be secure, not temporary like mine. I decided to speak to him like a friend instead of a business partner. I told him that he was doing the right thing, and that if he needed any help, I was there for him. I could give him money, just as I had been doing for Lump. I told him that if he stuck to it, things would get better.

I watched his eyes do an inventory of my house, and I knew at that moment he wanted what I had and wasn't going to take no for an answer. The problem was that Bear didn't have a clue about how this game worked. When he told me the rest of the story and that he had dropped out of school, class began that same day. Within a very,

very short period of time, not only was Bear able to buy a Happy Meal, but he also had probably stacked enough money to start thinking about buying a McDonald's franchise.

And speaking of franchises, I was preparing to go that direction myself. Despite all the energy and time it took to handle business in the streets, I had somehow maintained a determination to stay in business school. I had already learned how to plan, start-up, and operate a business. I learned the whole necessary legal process. I learned marketing strategies to drive business. I had also learned things that a real wholesale vendor would look for if you wanted to do business with them. In the real world of business, time meant everything. You had to open your doors on time, you had to pay your bills on time, and you had to order your product on time. In street business, nothing was on time, and some days you really didn't know how things would go. There was absolutely no stability at all. One false move and you could be robbed of everything you had, be sent off to prison for a very long time, or even worse —which often happened—your life could be cut very short. I wondered how this street business would affect my judgment when I switched over. Time and budgeting would be very difficult for a person who never had to fool with it. You see, my world revolved around me, but I would have to learn to revolve around the world. I had a talk with my uncle who was closing down his convenience store and asked if he wanted to go into business with me. I told him that Clairton could use a good restaurant and that I had learned everything I needed to know to make a business a success. He didn't give it much thought before he said yes. My uncle was in my corner, and he believed in me.

I started looking for a building that would work for my idea. We met up with the owner of a building, and I was proud to be negotiating my first real business transaction. He was an older white male with hair the color of snow. His glasses hung low on his nose as if they could fall off his face at any given moment. He gave us a tour at an accelerated pace, like he had done it a million times only for someone to tell him that they would think about it. He obviously didn't know whom he was talking to this time. I asked a few important questions that I had learned at school, such as what was the exact square footage, how long had it been vacant, and what was the average utility bill? After my questions, he seemed to look at me a little differently. Clearly, he had totally stereotyped my Jordan sneakers and Pelle Pelle jacket. He then began to talk price, and immediately had my attention.

He said it could be about $4,000, including the security deposit and first and last month's rent. He said he could do a two-year lease to see how things would go. I had learned some time ago that the advantage of any conversation was to listen first. Once you did that, you had more leverage when it was time to speak. So I let this man talk until I had enough information to plead my case. When he was finished, he pulled his keys out of his pocket as if to say he wasn't interested in wasting much more of his time. I cut straight to the chase. I looked him in the eye and said I was not at all interested in leasing his building. I squared up my shoulders again and told him that I was ready to purchase it. Within minutes, his red face turned its normal color, and somehow this man had new energy. It was as if his meds had just kicked in. We negotiated for about a week. I gave him a final offer and planned never to call him back, so when he called me, I knew my offer was good. Within a month's time, we remodeled and staffed a very nice café restaurant. It quickly became a comfortable place for locals to get coffee and breakfast in the morning, and the best soul food that one could taste in the afternoon.

Finally, I had something that made me feel proud. I wanted to continue school to pursue my degree, but I had already learned everything I needed to open a business. I also had more than enough money to operate any business I chose, so why would I need a degree? I simply just wanted the knowledge and to understand how things worked.

I had supported all the other local businesses for quite some time, so they started returning the favor. Not only would they support me, but they would also send business in my direction. I became really good friends with another restaurant owner who I went to high school with as well. We were proud of each other. Although we both were in the same kind of business, his was pizza and mine was soul food. He had delivery, and mine was dine-in only. They called him Fast Eddie and his slogan was encompassed in his name. When you ordered pizza, he would get it to you fast.

My favorite local business was owned by an old man named Johnny, a dry cleaners. All my clothes would have to be cleaned and starched every time I wore them if they weren't brand new. Johnny really appreciated that I would take in garbage bags full of clothes for him to clean. This man had been in business forever, and was probably old enough to be my great-grandfather. His hair was steel gray and combed back, still trying to maintain a hairstyle inspired by the Fonz. His plaid pants suggested that he thought they were still in style, and his wrinkled face had taken on a dark tint. He walked with a limp, but his pride did not allow the use of a cane. He would limp over to my restaurant and buy a plate just to reciprocate my support of his business. He also talked with me when I dropped off my clothes and would always throw out nuggets of wisdom.

And then one day he gave me a lesson that I would remember for the rest of my life. I had always been pretty careful in how I operated in the streets, and had gotten to the point that I did not handle the product as much. However, Johnny caught me off guard when I was picking up my clothes from his cleaners that day. He told the lady up front to watch the store as he directed me back to his office. He motioned for me to have a seat at his desk. I had someone waiting for me in the car, but I knew that this had to be important. Johnny had never invited me back to his office. He began by saying how much he liked me and thought I was a very smart young man. He said he was very proud that I had opened the restaurant, but that I needed to get rid of the other business that I was involved in. I put a dumb look on my face. I had no idea that he could tell what kind of life I lived in spite of all the money I spent cleaning my clothes. He then reached inside his desk drawer and pulled out a plastic bag with a chalky white substance in it that had been through his wash cycle. He told me that he wasn't going to ask questions, and he didn't want to know what it was, but he wanted to give it back to me. He thought he would give me some good advice with it. I was speechless as I grabbed the bag, stood up, and thanked him. As I turned to leave, he said one more thing. He looked me in my eye and said, "You can take a horse to water, but you can't make him drink."

Chapter Seventeen

Game Over

"IT AIN'T EASY BEING ME/WILL I see the penitentiary, or will I stay free?/It ain't easy being me/Will I see the penitentiary, or will I stay free?"

This time the music from Tupac was not coming from the stereo in my small project apartment. It was not coming from the Solo-Baric speakers in the back of my truck. It was coming out of the speakers of Def Sef's DJ equipment.

It was my birthday, and instead of having a nice little dinner where I blew out candles on a small cake, I decided that I would have a party that would make people wish it were my birthday every day. And the way I lived, it actually felt like it was every day. We had a pretty big yard between my grandmother and mother's house, so I figured it would be the perfect place. My aunts spent a small fortune at Party City on decorations, and they started a day early to prepare all the food. The yard was freshly manicured. Party lights were hanging on each tree, and kegs of beer were under them. I brought enough liquor to serve a whole section at a Steelers game. All they could drink. We had my aunt's husband Sam at the door for security, and the party was on.

I stood on the porch and listened to the words of that Tupac song, and it really had me thinking. Yeah, I was living the life, but I was smart enough to know that it would one day come crashing down on me. It was not like I hadn't seen people with the same lifestyle regularly going to prison. I thought about Johnny's cleaners and the words he had spoken to me in his office. I knew he was right. I asked myself, "Am I strong enough to pull away from this, or am I in way too deep?"

I stood there looking around at the people at the party and everyone seemed to be enjoying it. Either a drink or plate was in every hand. Tracy had come down from school with one of her girlfriends. She continued to pursue her education even after she found out she was pregnant. We talked about her moving into the house after she finished up her semester. I watched her joking with her friend and my aunts as they were enjoying the atmosphere. There were people from everywhere. Not only was I a well-known guy, but Def Sef was also one of the most popular

DJs in the Pittsburgh area. Word spread fast whenever he did a party, so the combination of him and me translated to a packed house or yard no matter where the party was thrown.

I looked at my Uncle Geno with a beer in his hand, doing a dance that only he could make up. It was a combination of army calisthenics and soul train, but he had the rhythm to make it look good. I hadn't seen him a lot lately, but when I did, he would always greet me with his favorite quote: "I love you, and that's from the heart." He may not have had a lot to physically give, but one thing he made sure to give was love. I watched my grandmother through the screen door with her apron and gloves on by the oven. I had taken her out of her comfort zone as she would only play gospel at her house, but now I had a live concert of worldly music (as she would call it) playing in her yard.

Everyone was dressed to impress. I looked across the yard and there were those white jeans again. Those things were starting to haunt me. A girl named Quinny was wearing them. She had a thing for wearing all white jeans, and well…I had a thing for how they fit her. She had to have had a dozen pairs of different designs, because every time I saw her she would have some on—some with zippers, some without pockets, and all of them without underwear. She would come in the restaurant with her friends and I would try my best not to stare, but it was impossible. She was about five six with absolutely no stomach fat, and would always have her belly showing. Her hourglass figure was held up by two petite legs, but healthy in the right places. Her most admirable asset was her apple bottom, which had no sign of dimples, marks, or cellulite. It almost seemed a little too big for her frame, but it somehow worked perfectly with her other parts.

My lustful gaze was interrupted by a series of loud noises. These sounds were clearly not coming from the speakers, and that was confirmed when I saw my grandmother's yard torn into total disarray. People were running, ducking, and screaming at the top of their lungs. I saw people hiding behind trees. I looked over and saw that Uncle Geno was literally lying on top of Tracy and her friend to protect them. The sounds were coming from a semi-automatic weapon. As cool as everything seemed to be going, the party was over and it wasn't even eleven o'clock yet. Thankfully, the perpetrator's goal was only to scare everyone. No one was injured as they drove past and fired shots in the air. No matter how good the food was, no matter how much liquor there was to drink, once people heard gunfire, they knew it was time to go. Within minutes, our houses were surrounded by sirens and red and blue lights. For years, it was my fear that the police would pay a visit to my house because of my lifestyle, but the first time they showed up was during a flamboyant birthday party. And what really made me feel bad was that I had brought danger to my own family.

The next day I went over with a little help to clean up the mess and put my family's peaceful abode back together. It took part of the day to do so, and when we were almost finished, my grandmother pulled me into the house. I hadn't made it to our little breakfast meetings in a while and she had a look of concern on her face. She took me into the living room, and instead of talking to me, she caught me off guard by immediately putting both her arms around my neck and just holding her stance for several minutes. She did not speak a word, nor did I feel she wanted me to say anything. I instinctively wrapped both my arms around her. I could already understand what she was trying to tell me. We had that kind of connection.

She was the first to let go, but by the time I released my hands, she had already reached into the front of my pants and disarmed me. I guess during her hug she was able to feel the handle of my 9mm Glock poking her in the stomach. She told me to wait right there, left, and then came back to the room without the gun. She had a bottle of olive oil in her hand. She unfastened the top of the bottle and poured some on both of her hands. Then she grabbed both of my hands and began to pray in a tone that I had never heard from her. I stood there and felt the power of God through her prayer. When she was finished, I did not feel the need, nor did I have the heart, to ask for my weapon back. She had totally disarmed me, but I felt that she had somehow given me more weapons to fight with. I knew in my heart that I wasn't where I needed to be, but I also knew that God was still working on me and He hadn't given up yet. I decided that even though my life wouldn't change overnight, I would at least start to think about going in a different direction.

The Side Pocket had closed down some time ago after a series of incidents that were life threatening, or even worse, fatal. I enjoyed the times I used to hang out there, but now I was not at all interested in spending an hour shooting pool to win $100. So I took on a new hobby. It was one that, if my luck was going well, I could walk away with $10,000 or $20,000 in my pocket. The downside was that I could also walk away $10,000 or $20,000 in the red.

My new hangout was Swamp's. Yup, this was the same candy store that I would stop at on the way to middle school. It was the same store where I would buy twenty-five candy fish and a couple of packs of Now & Laters. The owner still wore the same old-school apple cap with the mafia-like framed glasses. What I didn't know as a kid was that there was a secret place behind the candy store where the real business took place. And he had a pool table there, but had reconstructed it by covering up the pockets and putting twelve-inch high wooden walls around the inside of the table, making it a state-of-the-art craps table. His right-hand man was a guy they called Slant-Shoes. He was married to my aunt on my real dad's side of the family. Both Slant-Shoes and Swamp were usually there when a big game was taking place. If you were invited, then that meant you had plenty of money to gamble. So, of course, I became one of the special guests. I was one of the younger guys, but I earned the same respect if not more. The other guests were guys like myself, and guys who had long money and were riding around in new Saabs when I was in grade school. Boojie and E.T. were VIPs there as well. Their friend Ken Hicks was the son of the owner of this casino where we played regular craps or cello.

Mareese Comer

The pool table was usually filled with cash. And Swamp must have been well respected by everyone because, despite all the money that was often in the little room behind the candy store, there was never any sign of foul play. All of us in there owned guns. We knew that inside Swamp's, guns weren't necessarily needed, but once you stepped out the door, then you were on your own. And that's when a weapon might have been needed—especially if you had a lucky day.

I remembered that I had a few hours to waste, so I grabbed a few rubber bands (which was about $3,000) and decided to try my luck. I met E.T. and Boojie at Swamp's. Swamp and Slant-Shoes were already inside. I hadn't been there a full hour and I had already tripled what I had arrived with. Every time I threw the dice they seemed to land on seven or eleven. I didn't know what it was, but I could not lose. Even when someone else was shooting the dice, my side bets even turned into more money. Finally, E.T. said that he had had enough. He was by no means broke, but he understood that the dice were going my way so he decided to come back another day. I walked out with close to $8,000. I had gotten back every cent I paid for my birthday party and more, and it hadn't even started yet.

After the incident at the party, I decided to lay low for a couple of days, but then got the urge to roll the dice again. I called up Swamp and the casino was already in action. I had hit the jackpot a few days earlier, so I figured I would be smart and only take about a thousand or two and see what happened. Plus, it was late in the evening and I had a few other things that I needed to do. When I arrived, the normal crew was there. I hadn't been there long before I realized how happy I was that I had only brought back a portion of my previous winnings. Every time I touched the dice, I seemed to crap out. I got so frustrated that I threw my last $500 on the table and said I was shooting it. The way things were going they were all fussing at each other as to who would take the bet. They knew that luck wasn't on my side. I grabbed the red oversized dice and shook them with extra energy and a little longer than I normally did. I

236

put them up to my mouth, blew on them for good luck, and then let them go. The dice hit the back wall. One of them stopped on one as the other continued to rapidly spin. I held my breath as it slowed down. When E.T. yelled, I knew I had snake eyes as the other die stopped on one as well. So I lost everything that I had brought except a $5 bill I had in my back pocket. Losing never felt good, but I was not that upset. I was playing with the house's money.

I slapped E.T. and Boojie five, shook the hands of Swamps and Slant-Shoes, and was out the door. I walked through the fenced-in yard, grabbed my keys out of my pocket, and disarmed my car. As I was closing the latch on the gated fence, I turned around and was staring down the barrel of what looked to me like a chrome .32 revolver. I had not paid any attention to the two young guys who had walked past as I was walking out. But they had already been anticipating my departure. The tough guy without the gun pushed both of his hands into my chest and yelled, "Give me all of your money!"

I hadn't spoken a word yet, but what caught my attention were his sneakers. When I first glanced at the guys on my way out, the hoodies did not alarm me since I was still thinking about throwing the snake eyes. Had I paid more attention, I would have realized that there were no faces under the hoodies. They were wearing ski masks. But the sneakers are what caught my attention. Just a few days earlier I had seen two teenage kids hanging around outside Swamp's. Well, one looked closer to my age. I was coming out after hitting the jackpot and the kid with the worn-out white and black Air Force Ones asked me if I could spare a couple of dollars. I was so happy about what I had just won that I handed him a $100 bill. Now they were back for more money, except this time they were not taking no for an answer. And this time I wouldn't have a choice in what I would give them. They wanted everything.

I could not believe these kids had the heart to do this. Did they really understand whom they were messing with? I looked through the openings in the ski mask of the kid who was holding the gun. His eyes had a look of fear, so I thought that I might have a chance with him. I would reach into my pants and pretend that I was getting the money, but they would instantly learn that my gun was way bigger than theirs. But then the painful reality registered. There was no gun! Grandma had taken it from me a couple of days earlier and left me totally defenseless. It had been a long time since I started carrying a gun. I liked to keep myself in positions and places where I wouldn't need a weapon, but I also realized that my life warranted protection. The tough guy without the gun reached into both of my front pants pockets. They were empty. The guy with the gun finally spoke and said in a very cold voice that he was not afraid to shoot me, and I had better cough up the money.

I did not like this position at all. The problem was that I didn't have any money to give them since I had just lost it all. I was getting the sense that they thought I was playing games with them and refusing to give up my money. That's when the guy with the gun said that he was going to show me how serious they were. As soon as he finished his sentence, a Duquesne police car was turning the corner. There were neither lights nor sirens as they were simply patrolling the area. As soon as these guys saw the police car, they immediately took off running. The policeman then turned on his lights and pulled his car right in front of me. He got out of the car, came to me, and immediately asked if I was okay. He said that he saw the gun pointed at me and wanted me to come to the police station to do a report. I wanted to teach these kids a lesson on my own, so there was no way I would do a police report. Because of the life I lived, I wouldn't do a police report even if I was wounded. I had to think fast, so I immediately started laughing. I told the cop that it was just some kids playing a prank on me, and everything was fine. He looked at me as if he knew I was lying, but could not challenge my story.

I got in my car and my immediate thoughts were how I could teach those kids a nice lesson. Then my mind somehow shifted to my grandmother. She had taken my gun from me that same week and it just happened to be when I needed it most. But the more I thought about this situation, the more I realized that I didn't have the gun yet was still unharmed. The fervent prayers of the righteous availed much! It was not a coincidence that the police happened to be patrolling the area. It was my grandmother's prayers that had probably saved my life. And had she not taken the gun, I would have probably tried to play the hero and would have gotten shot, or better yet, became the shooter. Things were happening really fast. Yeah, I had money to buy almost anything I wanted, but I was beginning to feel I was missing something. I felt that I had to always maintain a certain frame of mind or else I would get swallowed up in a dirty game. I had started praying to God again, but had gotten so far away that He probably could not hear my voice.

I began to take things easier ever since Tracy moved in a few months ago. She had been spending some of her pregnancy at an apartment on her college campus so that she did not end her education. Then after summer classes, she finally moved in. This took some adjusting. Here I was, a guy who didn't live by any rules and had no real understanding of a serious relationship. Yes, I was sure that we loved each other, but we still had so much to learn about one another. Did we really know how to treat each other? Or were we just kids who had put themselves in a position where they had to act as a family and really didn't know how to play that role?

She enjoyed the finer things in life and didn't have any financial worries, but what I liked about her in the first place was that she wanted something from me. Would the fact that she grew up on a tropical island and got her fruit fresh off a tree clash with the fact that I grew up in a housing project and had to get my fruit out of a can? Would her being Catholic conflict with the fact that I was raised Pentecostal? Both of us had something deep inside that caused us to keep up a partial wall, but we were willing to give it a shot and look past these differences. We hoped that one day everything would work itself out because of the word "love." Yes, I was really trying to do something that I never done before, and that was to give my all to a person and trust that it would not be in vain. I wanted to be a real man, but did I really know how? Or was the excuse of never having a real male figure to learn that from really valid? I struggled with the question. I knew for sure who could help me figure this out and that was God. I knew that if I could get back to Him, I would be everything I needed to be and more. However, it seemed so difficult to do.

I had spent countless nights at the hospital with Tracy, as having twins was a difficult process. She experienced early pregnancy issues, and I would put everything on hold for days trying to make sure that the woman who was carrying my seed was doing okay. I always felt that if something did happen to me, then it would have been a result of my bad choices. But now my bad choices would be affecting more than me. Now I was sitting in a hospital room watching the Steelers and Browns game. Tracy was lying on her back with her watermelon belly sticking up in the air. My eyes were glued to the nineteen-inch tube television as the Steelers had just gotten a turnover. I began clapping like I was in the stands at the game when I heard a light whisper say, "Babe. Babe." The pain only allowed her to speak in a whisper, and when I looked back, I realized that it was time. She was rushed into the delivery room, where I would witness the birth of my first and second children three minutes apart. The nurse prompted me to rub Tracy's head to comfort her. Even though I was in shock, I felt that I was doing a good job until Tracy reached back and smacked my hand away, yelling, "Stop petting my head like I'm a dog or a puppy!"

I had no idea what a woman went through bringing a life into the world, but once a man witnesses this, they have a newfound respect for a female's strength. So in the blink of an eye, we went from teenagers trying to figure out life to a full-fledged family. We even had the puppy to go with it. Our twin boys brought new life to our home instantly. And looking at their innocent little faces made me realize that I had better make some changes, and I had better do it quickly before it was too late.

I hadn't spoken to my real dad in years, but I felt like the right thing to do was at least invite him to meet his grandkids. He hadn't been a part of my life, so maybe he wanted an opportunity to at least be a part of theirs. I had been hearing really good things about him as he had made some necessary changes in his life when it came to his addiction. He wasn't driving at the time, so I agreed to pick him up. When he was getting in my truck, I looked at this man in his long, black leather trench coach and matching Kangol hat. A beard covered most of his face, yet it was nicely trimmed. I knew exactly what he would look like before I arrived, but I had no idea who he really was. He sat in the passenger seat and we headed toward my house. After a couple of basic questions, the music became the only voice during the ride. I realized that neither of us really knew what to say, so we were probably trying to figure out what the other person was thinking. *Does he really feel bad about being absent in my life? Does he really hate me for not being a part of his life?* He broke the silence right before I turned on the street to my house, and said that he really appreciated me inviting him to see the boys. He said that it meant a whole lot to him. There was a big part of me that really wanted an explanation as to why he didn't attempt to be a part of my life, but we were already in my driveway and I didn't want to spoil the moment.

He went inside and met Tracy for the first time. She greeted him as if he had always been around. I took him upstairs and watched him hold each of my sons. I wondered if he had ever picked me up when I was a baby. The sad part was that I really didn't have an answer to that. I shook myself out of my daze and tried to let this moment be about the kids and not me. He stayed for quite a while, and then I took him back home. I figured that I pulled the trigger. Now it was up to him to choose if he wanted to be a part of their lives. And although it may be hard to make up for lost time, I did believe in redemption.

The money kept coming in, but everything else seemed to be going badly. I thought about all the men that I had looked up to as a child, and none of their lives seemed to be going well. Krafty, who was the first

Mareese Comer

person to supply me with drugs, was now in a wheelchair. His accident left him paralyzed. He always had a big Steve Harvey smile on his face, and was so unselfish with the money he was gaining from the life. Now that I was living that same life, I understood that his intentions were not necessarily to destroy me. It was just the life he lived. Did that make him a bad person? Absolutely not! In fact, he was probably a great man with a big heart who just got caught up in the game. My cousin Andre had been to prison several times, only to stay home long enough to await a new sentence. But would it ever come to an end? His brother Earl was not a repeat offender, but he had also spent time in prison. If only he had stayed out at sea serving our country, perhaps he wouldn't have had to serve time. There wasn't much difference with either of my uncles. Cornell had already pleaded guilty and was awaiting a reasonable plea bargain, and Uncle Mee-Mee was out on bond that took a large amount of cash along with property, only to delay an inevitable trip to the penitentiary.

I thought about these men and realized that they, along with almost everyone I knew who held a job as a street pharmacist, were either in prison or on their way. I also knew deep down inside that, although I had no run-ins with the law, it was just a matter of time before my number would be called. I had definitely pulled a ticket and was waiting in line.

There is a scripture that said that God judges the thoughts and intents of the heart. My thoughts were not bad as I really wanted to change, and my intentions were never to harm anyone. In fact, there were times when I felt that I hustled just to give it all away, as I would not just make life easy for myself. Life was good for my whole family. If they were behind on their light bill, it was no problem for me. If their water was about to be turned off, it was my pleasure to make sure it stayed on. And if their rent was late, then I made sure that it was paid. I never ever told someone "no" when they were in need. And maybe that was why I felt that I had so much luck in a very corrupt lifestyle. Or was that just my

242

way of trying to justify what I knew was absolutely wrong? It was clear that I couldn't pay for my sins with the sacrifice of the almighty dollar as the children of Israel did with their cattle. I did things for people because I had a good heart.

I will never forget going over to my Aunt Debbie's house and watching her son Corey get ready for football practice. I had known for a long time that there were no little league football teams in town but had not paid attention until I was looking at his blue and yellow football pants. I was thinking that we were in the city of Duquesne, where only white and red was worn. I had not seen a little league team there since I was a kid. It had dissolved many years ago due to the mismanagement of funds. I thought about all the parents who had to take their kids to nearby cities so they could play football. I immediately had a thought. My aunt was a very smart woman and she knew all the right people in town, so I told her that we should reorganize the league, and then kids could play football in their own town. She told me that it would cost a fortune, as everything would have to be bought brand new. There was nothing to work with since there hadn't been a league in forever. I then looked her in the eye and said that whatever it would take to make it happen, I was willing to foot the bill. She saw the look in my eyes and knew I was dead serious. By the beginning of the summer, we were fitting kids in uniforms in the basement of her house. She had worked it out with the city for us to play at the high school stadium, and they had designated a practice field for us at Polish Hill.

I felt that giving money to make this happen was a great deal, but let's be real. Money to me at that point didn't mean a whole lot because it came so easily. Donating thousands of dollars was not going to hurt me at all, so I figured it was time to give something that was way more valuable to me. My time. I told my aunt that I wanted to volunteer and coach one of the teams. She agreed, and I devoted my time to putting together a staff and planning a system that could help these kids become successful. The challenge was that some of these kids had not played football other than with a Nerf ball.

I found out about a kid named Windell Brown who was playing for a nearby town called White Oak. They said this kid was a touchdown machine. I remember thinking that we did not want to play against this kid, and we needed him on our team. I had never thought of recruiting at the little league level, but I figured this would be the first. I went to the Brown's residence and talked to his mother. I couldn't promise a new car or cash in a secret account, but I promised her I would give her son the experience of his life. I saw that his cleats were a little worn at the first practice, so I figured a new pair of Nike cleats would help him run faster. Whether our kids were that bad or this kid was extremely gifted is debatable, but he ran past the whole defense almost every time he touched the ball.

Bear was an assistant coach. He brought along his nephew Ty, who brought toughness to our defense. Don Chef, Avery, Little Jimmy, Courtney Dunn, David Daniels, Little Corey, and Little Carl—all kids whose names I could barely remember at first—made a name for themselves by the end of our first season. We went to Steelers games. We went to Pizza Hut after a win. We had Saturday morning film with Dunkin Donuts. We treated these kids like they were winners. Even though they were considered bad kids from a poverty-stricken neighborhood, we found a way to get them to play together as a team. In a league that had been around for years, we were in the championship game our first year. These were things that you could be proud of.

Selling drugs was never fun to me. I just felt that I had gotten in so deep that it was hard to turn back. But now I was seriously starting to think of a way that I could get out. The twins were growing fast. They were taking steps around the house and driving Tracy crazy getting into everything. So I took the pressure off by making sure that we always found things for us to do together. One night we were going to my aunt's cabaret party. Boy, were we going to be clean. We had gone to the mall and picked out a gown and an outfit to match for me. I even decided to go old school and wear a fedora. I loved when we went out together because Tracy always looked beautiful in any gown she wore. I knew I had the prettiest girl on my arm, and she knew that she was holding on to a boss.

She had warned me a thousand times that I needed to be home by eight o'clock so we could be on time. I knew we wouldn't go until about nine or ten but that was her way of ensuring that we even made it at that time. I was set on honoring her request, but I had to make one run and it was only to pick up money. I was on my motorcycle so it wouldn't take me long at all. It was about an hour away from Clairton, so I stopped by the projects to see a couple of faces that I hadn't seen in a while.

The first person standing in front of me by the time I stopped my bike was Little Frankie. He was now playing high school football and making some noise. I was one of his boosters and made charitable donations to him, hoping there would be no team violations. I put the kickstand down on the pearl white, purple, and bright yellow crotch rocket, and gave Frankie a hug with the grip of our hands separating our chests. I stood around for about twenty minutes, and then realized that it was already six o'clock and told everyone that I had to go. Frankie then suggested that I take him on a quick spin. This was something that I had done quite a bit. I told him that I had to take a ride about an hour away. He said that he had nothing to do, so he hopped on the back and we were out. We actually made it there in about forty-five minutes, so I was still on schedule to make it home at a decent time.

I went into the house, grabbed the money, put it under the seat compartment, and then we were on our way. I had traveled this road many times, so I was very familiar with all the lights and intersections. I knew where I could ride my bike past the speed limit, and I knew exactly where I had to be obedient. I was approaching the area where I had often opened up my bike to speeds as high as 140 miles an hour, but that day I would play it safe at 120. I was aware of an upcoming intersection where there was no traffic light and traffic was able to turn when the coast was clear.

It was now dark and raining, but the light drizzle did not affect the grip of my tires. Leaning with my chest on the gas tank in crotch rocket position, I noticed a car approaching the yield-friendly intersection. I was speeding at 115 miles an hour, but I knew she had to see my single headlight. "Should I try to stop?" I thought. But I was getting too close. I let out a sigh of relief as I saw her slowing down. "So she does see me! Oh, wait. She does not see me," I said out loud through my helmet. This driver had decided to try to beat me through the left turn, or the driver was paying no attention to my right of way. If I suddenly gripped my hand brake and pressed firmed with my right foot on the other brake, I was afraid that Little Frankie and I would fly off the bike. It was way too late to think anyway as I could not avoid the car. All I heard was a loud crash as if a bomb had exploded. I felt like Superman (except I did not have his cape on). I seemed to fly in the air for hours. I saw a slideshow of my life. Was this the end?

I felt a piercing blow to my right leg. I had landed on the guardrail. I grabbed my leg. Then I suddenly thought, "Oh, wait. I had a passenger on my bike. Where is Frankie?" I yelled out Frankie a couple of times, and then thought about the second loud crash that I had heard while flying in the air. "Please, God, let Frankie be okay," I said out loud as if he could hear me because of the urgency. I had not gotten up from the guardrail because I could not feel my legs. Suddenly, I saw Frankie crawling out of the grass on the side of the road. He said he was okay, but I could see the pain in his eyes. Within minutes we were surrounded by an ambulance and police sirens.

When they picked me up, I glanced over at the area where I had landed and realized that if it had not been for the guardrail (God), I would have flown over the same cliff that my bike had. The second crash I heard was my bike being shattered to pieces. By the time I was admitted to a hospital room, Tracy, my mom, and my grandmother were already there. I looked at Tracy and told her that she looked beautiful. She was already dressed for the cabaret. Frankie and I were both released with a few stitches, but we had hit a car head-on at 120 miles an hour and neither one of us had a broken bone. "The fervent prayers of the righteous availeth much." Tracy washed and doctored my wounded leg for several days.

As I was out of commission, all I had time to do was think. I sat on my couch with my splinted leg. I had to keep it still because of the stitches in my knee. I watched Curtis Martin break up the middle out of the fog to score a 60 or 70-yard touchdown against the Steelers. Yup, it was personal to him as he had to represent his hometown. I sat thinking that this was the kid who I had played with on the same McKeesport Tigers practice field. And I remembered him breaking that same exact run against us when we were kids. Now I was watching him on my big-screen TV playing in the National Football League. I had been following him the last couple of years and he had every opportunity to break Tony Dorsett's record, but he just stood on the sideline with his helmet on and did not go back into the game in the second half. I could not understand that at all. I had heard that he did not even play high school football until the 12th grade, which was hard for me to believe since he was so talented as a kid. Luckily, he made that one decision to play for whatever reason. He broke a few records, and then landed a roster spot at the University of Pittsburgh. The rest was history. I said to myself in a quiet voice, "That man chose to play the right game." The game he was playing seemed full of life, but the game I was playing could be deadly.

As if on cue at halftime, Mom and Grandma came in the door to check on me. They had just come from church and had not changed their clothes. They seemed to bring a presence with them inside the house. After hugs and kisses, they both asked how I was feeling. I said I was fine. My grandma started to speak and said she had sat back and watched me destroy my life long enough. She said she had spent countless days and nights on her knees praying for me, and believed that the reason

I had been escaping the hands of death was because the hands of God were upon me. My mother had her head down but didn't speak a word. Grandma continued and said that I needed to pay close attention to everything that was happening around me, and that I had better stop taking God's grace for granted. She said that in spite of how chaotic my life was, she still believed that God had great things in store for me. She said that I may be physically alive, but I was in a dead state and needed to be revived.

Tracy had already been talking about moving away to somewhere new and starting fresh. I was very hesitant since I was very close to my family and didn't know how they would feel about that. But then it was confirmed when my mother finally spoke up. She said that maybe I should move away. She told me to pay attention to how many people around me had died or gotten hauled off to prison. She told me that she didn't care how much money I had, she wanted no part of it anyway. What she wanted was for me to be safe and live a productive life. She then told me that I was way smarter than a drug dealer, and could probably make more money legally if I put my mind to it. Then she hit me with a blow. She looked me in the eye and said that I was doing the very same thing to other kids that had happened to me as a child. She said she had stopped using drugs because it hurt her so much to see us suffer. Then she said that I was bringing that same pain back to her because of the way I was living.

I took an extra long breath in and exhaled. I looked at the both of them and said, "Game over." From that moment my mind was made up. I was officially retiring from the game. I had wanted to do so for a long time, and had been saving up more money and not buying anything that wasn't a necessity. Now I just had a few loose ends to tie up.

I decided that I would shut down the restaurant and start preparing for my departure. It hadn't been doing particularly well anyway as I hadn't had the time to really focus on it like I needed to. So I got rid of most of the stuff inside and prepared to rent out the building. As I was getting the last couple of things out, a man walked in. It was a man who I was very familiar with. He was one of the first guys who I had sold drugs to when I started hustling. His name was Chick Green and he had gotten himself together a little while ago. I had even given him a job at the restaurant, but he still seemed to be struggling with this demon and couldn't stay clean. I looked him in the eye and I saw a defeated soul, but he looked as if something else was on his mind besides wanting to get high.

I stopped what I was doing and asked if everything was okay. He looked down at the checkered tile and said that his mother was dying and he didn't have the strength to go see her. He said that he had been avoiding family members who tried to get him to go. I sat there and thought about the reasons why he might not have wanted to go, and I felt the urge to encourage him. Although I had a few people waiting on me, I stopped everything I was doing and decided that I had to get this man to the hospital before his mother passed. I asked him to take a ride with me and he agreed. During the ride to the hospital, I made him an offer that he could not refuse. I watched tears roll out of this man's eyes. He probably had so many regrets, but on the way home, it seemed as if he were released from something. His mother may have been on her deathbed, preparing to go home to glory, but God was eventually going to get the glory out of this man's life.

I had a long talk with Tracy and decided that we would visit Mr. Mangrum in Colorado to see if that would be a good place for us to relocate. We planned the trip, but I had more than that planned. While we were there, we went into the Rocky Mountains on snowmobiles to one of the prettiest areas. We were surrounded by the beauty of God. I then got on my knees on the peak of the mountain and asked Tracy to marry me. She said yes.

We looked around Colorado and decided that it would be an excellent place to start over. We planned the wedding and went home to start preparing for the move. As good as I felt, I got a call on the way home from the airport. I received news that my friend Jeff Wade—the kid that I used to send to the store, the kid who used to drive my cars and detail them, the kid who always wanted to be around me—was now dead. And as much as he loved cars, who would have thought he would lose his life in one? He'd been in a terrible accident He was a very special young man and would always be remembered. I shook my head in disbelief. I was now sure that it was definitely time for me to go.

Game over.

Chapter Eighteen

New Look

The wedding was already planned so we went back to Colorado to look for a place to live. Tracy had already gotten all of her paperwork transferred and was planning to start classes when we arrived. My only plan at this point was to establish a productive life before I ran out of all the money that I had saved. And honestly, I was not sure what I would do in the Rocky Mountains, but one of the first things would be to find a good church to attend.

We looked at several apartments. While I had owned a house for several years, not having it in my name was detrimental to obtaining a lease. I was currently unemployed as well, which made it hard to convince any property owners to give us a shot. That was, of course, unless you were me and could pay off the whole lease up front. I figured it would give us some time to get on our feet, so we signed a lease for a comfortable three-bedroom apartment. We wouldn't have to worry about rent for the duration of our stay. At this point, there was no turning back.

The wedding was at the beginning of January. One may have questioned why we chose such a cold month when most people got married in the summer, but why would that matter when the wedding was in Nassau, Bahamas?

It was the most beautiful setting that one could imagine. We traveled to a place far, far away that we had never seen to make a commitment of forever. Did forever really exist when there was creation and end time? And was forever really possible in today's day and age? Well, I guess that would depend on the subjects and the situation at hand. And the situation at hand was that we were taking a vow before God.

"Better to not make a vow than to make a vow and break it," according to scripture.

We had unconsciously formed a union, and then consciously made a decision to become one flesh. Were we really ready? Had we really taken the time to make sure that both of us understood what we were about to do? Or were we just relying on the word "love" itself to carry us through whatever we would face? Was God a part of our decision? These were all the questions that I decided to think about after my arrival in the city where our ceremony would take place. Oh well, too late to turn back now. I really did love her and really felt in my heart that she was the one, but did we really know each other as well as we needed to, or were we just anxious to make our family official?

I liked it at the pyramid-looking hotel with all the Vegas-like lights, and thought that if there was such a place called paradise, this had to be it. Everything was beautiful everywhere you looked. I was hoping for the same with our marriage, but I knew there would be areas that were less attractive and lacked the same ambiance.

I stood in my separate hotel room, walking back and forth in my white pants, dress socks, and shoes, getting ready for the big day. For whatever reason, I had stopped in the middle of my preparation. I couldn't believe I was afraid. I knew this was coming, but it had not bothered me until this moment. Was I just getting cold feet? Was it normal, or was I really not ready? I knew that she loved me, but my question was, did I really know how to be a husband? This would be new territory for me. At that point, I couldn't think of many people in my family who had a happy marriage. And the fact that other than high school sweethearts, this was the first real relationship either one of us had ever had, let alone marriage. Would my extensive resume of women have an effect on us, or would her lack of experience with a man other than me become an issue?

These questions were far too difficult and I was asking a person who couldn't give me an answer, me. So I decided I would ask someone who would definitely have answers to all of my concerns, God. In my heart I was doing the right thing, but there was a fear that I would eventually fail. I had somehow been able to keep that locked up in a treasure chest. But then Tracy had gotten ahold of that key, made duplicates, and handed one to each of my boys.

I was sinking, but I picked my feet up fast enough not to stay in the same place. I looked forward as the blazing sun prevented me from opening my eyes wide. I saw my bride dressed like an angel in her luxurious, beautiful white gown that represented a willingness to give herself to me for a very, very, very long time. This promise was forever. Her veil was covering her face, but I was already aware of her beauty. What was it hiding? I wasn't afraid of what I knew, but what I didn't know. I kept walking, not allowing my footprints to go too deep into the sand. I took my eyes off of her for a second. Hmm, was that something that I should never do after I say I do? I looked at the beautiful ocean water to my left and saw how determined the waves were. None of them seemed to stop until reaching the shore. I saw the background of the sun and clouds. "What a beautiful picture," I thought. I refocused and looked toward the beauty in front of me, and I kept going. We were facing each other, holding hands, and refusing to look any other way as we were locked in each other's gaze. Would that continue forever? I saw everything that I wanted right in front of me. I heard the minister quoting this promise of forever that I had heard at weddings before, but I had never paid attention to all the words. I was able to hear them now. Was I going through the motions and relying on the word "love"? Our eyes spoke of inexperience and youth, yet we were so willing to try.

"For love never faileth," according to scripture.

After the honeymoon, we went to gather up our life in Pittsburgh. The apartment in Denver was already waiting for us. We just had to get there. I went around and had conversations with my closest family and associates and let them in on my plan. At first, I thought it best to just disappear into thin air, but I felt that my success in a very corrupt game was based upon my loyalty, respect, and honesty. I had to tell the people whom I trusted and who I knew had trust in me. I wasn't sure how they would take me bailing out when I kept them supplied at all times, but the game had been around long before me and chances were it would be around long after me. A couple of my friends thought that I had lost my mind. What they didn't know was that I felt I had lost my mind a long time ago and was actually trying to find it. A good place to start would be somewhere new. They couldn't understand how I had gotten to the point where I barely had to see the product anymore as I mostly collected money—and sometimes I didn't even have to do that. They wondered why I wanted to leave when things were so easy and I was making so much money. To show my loyalty, I told several of them to keep the money that they owed me as a gift since I would no longer be their source.

D-Wee and I had a very long talk, and I told him that after I had gotten myself settled in Colorado, he was more than welcome to join me. I told him that I wasn't quite sure what I would do when I got there, but I would figure out something quickly. I only knew one person in the state and that was Mr. Mangrum. But I knew God had given me that confidence that things would eventually work out for me. I was simply stepping out on faith. I also told him it was a sacrifice. Even if it we didn't feel it paid off for us, it would definitely pay off for our children. I went on to say that I did not want my sons to have to experience the life I had to see. I wanted to give them a fair chance to succeed in a very tough world. This was a man who I did everything with: vacations, shopping, hustling, clubbing, and sharing an apartment. We even had our children around the same time. My twins were only about a month and a half older than his son. He told me he would give it some thought, but he was unsure if Pretty P was willing to make the move.

We packed up the U-Haul truck with everything except the items that we were giving away to family. We were starting off new, so I figured there was no need of taking too much of the old furniture. I sold the extra car and traded in the truck for a brand new Expedition that would never touch the Pittsburgh streets. We loaded it right onto the trailer of the U-Haul straight from the dealership. I was really going to miss my family, but this was something that was very necessary. And I could always come back and visit. If I didn't leave, my fear was that they would be visiting me at the penitentiary, or worse, a grave.

Aunt Ron and I had gotten really close. I mean, she and Aunt Bam were more like older sisters to me growing up because Grams had taken care of me throughout my mother's addiction. We were all close in age, and we were also a very close-knit family. Aunt Ron was married with a couple of daughters, and they were growing up in the very same town of Duquesne that my grandmother had wanted to get away from years ago. She was a sweetheart. She had maintained a very strong relationship with God. She probably had almost perfect attendance at church since childhood. Aunt Ron never drank, got high, or even indulged in the party life, which you could see in her youthful features.

I had begun to talk to her about everything. No matter what, she would always listen to me. We became more like best friends instead of nephew and aunt. I would also capitalize on her hard work and credit history if I needed something done. I had always made it a point to show my family that I loved them, especially Mom and Grandma, but I was trying to figure out how I could thank Aunt Ron for everything that she had done for me. Then I came up with a brilliant idea.

They all came out to the house after we had everything loaded to say their good-byes. We had prayer service in my empty dining room as Grandma grabbed my hands and we all joined together. Yes, they were going to miss me, but this was when I really saw how much they loved me. They did not want anything to happen to me, so they were okay with not seeing me regularly as long as I was safe.

I called Aunt Ron into the kitchen as I had already told my mom the plan. I gave her a hug and told her that this area had one of the best school systems in Pittsburgh. I said I thought her kids should be a part of it. I handed her the keys to my house and told her it was now her family's home. She looked at me in disbelief as if I were joking, which I did so much with her. But when she realized that it was not a joke, her eyes began to water as she thanked me with the tightest hug. Although I knew my income was not coming from the right place, every time I gave someone something it was always from my heart.

On our way to the airport I took notice of everything. We would be arriving in Denver before our belongings, but I wondered if my body was going to arrive in Denver before my mind left the place I had known so well. I looked at all the mountains of trees and how green it was everywhere. I took notice of the tunnels that I had driven through almost every day, yet previously was overpowered by rap music—or maybe it was the fact that I wouldn't be seeing any of it again for a while. I stared at the many suspension bridges. I hadn't noticed any during my visit to Denver. I stared at the three rivers that flowed consistently, and I looked at the hill of Mount Washington and noticed how amazing the incline cable car was traveling up the mountainous hill. Oh, I had ridden it a few times before, but today it looked as if the ride was more exciting. I looked at the stadium where our proud gold and black terrible towels waved every Sunday. I was going to miss this place!

Then suddenly the city disappeared and I was in another tunnel. All the memories were now in back of me, the life that I had enjoyed and the benefits. However, I despised what I was doing. Was I escaping the consequences of my actions, or would I still have to pay for my sins? I had always believed in myself, but I was now putting all my trust in God. No, I was not sure of the plan in Colorado, but the one thing that I was certain about was that I was giving my whole life over to God. I watched my tiny four little Air Jordans walk through the airport toward the gate and felt that this decision would one day allow those little feet to take my sons anywhere they wanted to go in life.

The first week was kind of mellow as we sorted through our belongings while we waited for the new furniture to arrive. We hadn't gone to many places, but I knew I eventually had to figure some things out. The biggest part was done as we made the move. They said that if you took one step, then God would take two. Well, there were a whole lot of steps between Pittsburgh and Colorado, so I was really depending on Him. I decided that we would visit the church that Mr. Mangrum had taken me to when I was in Colorado as a teenager. It was different than what I was used to, but I still remembered how comfortable I felt. After all those years, I quickly noticed that it really hadn't changed. Living for God wasn't brand new to me. That was all I knew growing up. But I had gotten so far away, and I was hoping that God would bring me up to speed. I had walked away from a life of luxury toward a life of the unknown. I did not know anyone or anything in this state except an old Sunday school teacher from when I was a child. I had no idea what to expect. We continued to attend Marilyn Hickey's Ministries on a regular basis and I felt myself getting more and more connected with God. My prayer was that he would direct my steps so that I would know exactly what to do in Colorado. And then one day it came to me.

I had stopped my frivolous spending, but I still had a habit of shopping. I was starting to believe it was therapy for me. I also needed to know where things were just in case there was a special occasion and I wanted to be fly. The closest mall to us was the Aurora Mall and I decided to check things out. I quickly noticed that there were Mexican people everywhere, just as I had observed when I was in Colorado years earlier, except at this mall there was now a mixture of African Americans, unlike my experience as a teenager. I walked through the mall thinking about how everything looked so new. When I walked into a store in

Pittsburgh, I was treated like a celebrity. Now I was just a regular person. I had left everything, including my VIP status, in hope of becoming a productive citizen.

I went in about three or four stores that were supposed to have the best selection of urban wear. I even talked to the employees of each store and got the same advice: Aurora Mall had the best clothes that Denver had to offer. I asked if there were any mom and pop stores around town that sold urban wear clothing, and there were none. Back home we really didn't shop at mall department stores as there were always stores like Mo Gear or Stylegate. They stayed updated with the newest fashions. But this place had absolutely nothing.

I was still trying to figure out what I was going to do to become a productive citizen. My first thought was to find a decent job and try to conserve the money I had saved until I figured out a career that would help keep us afloat. In the back of my mind, I also had the idea that I would eventually pursue starting another small business. If I chose that option, I had no idea what direction I would go. I had decided after closing the restaurant that I would not go in that direction again, but I wanted to do something I enjoyed. Was it wise to start a business now while I had the start-up capital to do so, or should I be patient until I was really sure?

As I was walking through the mall, I suddenly had a revelation. Since it was clearly difficult to find some decent clothes, why don't I start a clothing store and bring some of our East Coast styles out West? I had watched Morris make a fortune in Pittsburgh with his businesses. He had even expanded to three different locations. I also felt I would have an advantage over Morris because I had clearly been a consumer for so long. I knew how to start the business, and I had a great eye for selecting merchandise. However, I had no idea how Morris was able to get his product. I wondered if he traveled to New York to buy wholesale from one place or if he had to deal with several companies. I wasn't quite sure how that worked. One thing I knew was that Morris had the answers, and I knew he had grown to like me. He would also be open to help if he understood that I would not be competition since I was way across the country.

I had continued to ask God to give me some direction once I got to Colorado. Maybe that was it. I made a decision at Aurora Mall that same day that I would open up a clothing store and bring in some designer clothes that Denver was not used to. I started looking for a building immediately, but I had to make a trip back to Pittsburgh so I could pick Morris's brain. My plan had been to not go home for about a year. I wanted to get settled in my new life first, but this was a strictly legit business so I felt it was safe for me to go.

Within three weeks, I was on a flight back to the 'Burgh. I only let a few people know, like my mother, D-Wee, and Bear, that I was returning. They were clear that our old business was finished and said they would always be happy to see me. Plus, I wanted to let D-Wee in on the idea so perhaps it might motivate him to start a new life as well.

I arrived at Morris's downtown location. Without saying a word, the Dennis Rodman look-alike picked up the phone and within minutes Morris walked through the door. He greeted me with a huge smile and immediately told me about some new leather jackets he had gotten in that he knew I would love. I smiled but got right to the point. I said it was very important that I talked with him and I preferred somewhere quiet. A look of skepticism came over his face, but he agreed and prompted me to follow him to his office. We walked a couple buildings over from his store and went up some long stairs. Eventually, we were inside his office.

There were several desks and computers, and paperwork everywhere. A heavyset white lady with a mole on her cheek said a warm hello as soon as we entered. Morris told me to have a seat at a large wooden desk in the back of the office. In my mind, Morris would have had some elaborate high-class, attorney-like workspace, but his desk was part of the war room. I did, however, notice the very comfortable chair he had.

He leaned back, folded his hands across his lap, and asked, "How can I help you, my friend?"

I was well aware that Morris knew exactly the life I had lived as I had spent a small fortune in his stores. In fact, I believed that guys like me were exactly the niche that he targeted. I sat up in my chair, looked across his desk, and told him that I really needed his help. I told him that I had moved to Denver to start a new life and quickly realized that they were lacking the clothing that we wore on the East Coast. I told him that I had been saving up money and wanted to start a clothing store. Morris also knew that I was not a regular street guy and had an understanding of business. He knew about my restaurant. As I was continuing my spiel, I noticed the biggest smile that I had ever seen come across Morris's face. I didn't know how to interpret this smile, so I decided to slow my speech down. Maybe I wasn't making any sense.

When Morris finally spoke, I realized that I was making all the sense in the world. My goal was to start making some legal tender. He began by telling me how happy he was for me and that he thought I had made a very wise move. He told me that when he was planning his trip from Israel, he had discovered two places that were wide open for urban wear clothing. He said that he did not want to be in New York, Los Angeles, or Chicago, but somewhere he could corner the market. He went on to say that he ended up choosing Pittsburgh, but the other untapped market was Denver, Colorado. I said to myself, "Thank you, Lord." That was confirmation that I was headed in the right direction.

Morris was so excited for me. He said he also wanted to show his appreciation for all the money I had spent at his business, so he agreed that I could come to his office every day that week and he would cover everything that I needed to know about opening my business. He told me the secrets to getting accounts with major clothing vendors. He told me that he dealt with every clothing vendor directly, thus making it easy for him to get clothing on time and reorders. He then told me that it was imperative that I attend the Magic show in Las Vegas, which threw me for a loop. Why in the world would I need to go see something like Siegfried & Roy to open up a clothing store? What did a disappearing act have to do with anything? He must have read the look on my face, so he explained that the Magic tradeshow was held at the convention center and was the biggest clothing show in the world. Hundreds of vendors present samples of their clothes that would be manufactured in the upcoming seasons.

"Oh," I thought. He explained everything that I needed to do to sign up for it. He took things a little further and told me how it may be difficult for me to get certain accounts since I would be a brand new store. He said, however, that he would do all the orders for me in the beginning for only a five percent markup fee. I wanted to negotiate that to a two or three percent markup, but in my mind, I wouldn't need him too much longer. I was determined to land my own accounts. After a week's worth of lessons, I was headed back to the Rocky Mountains.

When my mind was made up about something, there was no stopping me. I was just proud that my mind was made up to do the right thing, knowing there would always be obstacles when trying to achieve any goal. I spent the next couple of weeks looking at buildings and locations that would be good for my new business. My first problem was that most of the shopping plazas where I looked, unfortunately, wanted proven chains as tenants so they would not have to worry about them surviving. My second problem was that my restaurant had not yielded the kind of numbers that would impress a would-be landlord. I knew that a location was an absolute need. I also had to consider that I needed the capital for merchandise and possible renovations. I did not have the credit needed to obtain a sizable loan from the bank, so I had to make things work on my own. I figured that the clothing store would be a safe investment since I knew how much money people spent on looking good. The key was making sure that I purchased the correct merchandise. I also had Morris to help me along the way.

After looking at several buildings and filling out numerous applications, I realized that I had a real challenge ahead of me. Each time a door was slammed in my face, it just made me want to knock on more. I could not give up. I believed that I had made the right decision, and I was trusting that God would eventually open up the right one for me.

I sat at my large oak dining room table with both of my hands on my head. I was looking through the yellow pages, but I was not looking for commercial property. This time I was trying to locate a barbershop that would be appropriate for the boys and me. I had stuck with the same barber in Pittsburgh for many years and was hoping to find one that could come close to how particular I was about my fade. After calling a couple of numbers, I finally found one that sounded like what I was looking for. I was told that it was in a neighborhood where a lot of African Americans lived, so I figured it would be my best bet. A lady picked up the phone and answered, "Montbello Barbers."

I could hear music and a lot of people in the background so I did not ask if they cut black people's hair. Instead, I said that I was new to the area and was looking for a good barber. The lady then introduced herself as Debra, the owner, and said that she would be more than happy to take care of me. Now that was new. Over all the years that I had gotten haircuts, I had never had a woman cut my hair. She gave me directions, and I figured I would go and be the guinea pig before I took the boys there.

I walked into the shop and the place was full of life. Every barber had a person in their chair, and there were several people waiting. I took a seat, which I had not done for many years. Every time I went to the barbershop, I was able to get right in the chair. If there were people in front of me, I would just pay for all of their cuts. I quickly had to remind myself again that I was a regular person now. There was a bald-headed guy with gold teeth who greeted me when I walked in the door. He said his name was Mickey, but no one else said a word to me. So I just patiently waited my turn. Within fifteen minutes, a light-skinned lady looked at me and pointed to her chair. Her short, permed, jet-black hair looked as if she had just left the beauty salon. The only indication that she was a barber was the jacket she had on and the tools she held in her hand. I gripped the handles on my chair, as I was hesitant to respond to her suggestion. It was my first time there so I would be taking a chance even if I said I was waiting for one of the guys. I slowly got up and sat in her chair.

She told me her name was Shaun, and asked how I was doing and what I wanted done to my hair. She nodded as if what I explained was a piece of cake to her. She then asked if it was my first time at the shop, and I told her that I was new in town from the East Coast. She continued to converse, clearly very comfortable in her craft. There wasn't a moment where she had to think about what guard or clipper she needed to complete the job. I was already relaxed in her chair as she had a very welcoming personality.

She then asked me what brought me to Denver. I quickly said that I needed a change of pace and was planning to open up a clothing store. She told me about a vacant building that was in the same complex as the barbershop and said that I should take a look at it while I was in the area. I was very appreciative of the information and planned to go as soon as she finished with my haircut.

She brushed off the loose hair and put the liquid that stung so bad but smelled so good on my head. Then she handed me a mirror. I could not believe it. She had given me one of the best haircuts that I had ever gotten! She nailed it on the first try. I reached in my pocket and handed her a fifty-dollar bill. I told her that I would be back for sure.

I drove to the other side of the building where she had told me to go, but something else caught my attention. There was a building inside the complex that had the words "Now Faith" on the front of it. It looked to me more like a movie theater. There was a black and white sign that looked like where they would list featured movies, but in that space were service times instead. And the featured show was "Marvin Sapp." "So this is a church," I thought. I had loved Marvin Sapp since I was a kid.

He was part of the group Commission. Maybe this was a church like the one I was used to. I made a mental note of the concert on Friday at 7:00 p.m. I figured that would be an excellent time to visit the church.

As I looked at the vacant building, all I could see was just an empty space. There was no remaining identity of what the former business was. There was no real estate agent posted on the window. It simply said call the number listed if interested in the space. I took down the number and planned to call right away. I left a couple of messages that week, but I never got a return call. I figured either the space was already taken or they may not have had the chance to get back to me yet. I hadn't totally ruled it out, but I continued my pursuit.

I did make a decision to go to the Marvin Sapp concert. I was curious as to what kind of church he was performing at. We were very happy with Marilyn Hickey Ministries, but I thought a small church like the one I was raised in might be a little better for us. Plus, it was very important that I really stayed in tap with God, as I did not want to go back to any of my old ways. Tracy had class late that Friday evening so I decided I would just go to the concert by myself. I pulled into the parking lot and could not find a parking space. It was completely full. I parked over on the side where the vacant building was that I had looked at earlier in the week. The sign was still on the window, so maybe they just hadn't gotten back to me yet.

It was after 8:00 p.m. when I got inside the church. When I walked in, I immediately felt the presence of God. I knew I was a total stranger to the place, but I felt like I was home. There were people singing and dancing as if they were the only ones in the building. A seat was as hard to find as parking. I eventually found one all the way in the back on the right side. Marvin Sapp hadn't even taken the stage, but the praises of God were already going forth. Right then, an older man took the stage, looking as if he was dressed to be the main attraction. His heavy frame carried his suit like he was a model for a top designer suit company. The suit was navy blue with tan pinstripes, highlighting his Mauri Gators.

As he held on to the microphone, you could see the glitter coming from around his wrist. A look of boldness, but also humility, shone in his eyes through what looked like Cartier frames.

He announced himself as the Apostle Leon Emerson. From his demeanor I could tell that he was the leader of this establishment. Now, this was very new to me. I was used to seeing the old-school pastors in robes and white-collared shirts, which told you they were in the ministry. I was very impressed with his attire. I also had a couple of pairs of Mauri Gators in my closet. However, I was really impressed by his energy. He had a presence when he hit the stage that said he was a man after God's own heart. He continued to speak and invited everyone to come to services on Sundays or Tuesdays. I made another mental note that I had to come back and visit during regular services. If I liked it, maybe our family would join.

By the time Marvin Sapp hit the stage, the whole place seemed to be on a natural high. The tears began to flow, arms were raised, and you could see God moving in the whole building. The experience was so surreal. I had a feeling that the life I just left was never able to give me. I made up my mind that I at least wanted to give this church a try. I told Tracy about the whole experience, and I was so happy that my life was headed for a great change.

On Monday morning, I got up motivated to start looking at more buildings. I had a couple appointments set up and I believed that God was really going to help me out with this. After I looked at one building, I received a call from a lady that said she had gotten my message about looking at a property. I had no idea which location she was referring to as I had made plenty of calls. I told her that I was still interested and was available as soon as she could show me the building. She said that I could come by that afternoon. I agreed and set a time. I still continued with my other two appointments. Only one of the other owners seemed as if he was open to giving me a shot, but the inside of his building would have needed a ton of work. That was probably why he was so open-minded.

I followed the directions from the lady who had called earlier and I quickly noticed that I was headed toward the barbershop. It had to be the building that was suggested by the barber. The address was different than the one that I had written down from the window, though, so I figured they had an office space within the complex. I drove through the complex twice and could not locate the unit number that she had given me. I pulled into one of the parking spaces in front of the church that I had gone to Friday for the concert. I grabbed my phone to call. Just as I was dialing the number, I noticed the numbered white stickers above the entrance of the church. That was the address! It seemed really odd to me. I wondered if I had written the wrong information down. I decided that I would at least check things out and maybe someone could direct me to the landlord.

There was a small doorbell on the side of the door, so I pushed it twice and waited. A black lady in casual business attire opened the door with a huge smile. I told her that I was looking for the landlord who was responsible for the vacant unit in the complex. She maintained her smile and said that I was in the right place. She reached out her hand and told me that her name was Charlet. She instructed me to follow her to an office in the rear of the sanctuary of the church. I followed her through the same church I was in just a few days earlier when I was listening to Marvin Sapp. I looked over at where I had been standing and remembered asking God to order my steps and direct my path.

I also remembered that I had broken down during the concert. I would never forget the feeling. Something had come over me as Marvin began to sing, and all of a sudden, tears began to flow from my eyes. At first, I tried to stop them, and even wiped my eyes quickly. But my hand and the tissue that the person next to me had given me were not enough to absorb the tears. So I just let the tears go and asked God to forgive me for the life I had gotten into. I told Him that I was surrendering everything to Him. Now I was walking through the same exact place to talk about a lease for my new business. If I couldn't see the hand of God moving, then I had to be really blind. I had been directed to a barbershop to be directed to a Marvin Sapp concert to be directed to a landlord who would give me an opportunity to start my business.

Charlet walked me around the building after we discussed all the details of the lease. By the time we got back to the church, the man who had spoken before Marvin Sapp got up to sing was there. He was the pastor of the church. He introduced himself, and I noticed right away that this was a great man of God. He wanted to make sure that I was serious about the lease, and that I was in a position to start and operate the business. I could tell he had a heart that really wanted to help me. I could feel it.

I left that same day with a signed lease to the new location of my clothing store. I said a quick "thank you" to God as I was walking out of the sanctuary. I told myself that it was time to get to work. As I was pulling away from the church, I decided I would call D-Wee and tell him the good news. However, before I got a chance to relay any information, he had some news for me. Bear had been arrested and was now in prison. He explained that he was over at someone's house during a drug sting. I knew that just because I moved away, things wouldn't stop. But I was hoping that I could figure something out quickly, and once I got myself together, then maybe I could help my friends find a better way of life. I had moved away before something bad happened to me, but that did not mean I didn't care what happened to my friends.

This news really bothered me. I thought back to the day when Bear was over at my house and made the decision to leave college and become part of the vicious game. Had I really tried hard enough to convince him to stay in school? Or was I replaying what my uncles did to me, telling me not to become a part of the life while simultaneously showing how glamorous it was? I couldn't help but feel bad. I was probably responsible for his trip to prison. The least I could do was get in touch with his family and see if he or his daughter needed anything.

After D-Wee had given me all the information about Bear, I finally told him that I had found a building and already signed a lease for the new store. I told him that my offer still stood for him to move to Colorado to start a new life. I told him how great he would be at selecting merchandise since he had such a good eye for nice clothing. I also told him that if we put as much energy into the business as we did in the streets, then we were destined for success. He told me that he was not sure about a permanent change, but he was willing to come stay for a while to see how things went. If they worked out, then he would bring his family and make Colorado his home.

So within the next few weeks, D-Wee loaded up his truck and headed to the Rocky Mountains. I was excited that he had made the decision to try to change his life. I was also excited that I would have a business partner that I could completely trust. We didn't understand everything that it would take to make this business a success, but we were determined to figure it out. We spent the next few weeks renovating the space. When I was in Pittsburgh, getting things done was so simple. I knew plenty of people who were always looking for this kind of work. But I didn't know anyone in Denver, so I had to resort to the Yellow Pages. Since I had nothing else to do, I became a laborer who at the very least could hand over a hammer and a nail, or any other tools, to the people who actually knew what they were doing. It also gave me a little leverage on getting a good deal. Within three weeks, the building was new. I had worked on all the legal issues during the renovations. Now all we were waiting for were the boxes of clothes from Morris, which were already on the way. I had also gone to New York for a weekend just to get a few other things wholesale so that the store was full when we opened the doors.

We stood in the building, hours away from our grand opening. I had to say that the place looked amazing. The carpet was new—charcoal gray with small white specks. The slot wall that surrounded the whole interior was painted a relaxed yellow, or Steelers gold, with black inserts in the slots. All the waterfall fixtures hung neatly, separated by about two feet. And all the racks and counters were strategically placed. The checkout counter had a top-of-the-line computer and software system with a bar scanner and receipt printer. Everything about the store said it was professional and we knew what we were doing. Every rack and fixture had clothing hanging on it, thus customers would have more than enough to choose from. We had spent the whole night before tagging and putting everything in place. We were ready! Since we would be bringing a new look to Denver that was exactly what we called it: New Look.

We had taken Morris's advice and made a trip to Las Vegas to check out the Magic show. When we arrived, we finally realized how big the clothing industry really was. There was everyone from Versace to Fruit of the Loom at this show. And Morris was right. If you wanted good prices and merchandise on time, then you had to be a part of this show. Not only did you meet representatives from popular clothing lines, but it also gave you an opportunity to see what the new lines were all about. We met Russell Simmons at Phat Farm, P Diddy at Sean John, Jay Z at Rocawear. We had no idea how exciting this would be. We had found a new career, and we loved it. Plus, even better, we wouldn't have to look over our shoulders.

The store began to catch on really fast in Denver. We had quickly gained the reputation of having the best and latest urban wear. We not only attracted the ballers from the streets, but we were also now attracting ballers from the NBA and NFL. Chauncey Billups, who was from Denver, immediately gave us his support by bringing all of his NBA friends in to shop. We did not disappoint them. Every time they showed up, we had new boxes of clothes to open. It got so bad that we didn't have time to enter our clothing into the inventory system, so we would just keep the tags and enter them afterward.

We had also done a fabulous job on marketing as we ran TV commercials on BET and TNT through the local cable company

Comcast. We had flyers distributed at every major event. Our name was spreading like wildfire. I made it a point that if there were a party or event where I knew there would be celebrities, I would show up with business cards. I was told about a Broncos party that was supposed to be a popular event, so I showed up with all my pockets full of business cards. At the event I was suddenly standing across from Terrell Davis, the MVP running back of the Denver Broncos. He was getting all sorts of attention, and I had to find a way to get him a business card. I saw him hugging two ladies as if he was saying good-bye, so I had to make my approach. I walked up to him with my card in hand and told him that I was the owner of a new clothing store and thought we might have some things he would like. He took the card from my hand and looked at it. His eyes immediately lit up. He then said that he had already heard about our store in their locker room and would definitely check us out. I wasn't sure if he was just blowing me off or if he had real intentions of coming in, but I felt good that I at least gave him an invitation.

The next week the shop seemed to be picking up more momentum. We were making sure the orders kept coming in. I was sitting in the office looking over some invoices when the phone rang. I could see on the monitors that Dani was busy with customers. Dani was the beautiful bilingual Mexican girl who I had hired so we could communicate with our Mexican clientele. She was perfect for the job. I watched her handle the customers with a smile as I picked up the phone on the second ring. I said, "Thank you for calling New Look. How can I help you?"

A deep voice came through the receiver and a guy asked if he could speak to the owner. I quickly responded by saying that I was he. I asked to whom I was speaking.

The voice said confidently, "TD."

"TD?" I thought. "It doesn't…ohhh, TD."

It registered that I had Terrell Davis on the line. He was definitely a man of his word, and I was happy to have him on the phone. He told me that he was on his way from the airport and was going to stop by.

Within fifteen minutes, I had the Super Bowl MVP standing in my store. He was very impressed. He picked out several outfits and was very comfortable as he walked around the store in his socks. He talked about the Broncos, but what he was most proud of was his undefeated season of Pop Warner little league football in San Diego when they didn't allow a team to score on them the whole year.

I wanted to show my appreciation so I went to the back and opened up a brand new box of leather jackets. I gave him one on the house. He seemed very pleased with his visit and said he would be back. He kept his word. And I even got a call from him before he returned to tell me that he went to see a new movie while wearing the jacket I had given him and it was coincidentally featured in the movie. We already felt that our store was official, but that put the icing on the cake.

The store had gotten so busy that we had to consider hiring more staff. I had no family in Denver, at least that I was aware of. I was about to close the shop one night when this guy walked in and purchased a velour sweat suit from me. I paid no attention to the guy as we were trying to close the store. The fellas and I went to a sports restaurant called Jimmie's that evening and I noticed the man wearing the sweat suit that he had purchased earlier. The fact that he was wearing it that night did not grab my attention, but when he returned it the next day, I immediately put it together.

Now, I knew that the customer was always right, but what do you do when you know they are dead wrong? Well, I made some small talk with him and told him how I enjoyed this sports bar the night before. He must have realized why I said it and suggested that he try on the sweat suit again and it might work. Within about ten minutes of conversation, I found out that he was the son of my uncle from Philly. I could not believe how small the world was. What a coincidence. Needless to say, JV became one of our employees. With him knowing everyone, and the high school kid Justin having a large network of friends, our staff was a marketing machine. I could not believe what was happening. I felt like I had hit the jackpot. This was the best decision I could have made.

I also tried to stay focused on my relationship with God, as I knew it was His hand that had opened up the doors for me. Was the instant success of the store pulling me away from Him? And was it affecting my family?

Tracy had decided to take a job with the airlines, which put a little stress on me with the boys since she had to go away for days at a time. However, I loved my boys, and having them at the shop all the time was no problem. The way I looked at it, one day I may be handing them the keys to it, so it was good that they could see how things worked. I was always optimistic, but to be honest, I knew that the focus on my business and Tracy being gone as a flight attendant was really starting to affect our marriage.

Chapter Nineteen

BAWLIN'

ACCORDING TO SCRIPTURE, "GODLINESS WITH contentment is great gain. For we brought nothing into this world, and it is certain that we can carry nothing out. And having food and clothing, we shall be content. But those who desire to be rich fall into temptation and a snare, and into many foolish and harmful lusts. For the love of money is a root of all kinds of evil."

As the business continued to grow, I found myself getting further and further away from God. It was like I had gotten close to Him, and as soon as he poured out His blessings, I began to slowly but surely drift back to my old ways. Yes, hustling clothes was far safer than selling drugs, but neither of them was worth selling your soul.

I realized how much I liked the energy I got from making things happen. Yeah, I had changed cities and I had gone legit, but hustling was still inside of me. Something else that I also quickly noticed was something that I actually knew. Besides the high school kids who borrowed their parents' credit card or the professional athletes who we attracted, we seemed to bring out a plethora of people who lived the same life that I had just left. Why hadn't I even considered that one small detail? If my friends in Pittsburgh and I were Morris's niche, then I had to know that Denver wouldn't be much different. Although I was not committing a crime, I was still dealing with the hustlers. I hadn't even thought about if it would have an influence on me.

I still attended church as I had joined Now Faith, but I was not consistent at all. I would be lucky to make it once a month if that, and when I did show up, I felt like such a hypocrite. I was going to nightclubs to promote the business. Therefore, it put me right back in the same atmosphere that I had left back in Pittsburgh. Yes, I changed my address, but I was really starting to wonder if I had really changed. A lot of people move to start a new life. I do believe that a change of location is very helpful, but the problem is that whatever temptation they were running away from would still be available wherever they were going. True change had to be within. Exterior circumstances had very little to do with it.

One thing I learned from my past was that contentment did not exist. The more money you made, the more you wanted. The more product you were able to buy, the more money you were able to make, therefore, you wanted to purchase more product. And the product went so fast that you had no problem with investing everything you had and not worrying about the next day. You just knew that once the product was in your hand, then life would be good.

The cost of living was not even considered as all the focus was on purchasing and selling the product. And whatever money wasn't wasted on living the life of partying, cars, and good food would then be used to pay the bills last. That was one principle that I feared would hurt me if I carried it over to real business.

My "just do it" attitude had been in place for so long. It had never disappointed because I always had the cash to back it up. Business was excellent, especially for the first year, but it was peanuts compared to what I brought in from the streets. But just as I had functioned in street life, I now wanted more. My 1,100 square feet was just not enough, so I obtained the building next door and knocked out the middle wall. I doubled my orders with my vendors thinking that would double our revenue. I had invested almost everything into this business. But unlike when I was in the game, my personal finances began to struggle. D-Wee and I hadn't even taken a salary in hopes that the store would do well enough to replenish our initial investments.

Things got so tight that I started to take from the business account to cover some of my personal bills. I had made the move and was trying to live right, but this was something that I was not used to. Since the very first time that I had climbed out of my project window as a teenager, I never had to worry about money. If I wanted something, I bought it. If a bill needed being paid, I just paid it. There was nothing to think about.

Well, now I had everything to think about. Had I tried to develop this business way too fast? My biggest mistake was assuming that I could change product and go legit while still reaping the same kind of profits. What made me feel better were the consequences in each of these worlds. In a legal business, I would have financial losses, or at worst I could lose the business. But in the streets, I could lose my life. I tried to stay optimistic, kept working hard, and prayed that things would eventually work out.

As glad as I was to get away so that my kids would have a better life, I did feel bad that I had taken them away from their family. In Pittsburgh they would always be around other kids. There would always be a birthday party or cookout for us to go to. In Denver we had none of that. I made it a little fun for them by putting video games and toys in the back office of the store so they were not bored while they were there. I also made it a point to take them to events, whether it was Disney on Ice or a circus. And unlike Pittsburgh, I did like the fact that Denver had an NBA team.

I remember dressing my sons up in their matching khaki Polo jackets and pants and taking them to their very first Nuggets game. Tracy was out of town working flights, so I decided that it would just be the boys and me. As we walked through all the people, I could see their little eyes taking in the whole atmosphere and wondering where they were. They probably weren't too worried, though, because they were with their dad. And at that point, they probably felt like celebrities, as people were so in awe of twins wherever we went. We got to our seats and the only thing that grabbed their attention was Rocky, the mascot, and cotton candy, which they wouldn't stop eating. I watched these two little guys communicate with each other as if they had their own language. It would have been really hard if we had just one son, but having each other made it easier on them.

The Nuggets were losing badly. I thought it would be smart to get ahead of the mass departure of fans so we headed toward the exit. I also wanted to make sure that I got the boys a souvenir. When we walked in the team store, I repeated my rule that I always used when we went into any store: "You can pick one thing that you can get, not two." I always wanted them to make decisions. They understood the rule. I knew it would be tough on them at times, like when they had a race car in one hand and some M&M's in the other. But they had to make the choice. I was wondering if that rule would one day bite me in the butt when they were old enough to point to a car that they could actually drive.

It was apparent at a very young age that they wanted to be different. We dressed them the same every day, they always ate the same food, and sometimes they even sat on their potties in the restroom at the same time. Everything they did was the same. But as we were in the souvenir shop, their differences showed. One of the twins immediately grabbed Rocky, the stuffed animal, which made sense since they had enjoyed the mascot more than the game. The other twin chose the mini Nuggets basketball. Before I made the purchase, I looked at both of them to confirm that I was buying what they wanted, as I always did. They both gave me their approval. I was happy that we were in and out; they had made their choices quickly. But we hadn't made it twenty steps out of the store before the twin with the Rocky stuffed animal was reaching for his brother's basketball. His brother wrapped his hands around the ball as if it was a football. I separated the two and reminded the twin that he had chosen Rocky. Therefore, he had to leave his brother's choice alone. I guess he didn't like the answer I gave him, so within the next couple of steps he decided to throw Rocky on the ground. My first thought was that there was no way I could approve of animal cruelty, but my second thought was that it was an excellent opportunity to teach my son a lesson. So I picked Rocky up off of the floor, brushed off his face, and politely asked my son if he wanted it. He looked up at me with his eyebrows knitted and quickly said, "No!" I asked if he was sure. He confirmed his answer by saying that he didn't want it. So I smiled and said okay. The next little kid who walked past us without a toy in his hand, I reached down and handed Rocky to him. I figured it was done at animal shelters all the time. If a pet owner did not want their pet, then they would find a new owner who appreciated it. Usually the new owner didn't have to pay anything and instead just had to love the pet. The little boy with scraggly blond hair brightened up, and his parent thanked me for the kind gesture. That immediately got my son's attention as he was reaching back for Rocky while we were walking in the other direction. He continued to pout all the way to the car. I was willing to bet that it would be the last time I would have to go through that again.

Other than the normal lessons that a parent had to give, they were really excellent kids. We had enrolled them in a day care that was within walking distance from our apartment. They seemed to have adjusted pretty well—especially since the kids at day care were the only other kids that they had to play with during that time.

As I was picking them up one evening, I got out of my Expedition and heard a deep voice say, "Nice truck." I smiled as I noticed that a tall African American man with a touch of gray in his beard was getting out of the same kind of truck. His physique implied that he might have played a down or two in his past. The toothpick in his mouth and the collector's coin that hung from his chain translated his wisdom and savvy. I slowed my step and held the door for him as he approached. My assumption of him doing grandfather duty was totally wrong, as he was there to pick up his son. We quickly discovered that our sons were the same age and in the minority of their class. We continued our light conversation as we exited the day care. Our sons never stopped playing with each other. When we got to the parking lot, he reached out his hand and introduced himself as Mr. Faison. I shook it firmly and gave him my name. He told me that he also lived within walking distance from the day care and that he had a huge yard. He invited me to bring the boys by so they could play with his son. I accepted the offer, as I knew the boys needed some friends their age. We exchanged numbers and planned to make something happen as soon as possible.

The following Saturday I got a call from Mr. Faison. He said that he was throwing something on the grill and suggested that the boys and I stop by. I knew Saturdays were our busiest day at the shop, but at that point, I had staff to cover it. I figured it was a great idea, and I could give the boys a day where they could unwind. I took down his directions and told him that we would arrive around one o'clock. When I gave the boys the news, I could already see their excitement. We loaded into the truck and made the trip that could easily have taken five to ten minutes to walk.

Mr. Faison's house was probably as big as one of our apartment buildings. I did a double take at this massive, white and red brick ranch home. I looked at the address to make sure it was correct. But when the garage door began to open, I immediately noticed the identical truck inside and knew for sure that I was at the correct place. His son came charging out before we had a chance to get out of the truck. I took it that he did not often get the privilege of having company the same size and weight as him.

I could already tell the first time we met in the day care parking lot that Mr. Faison was a hard-working, productive citizen. It was the way that he walked with confidence and how he spoke matter-of-factly. However, I had no idea that he was successful to this extent. When I looked at his home, I could only wonder what this man did for a living.

I was one hundred percent sure that it had nothing to do with breaking the law. Up until that point, I couldn't say that I had ever been closely associated with a man who was able to build success without illegal activity (besides Morris).

They invited us in with open arms, and the boys enjoyed every second of it. I knew we would have a conversation to find out more about each other and that point came sooner rather than later. As we were sitting watching the boys chase each other on their professional-style basketball court, he popped the big question: "What do you do for a living?"

With pride and without hesitation, I told him that I was a small business owner. I told him it was a clothing store that was starting to catch some momentum. He smiled without showing his teeth, not letting the toothpick fall from his mouth. People believe that a smile is used when a person is happy, but a smile could be used to say many things. This smile told me nothing at all. That is until he began to speak. He took his time with his words as he told me that he had been a very big business owner who had started out small. He had built his company to over 100 employees and got to the point where he could sell the company for a nice chunk of change. He said he was retired and was just trying to find something else to do with his time. All I could say was, "Wow!"

I went to school for business and dreamed of becoming a successful businessman. Now here I was sitting across from the real thing. At that point, I couldn't tell him that I feared losing my business. It wasn't like I wanted anything from this man financially, but what I could use was his wisdom. If he had built his business from the ground up and was able to sell it for a small fortune, then he would certainly have the knowledge to help me stabilize a business that had great potential. Was this a coincidence that we met, or was it God answering a prayer that I had too much pride to even pray to Him about? It is said that God knows our heart, and knows what we need even before we can ask. Lord knows I was in need of some help.

We continued to get the boys together, and he eventually made a trip to my shop. The moment he walked in, I could tell that he was impressed as I watched his eyes survey the square footage of the building. After doing a complete walk-through with a slight smile again holding the toothpick in his mouth, he stopped in front of my checkout area and reached into the candy jar on the counter. He looked up at me and said he was very impressed. One thing I was confident about was that we had gone first class with this store. We made sure it was spotless at all times. So whether it was an athlete, hustler, or big business owner, we always got compliments on how professional it was. And as organized and neat as the showroom floor was, the most important space in the building was starting to look the total opposite.

Most people think the most important part of a store like ours would be the merchandise and what people saw when they entered the business, but the most important space was where you controlled the numbers: the office. That's where the bills got paid, invoices were kept, and data was tracked to understand exactly where the business really stood. It didn't matter if the store was full of good merchandise and items were flying out the door. If the office was not managed correctly, then that business was destined for failure. There was no way I could let that happen! I had rolled the dice and left everything in hopes of building a life where I didn't have to look over my shoulder. But was I in way over my head? Our problem was not that we were in debt at this point, because we actually owned all of our merchandise. However, doubling my orders only put the business under more pressure. Therefore, as quickly as we made a profit, it was going to new invoices or current bills.

Many athletes shopped at my store. It was a business that had great potential, so I thought that maybe opening the door for some investors might be a wise decision. However, pride goes before destruction, and a haughty spirit before a fall. Did I have too much pride to ask for help? Was I too embarrassed to tell Mr. Faison the truth so that he could help me?

I decided to write him a letter and try to explain my dilemma. I had to be careful with my words, as I did not want him to think I was interested in his money. I hadn't asked anyone for anything since I was a kid. I had jumped into a life that allowed me to financially take care of everything I wanted. In my mind, I was not about to ask for a handout. I also had a fear of opening the doors of a business that D-Wee and I had built on our own, so we wanted to be the ones who reaped all the benefits.

Mr. Faison read my letter and said he would consider how he could be of assistance to me, but he needed some time to give it some thought. That was totally understandable, but the clock was ticking for me. I had to figure out something fast or else my business would be in trouble. And if my business was in trouble, then that meant I had brought my family all the way across the country just to fail.

I had spent so much money on this project that it was becoming hard to keep it afloat and still take care of my household. I had also discovered upon engaging in some small talk with a couple of my regular customers that the price of the forbidden fruit that I had hustled for so long was way cheaper in Colorado than I had ever paid when I was in Pittsburgh. My problem would be transporting it from here to there. Getting rid of it would definitely be a nonissue.

I had made all the necessary steps for change, but had I truly changed, or did I just change my address? I couldn't believe that after all that I had accomplished, I was now thinking the unthinkable. Could I actually pull off a move that would put this business over the top along with giving me a little cushion to take care of home? I would only need to make one more move and that would be enough. Afterward, I could just continue to function as if it had never happened. I would tell my friends back home that it was just a one-time deal and I was totally done for good. There was a fight going on in my head. A part of me was saying that it would be foolish to turn back now; the other part was saying that it would only be the one time.

I hadn't had the talk with Mr. Faison yet, but I was already beginning to have conversations with the wrong people. I hadn't fully made my decision, but I couldn't believe that this was even a consideration. Having those negative conversations only put more pressure on me as I was now getting phone calls from guys in Colorado who were anxious to capitalize on my strong network of hustlers. Once they knew that they could make more money on the East Coast and I had the resources to make the product vanish in the blink of an eye, they were all for it. I always paid for my product, but they were willing to take a down payment, which I was not comfortable with at all. If I were going to do it, it would have to be my right hand man and me.

We finally put together a deal that was going to put us over the top. This was something I had told myself I would not do again. As in Romans 7:21, "I find then a law, that when I have a will to do good, evil is present with me." The very thing that I know not to do is the very thing that I do. So it is no longer me that does it, but sin that dwells in me.

I was having second thoughts, but once you had certain conversations in this kind of life, it was very difficult to turn back. At that point, the only reputation I had in the state of Colorado was as a young business owner. I did not want to ruin the good work that I had done. But I was beginning to fear that it would all go down the drain if I didn't do something about it.

I had trusted God all the way up to this point, and I was wondering why I was now relying on my own strength (or weakness, for that matter). I kept telling myself that if I made only one more move, then things would be okay. I had made it crystal clear to my friends in Pittsburgh and my new friends in Denver that this was only a one-time deal. I was dead serious about it. I also made a promise to God that after this I would be done for good.

The next couple of months seemed to go by in a blur. It was like I had blacked out. I was a normal person who had turned into a demon and lost control. Sometimes when having a wonderful dream, you wake up a little too soon and get upset. Maybe you are on some beautiful island or at a resort and everything looks so pretty. Or maybe you are with a loved one who has passed and so you wish you had slept a little while longer so you could spend a few more minutes with them. Maybe they would have told you something that you really needed to know. But then there are other times where you are running from a ghost or falling from a cliff and aren't sure where you are going to land. Then you wake up in time before an unavoidable calamity. In those cases, you are so happy that it was a dream or a nightmare that you were able to wake up from.

I looked down at my feet. For some reason, all I could take notice of were my socks. I had worn these socks many times before, but today for some strange reason they reminded me of many years ago. I was on my way to my little league football game, changing my church clothes in the back of Mom's Gremlin hatchback, and I had forgotten to change my socks. It was how I got the nickname Church Socks, which stuck forever. It was game time and my performance may have been enhanced by the luck of those socks. I continued to wear those church socks for good luck in every football game I played. Even in high school the orange, black, and white team socks may have been visible, but the church socks were always underneath. I even had them on the day I won all that money at Swamp's years ago. They were my good luck charms—a reminder that God was with me no matter how far I drifted away.

I was still staring down at them. Yeah, today was game day. I was hoping that they would bring me some luck, or better yet, a sign that God was still with me. Out of all the years I had done dirt in Pittsburgh, I had never seen what the inside of a prison or jail looked like. I had moved far away to avoid such a tour. Did the move really change me, or had I just run from a temptation that I never truly dealt with? Was I hiding from something that was somewhere still deep inside of me and I felt that moving away would be the only cure? Most of all, was I just absent from the game and not yet truly delivered?

Mom and my real dad had been strung out on heroine and crack cocaine. Neither of them ever moved away. They were around the heavy temptations of drug-infested neighborhoods, yet refused to turn back to a life of addiction. They were truly delivered from the demon. I was just running away to another part of the country that was actually even worse when it came to the temptation of this kind of life. My mom and real dad were proof that true change, or better yet deliverance, had to take place inside of you. Moving away may just delay an inevitable relapse if you hadn't really dealt with the addiction. Most people in that life viewed the users as addicts, but the hustlers were even worse. They were eventually on their way to prison, or in most cases, they would change over from the high of the almighty dollar to getting high on their own supply, or in some cases even death.

So who was worse, the user or the hustler? In my eyes, they were no different. Yeah, the hustler may have had the disguise of fancy clothes, jewelry, and exotic cars, but their spirit and soul were no different than the user's. Both of them were in need of true deliverance before it was too late.

Many years ago I had made "the vow." I was standing in my mother's room holding a crack pipe that I had found in her dresser drawer. I had vowed that I would never use drugs. Until this day, I had never used any of the drugs that I had handled because of that vow I had made. Most drug dealers eventually started to sample their own product, or another form of drug that they felt was less embarrassing or offensive than the drug they sold. But I was different. Because of what I saw my mother go through when I was a child, and because at times she made me feel like nothing, I had made a vow.

It had not been broken. I was totally drug free and hadn't even thought of using. I now stood there, wishing my vow had been twofold. Had I vowed not to allow drugs to use me, then my life wouldn't be in jeopardy. Plain and simple, I was an addict. I had never sniffed a line or had a needle stuck in my arm except at the doctor's office. My addiction was to an easy way of life. It seemed to be easy on the way in, but hard on the way out.

Yep, it was game time! If only I could rewind life, I would be at my little league football game, waiting for the referee to blow the whistle and make a call. This day, the game wouldn't be that simple. In fact, it was quite serious, as the field I was playing on was a federal courtroom, and the referee who was waiting to make a call was a judge. I picked my eyes up off the floor, looking away from my socks and up at the honorable judge who was about to announce my fate. Was I finally paying for all the transgressions that I thought I could run away from? They say you reap what you sow. Was I now about to reap all the bad seeds that I had sown over the years? I looked to my right and saw a poker-faced attorney who was said to be one of the best in the state. Would his thirty years of practice and the small fortune that I had given to him do me any good?

I looked back at two women who knew me when I was off the field and away from the locker room. They knew that there was so much more to me than the game I was playing. Both of them smiled at me, but their smiles said something different. My mother's smile said that there was still hope and to not give up. Tracy's smile said that she was so afraid for me, but also afraid for her and the kids.

I then thought about my boys and how I had spent so much time with them, how I had made it a point to teach them so many lessons. How would they feel when I was not around to take them to a movie or a basketball game, or just fix them a bowl of cereal? These were things that a drug dealer never thinks of until standing in my position. I tried to square my shoulders, but they kept going limp. I tried to keep my head up, but it just seemed too heavy. I felt too embarrassed to even pray to God, so I just whispered the words, "Let your will be done."

What had seemed like a great plan went totally wrong. And now my best friend D-Wee and I were in position to be sent off to federal prison. Everything had been thought out so smoothly. You would never have thought after all the years we avoided the police that we would get caught red-handed for possession of a controlled substance. Yup, we had enough illegal products to send us over the top, but we had not thought about how far it could sink us to the bottom. I thought about my friend and how we had done so much together. Now we were going to prison at the same time and for the same length of time. What about his son and his family? There were a million things running through my head, and I had absolutely no control over them.

During the proceedings, I had watched lips move but had not heard anything. My body was standing in the courtroom, but my mind was somewhere far away. And then it happened. I could see the judge as if he were moving in slow motion. He picked up the wooden gavel and raised it to the side of his ear in preparation to slam it down and confirm my fate. Everything was still in slow motion. His voice dropped like the voice of Count Dracula when he said that I was sentenced to six years in the federal penitentiary. Immediately after the loud slam, the volume in the room seemed to be turned on. I heard sudden whispers and sounds of deep breaths. But me, I was actually holding mine in disbelief.

I looked back to see smiles from the two women who I was close to in heart, but was about to be physically so far away from. Both of the smiles were now gone. Mom had a stoic look that said she wouldn't ever give up on me. Tracy's smile was replaced by a flood of tears that spoke volumes. There were no hugs good-bye, and the handcuffs holding my hands behind me prohibited me from even blowing a kiss. But would that have even been necessary? "Six years?" I thought.

I found it pretty strange that I was getting sentenced to almost the same amount of time that I had been hustling. It was like God was making me pay for every day that I had lived the life. I couldn't help but think that I could have stayed in Pittsburgh if I was going to come all the way to Colorado to go to federal prison.

I was escorted out of the courtroom and transported to my new residence, where I would be living for several years. And instead of a number on the back of a football jersey, I would now have several numbers accompanied by letters on the front of my prison shirt.

Galatians 5:9 says, "A little leaven leavens the whole lump." In other words, all the good I had done by walking away from the game and moving away for change was now ruined by one bad decision. But would it have really been one decision? Or, if everything had gone perfectly fine, would I have been on my way to continuing the lifestyle that I thought I had left behind in those tunnels in Pittsburgh? To make matters worse, I had brought my family across the country just to abandon them. I could not think of a time in my life when I had felt worse. Not only was Tracy left to figure out things for her and the kids, she was also left to clean up some of the mess that I had left behind. She considered trying to keep the business going, but we decided that it would be way too much to handle—especially since my bad decision was supposed to be the fix-all for the struggles of the business. Instead, it made things worse than I could have ever imagined. She was forced to liquidate a business that she knew very little about. All I could do was tell her to do the best that she could and that I was more than appreciative of her efforts.

So within the next couple of months, the business that I had worked so hard for was now gone, and so was I. Tracy and I stayed in contact as I called almost every day, and she showed up faithfully to visit me. I had watched her go from a very strong and determined woman to one with a look of hopelessness. I had also noticed through the thick visiting window that she had lost a substantial amount of weight. She tried her best to smile at me, but I could tell that the stress was slowly eating away at her. And to add insult to injury, during one of her visits she informed me that she had found out that I had kept in touch with some of my lady friends from my past life. Although those friendships were obviously not physical, as the women were way across the country, it was enough to make her want to give up on me.

The fact that we had been so caught up in our own lives, and were slowly drifting away from each other, was not an excuse to keep friendships with women who I had been involved with in the past. But that was what I did. And I knew it was the friendship and the conversations that I had sought, but why hadn't I sought that in the person who I had taken vows with? After some very tough conversations, Tracy finally told me that she loved me and was going to be there for me every step of the way. She said it might take some time to truly forgive me, but she believed that we could work through it.

I was fortunate to be sentenced to a prison in Colorado since in the federal system you could be shipped to any part of the country. D-Wee was hoping for the opposite. He wanted to get closer to the East Coast so he could be close enough for his family to visit him. He was shipped off immediately while I was set to do my time in Colorado. This was the less glamorous part of the game that most drug dealers were never able to think about. They were introduced to a life of luxury only to leave their family behind with a struggle, along with broken hearts. As I sat and thought about the whole picture, I could clearly see that things did not add up. There was no amount of money worth leaving your loved ones behind.

That was until almost my second year of incarceration. Everything would suddenly change for the worse. I already felt that my life couldn't get much worse than it was, but I was definitely wrong about that. You would be amazed by some of the things that people could get hold of behind prison walls. And if you still had money outside of these walls, then you were somehow able to make things happens.

I met a guy from St. Louis who just happened to be one of those guys. When he offered me what I thought was an opportunity to make unmonitored phone calls for as long as I needed to talk, I was all for it. Yup, this guy had a cell phone inside of prison. I would return the favor by buying him something from the commissary list. I wasn't overly concerned with the unmonitored part, as I really had no conversations that would have gotten me in trouble, but being able to talk as long as I needed was what grabbed my attention. Things went pretty smoothly for a while until one day when I was called to the security office, handcuffed, and thrown into what we called the hole.

At first, I thought they were making a mistake. I was certain that I hadn't done anything wrong. I was already having a bad week as I had called home and gotten the news that my Uncle Geno had been murdered. He was on my mind that whole week. I was well aware that his life had been taken over by drugs and alcohol, but I could not allow those elements or substances to overshadow the real person that he was. Yes, he was bound by a demon, but he was by far the most loving and loyal person that I knew in my entire family. You could not have a conversation with him without him finishing it by saying that he loved you. And it was from his heart. He may not have had a lot of material things, but what he did have was much more valuable. That was love. He may not have bought his only daughter Neak a brand new car, but she knew without a doubt that he loved her. In spite of his addiction, he would make sure she was always okay. I thought about how hard my grandmother was probably taking it since he was her first child. I knew she was a very strong woman of God, but I knew he was her heart and it was probably now broken. I was told that he was stabbed to death and found by the train tracks that led to the closest hospital. I wondered if he had tried to make it there on his own while ignoring his wounds. I wondered if he had even tried to get to the main street so that someone would notice him. According to reports, he had walked quite a ways before falling to his fate.

I couldn't believe that I could not be present at his funeral. This was really killing me. Oh well, I guess I would have to be content with all the memories of when he was alive instead of lying in a casket. One thing that I would never forget was that, although he may have been discharged from the army, my uncle would always be a soldier in my book. God judges the thoughts and intents of the heart, and I knew for sure he had a good one.

So now I was locked up again—as if I were not already in prison. I had been doing great, but now I was in solitary confinement. That same day, I was served with a write-up that pretty much explained that one of the numbers on my approved phone list had been matched to a number retrieved from a confiscated cell phone. All I could say was, "Oh, boy!" They informed me that it was quite serious as it was a breach of security. They said about eight of us had gotten in trouble for it. Then I was told that it was possible that I could be sent to another prison in a different state. I could not believe what I was hearing. I could not imagine not being able to regularly see my family. Everything was becoming way too much to bear.

The cell was dark and dim with cemented floors and bars on the windows. Just a short time ago, I was so particular about the fluffy carpet I stepped on or how many feather-soft pillows I could fit on my bed. I controlled the climate of my home simply by pushing the buttons on the thermostat. Now I was in control of none of that. I stared in disbelief at what I had reduced myself to. I sat and waited for my fate. Would I be shipped far away? Although I had been incarcerated for almost two years in a prison camp, this was actually my first time inside a prison cell. The prison was built many years ago, but this was probably the only part that hadn't been upgraded.

It was called the hole because when you were in a hole, there was very little light and mostly darkness. The view was depressing when your eyes were open, and only your imagination would give you a more comfortable sight. Not only was the water tap on the sink stainless steel, but also what you sat on to relieve yourself. The hard metal frame of the bed lacked the luxury of a mattress and made it hard to sleep in one place. Yes, I was in the hole and things were considerably worse.

The first couple of days I sat in silence. Although the only one I could have spoken to was God, I still refused. I knew I probably couldn't hear Him at that point anyway, so I just stayed silent. I paced the floor back and forth, running out of space within three or four steps. I kept asking myself, "What have I become? And how had God allowed me to sink so far in that dark, dark space called solitary confinement?" It was probably equivalent to the state of my mind and spirit.

I started to ask myself questions since I was not talking to God. My problem was that I could not answer any of them. On about day four, I requested a Bible. I figured, although I hadn't been speaking to God, at least I could read the word and see what I could get out of it. So I started reading the pocket-size New Testament Bible that they had given me. The small print and very little light made it difficult to read. But was it the lack of a power source in terms of electric energy, or was it the lack of a power source in terms of God? I continued to force feed myself the scripture in spite of not really understanding anything. I read through Matthew and Mark, then Luke and John. By the time I had gotten past the Gospels, I felt that I had lost my mind in this hole. Was I hallucinating? I was reading different books of the Bible, but I felt like I had just read the same miracle or parable days before. I was not aware that all four Gospels were the same account of the life of Christ, but told differently, and I really thought I was going crazy. By the time I got to Revelations, I was in a state of confusion. I read the entire New Testament. Every word, every comma, every period. Yet, I was in the same exact place I was before I requested it. Why hadn't it made me feel better? Then, about the third week, I got the answer.

I remember pacing back and forth, still asking myself questions. Finally, I decided to ask God a couple of things. Why was I mad at Him anyway? It was because of my own decision that I was now in this cocoon. So I began to talk to God, and before I could get out a full sentence, something came over me in that cell. I could barely pronounce a word as tears had overtaken me. I had totally broken down, and I began to cry out to God to ask Him to forgive me for my stubbornness. I remember praying in that cell until I had emptied out all the tears that I had inside of me. I confessed all of my faults, and I asked God to come back into my life like never before. After that prayer, I felt a peace come over me. I decided that whatever happened to me, I would trust God and know that I was in His hands. The next couple of days I continued to read the Bible, but now I understood what I was reading. I knew I was in a bad situation, but something happened to me in that dark cell. I found myself bawlin' outta control.

At first, I began to pray that God would show me favor and somehow I would not be shipped away from my family to do the rest of my time. But then I read a scripture that said all things work together for the good of those who love God and are called according to his purpose. So I just waited patiently to find out what was going to happen. After being in the hole for weeks, they came and gave me the news that I would be shipped off to a prison in a different state to finish up my time. I immediately felt a feeling of gloom come over me. I knew it was actually for my family. As for me, I had a new confidence that my steps were being ordered by the Lord. If he was allowing this to happen, then it must be for a purpose. It was my duty to find out what that was. It was also difficult because I was being shipped away the week before Thanksgiving. I had no idea what to expect or where I was going. I just knew I was leaving the state of Colorado. I didn't even know how I was getting there until we were lined up shackled in front of an airplane that they called Con Air.

I had flown many times, but I this was the scariest flight that I had ever taken—particularly because I was handcuffed and shackled to the plane. If it happened to go down, there was absolutely no chance of survival. I used to pray all the time before I took a flight, but for this flight I felt the need to pray continuously until it landed safely. After making a connection in Oklahoma so I could be processed for wherever I was going, I finally landed at a prison in Minnesota. This was where I would be doing the rest of my time.

I had already made up my mind about something while I was in the hole. Wherever I ended up, whether I somehow stayed in Colorado or was shipped off to another place, as soon as I hit the prison yard, I was going to devote my time to learning more about myself. Most of all, I wanted to learn about God. At that point, it was pretty obvious that I did not know enough about either of them.

So there I was, dropped off in the middle of nowhere, with about 500 people who had one thing in common: breaking the law. Other than that, it was like being in a foreign country where you didn't know a soul and couldn't even understand their language. After being processed in, I walked across the yard observing my new atmosphere. I felt totally lost. I was directed to the room (or cell) where I would be laying my head for the duration of my stay. The room was pretty big considering the resort I was staying at, but the walk-in closet was small compared to one in a nice home.

The very first thing that I noticed was the floor. It was cheap, lightly speckled brown 12 x 12 tile, but somehow it had the shine of glass. It seemed like a luxury to me as I had just spent thirty days walking on a cement floor. Although the other occupants were not in the room, I took note of how someone had really taken pride in the place they called home. I threw my belongings on the bunk and said a quick thank you to God for the paper-thin mattress. I then headed straight for the chapel. I had absolutely no time to waste. I figured that by the time anyone knew my name at this place, they would be clear that I was a man of God.

The chapel was amazing. I quickly noticed that they had a very large library and very extensive resources to learn about God. I hadn't been there for ten minutes when I was approached by a guy named Chico. I would later learn that they called him Bishop because of his knowledge of the word of God. He was also taking college courses while in prison to become a minister. He welcomed me to the chapel and invited me to a study what was happening at that moment. I started to decline, but I figured I had nothing to lose. When I walked into the room, I could not believe my eyes. There were about ten brothers, mostly African American. There were a couple of white guys as well, all sitting around a table with their Bibles open. They also had notepads, highlights, commentaries, you name it. I could see instantly that these guys were serious about the word of God.

Before I could get to my seat, I was attacked with handshakes from each of the brothers. They welcomed me to the body of Christ. I had never seen anything like it. I sat quietly through the study. I could see why Chico was called Bishop as most of the questions were directed toward him. He would not answer any of them without flipping through the worn-out Bible to go right to a scripture that would support whatever the question might have been. I was so impressed by how excited these men were about the word of God. I was so happy to be there, and decided that I would attend every study, every service, and every event that was lifting up the name of Christ.

After the study, they informed me that they had a treasury of everything new people might need when they first arrived. It was the way they paid tithes since they didn't have access to money. When someone would get money from their family or got paid the minimum prison wages, they would buy extra toothpaste, soap, or other hygiene items and throw it in the treasury. And when a new person hit the yard, they would bless them with a hygiene package. Bishop made it clear that it didn't matter what race or what belief that person may have been. Their motto was simple, "They will know that we are Christians by our love."

On the way back to the unit the topic of the study was continued, which was all about how hard it was to control the flesh. I listened to Chico and another one of the brothers, who they called BaBa (the A being pronounced like the word aw), having a debate as if they were arguing which was the best football team or who was the greatest basketball player of all time. However, they were actually debating about the word of God. This was something really new to me, and I knew right away that God had sent me to the right place.

We walked to the front of the unit I was assigned to. Chico shook my hand and asked if there was anything that I wanted him to pray for. He said he was going to lift me up since he knew how hard the transition was. Without hesitation I said that I wanted God to give me strength. His whole expression changed instantly. His eyebrows puffed up like I had made him angry by my request. He looked me in the eye and asked if I was sure. I looked back at this middle-aged black man who had light brown skin, droopy cheeks, and eyes that conveyed wisdom. I then ask if there was something wrong with my request. He said not at all, he just wanted to be certain that I wanted him to pray for strength. He explained that, just as I had gotten stronger lifting weights from the resistance, I needed to understand that most times we got our strength from the things we were going through. And if things got tough, then I needed to continue to trust God and know that he was indeed strengthening me. I thought that I sure hoped things didn't get any worse than this, but I would definitely trust God.

So from that moment I began to walk blameless before God. I dedicated everything to Him. I lived at the chapel as I went to every study service. I even went other times just to do some personal study. I had never felt a peace like this in my entire life. The pastor who came in on Sundays even baptized me. I was on fire for the Lord. I got a job in the laundry department with Chico, BaBa, and a brother named Tee. All we did was study the word together for almost eight hours a day between changing loads. My only other activities besides work and God were working out every day and participating in sports.

Bear, Lump, and Mo-Joe may have gone undefeated in flag football, but I was undefeated in prison flag football. Sad, but it was so much fun, and it was amazing that there were people on my team that had made it to play college football. We had a receiver that played for Nebraska and a running back that played for San Diego State. Both of them had done well with their lives until falling for the same exact temptation that I had.

And speaking of my childhood friends' undefeated high school season, all of them seemed to have taken a loss. Bear was already in prison. Mo-Joe, I was told, also had a run-in with the law. But what surprised me was what I heard about Lump. He had played four years of college ball and had gotten a huge contract to play overseas in hopes of eventually landing a potential NBA contract. He was doing really well until he decided that the overseas contract was not enough money, so he teamed up with a few of the guys who I used to shoot dice with at Swamp's. Within a short time, they were indicted by the Feds and sent off to prison. E.T. was not as fortunate, however. When I heard about his story, it really did something to me. They said he was coming out of Swamp's and was apparently being robbed. Whether he resisted or not, he was shot in cold blood and his life was over. I couldn't help but think back years ago when I was coming out of the same gambling shack with a gun pointed at my head. In my case, a police car happened to be patrolling the neighborhood.

Why were things different for me? E.T. was a great guy who I liked a lot. He had lived the same life that I had, but his life had been taken. Sometimes things were so hard to understand, but as my grandmother would always say, "Never question the hand of God."

Tracy understandably did not take the move well at all, and our conversations seemed to be very uncomfortable at times. I was happy that she was attending church and singing in the choir. I was not familiar with the new church she had chosen, but I had heard good things about it. So while God was working on me, I felt like He was working on her as well. That was until one day when I was hit with a blow that knocked me off my feet. All I could see was the referee standing over me counting in slow motion. I wondered if I had the strength to get up, or if I should stay down. And if I did get up, would I even have the strength to continue fighting?

I went to our normal mail call, where everyone showed up to see if they were still loved by the outside world. A picture or a letter meant so much to someone under these circumstances. Today mine was a large envelope. It was white and trimmed in green, but what got my attention was that it was from an attorney's office. What made it even stranger was that it was not from my attorney. My first thought was that I had done something in my past that was catching up to me (to go along with my present consequences). People didn't wait to get back to their cell to open their mail. They pulled out pictures and read their letters, paying no attention to where they were walking as their bodies just knew which way to go. This piece of mail was a little peculiar, so I decided to wait to open it by myself. When I got to my room, I opened the large envelope and suddenly lost my breath. It was like I was being suffocated and couldn't find air to breathe. There, inside that envelope, were papers for me to sign approving the request that Tracy had made to file for divorce. I could not believe what was happening. I hadn't been at this place six months and she had already filed for divorce. To make matters worse, she also informed me that she had started dating someone. What I couldn't understand was why, when I had totally begun to get myself back together with God, the enemy was attacking me. The pain was unbearable, but I had to maintain a look of strength considering where I was. Was this what Chico was talking about? Maybe I shouldn't have asked him to pray for me. After a little thought I decided that, if that was what she wanted, then I would sign and send them back to her. So I signed the papers, had them notarized, and put them in the mail. I made up my mind that I would let nothing—even this terrible news—throw me off what God was doing for my life.

I started studying more, praying more, and taking my walk even more seriously. Men would come to me for prayer, and I would be glad to lift them up. I also started a nightly study inside the unit. It started with three people, but within weeks the room was not big enough for our study. I felt like God was beginning to speak to me. I was free spiritually, although bound physically. I remember going to the chapel and finding an old box of videos of T.D. Jakes. I began to watch them every day and take notes, as I was amazed by how this man was able to bring scripture to life.

Within a week, they made an announcement that everyone had to go to their unit for a while as they had a very important guest who was coming on the yard. My thought was that it was a politician of some sort and they wanted him to feel safe. However, they announced shortly after that we could move about normally. That's when I saw this big black man escorted by several people. He moved about the yard like he was not intimidated by his surroundings. I could see the shine from his bald head as he walked securely in his long, black trench coat. And then I was close enough to not only recognize who he was, but also to actually shake his hand. It was T.D. Jakes in the flesh—or better yet, the spirit. I was told that he was there to visit an ex-professional athlete who was now incarcerated. I had just started studying his tapes a few weeks ago and had made a mental note to go see him when I was released. I felt he had come to visit me while I was still bound. Coincidence or what have you? There are no coincidences with God.

I continued to walk firmly in the ways of the Lord and had gotten much deeper in my studies. I had learned so much within a year's time about the word of God. I also continued to watch videos of various preachers at the chapel. One day I found a box of videos by a bishop named Noel Jones. I had never heard of this man, but I thought I would give him a try since I had already dissected the T.D. Jakes videos. I wasn't sure if this man was just that powerful, or if I was just at a place spiritually to be receptive to his words, but I hadn't made it past the first video before tears ran down my face. This man had a power that I hadn't heard. He forced me to study at a whole new level. I had no idea what a theophany was or what getting to the substratum of the text meant, but my spirit immediately connected with this man. I allowed him to teach me through his videos. I sat with a notepad and dictionary while watching him. I also discovered that he had a show on BET called *Fresh Oil*, so I would get up every Wednesday morning at 5:00 to watch him. I was being transformed by the word of God. I made another mental note that I wanted to meet this man and attend one of his services in California when I was released.

So much had happened to me over the last few years, and I was feeling like a new person. If any man be in Christ, he is a new creation. Old things have passed away. Behold all things have become new.

Chapter Twenty

THE REAL WORLD

In 1 Corinthians 10:13 it says, "There hath no temptation taken you but such as is common to man: but God is faithful, who will not suffer you to be tempted above that ye are able; but will with the temptation also make a way to escape."

I began to learn that some scriptures were literal while others were figurative. There was no way I was escaping from this prison. The fence was just way too high and the circular barbed wire that accompanied it was just way too sharp. Yes, I had fallen to temptation at a very young age and had to deal with the consequences, but my time was now coming to an end. I was being released. No escape route would be necessary. I would simply walk out the front gate.

I had spent the last couple of years locked up physically, but I had been totally free spiritually. I understood that no one was perfect except God. In my mind, however, I had been pretty darn close to it. I had gained respect from the most feared criminals. It had nothing to do with what gang I was from or how much weight I could lift in the gym. It all had to do with lifting up the name of Christ. I also believed I earned respect because I had not only talked the talk, but more importantly, also walked the walk. One could argue that this may have only been possible because of my limitations, but I would beg to differ. People in prison still got drunk, gambled, got in many fights, had issues with homosexuality, and took drugs. Many people talked the talk to their family over the phone or through letters, but when you actually walked the walk in that type of environment, then you were well respected. I was very proud of my stripes, and even more impressed with the way I had earned them.

But my time was up. I opened the box of brand new clothes that my family had sent me. The lady who had given it to me warned me to never return. She also informed me that ninety-something percent of people did return. I decided I did not want to become a part of that recidivism rate. I also realized that I had passed one test, but the true test was about to begin upon my release.

I had been separated from everyone that I loved, and hadn't even gotten a visit from anyone during the last two years of my stay. But I had gotten closer to God than I had ever been. I couldn't believe it had been two whole years since I had seen my boys. Yeah, I heard their voice over the phone as I still called them in spite of the decision that their mother had made. I knew none of it was their fault, and I still had to be a responsible father at the end of the day. When I disappeared from their lives, they were mere toddlers. Now I would return at the end of their grade school years. They couldn't tie their shoestrings when I left, and now they were choosing what kind of shoes they wanted to wear. I wondered if I had created a strong enough bond during the first couple of years of their lives that would help us reconnect. I hoped that they would remember how much I loved and cared for them. I also knew that things would be even more challenging now that their mother and I weren't together, but I had made up my mind that I would not allow them to suffer because of it.

So here I was, walking out of this place a free man. Well, sorta kinda. I still had to report to what we called the halfway house. It was a place that reminded you that you were only fifty percent free, and designed to help you transition smoothly into the community—especially if you didn't have family or a place to go. It would allow you to work and save up enough money to get yourself established.

I arrived not having a clue of what I was looking for, but I knew it would be much better than the accommodations I had just left. I approached the red brick building that was secured only by a black iron gate in front. Unlike prison, the only thing that prevented an escape was the decision itself. It was nothing more than an apartment building with rules and regulations. Those rules pretty much stipulated that anytime you were away from the building, they had to know exactly where you were and how long you would be there. And bedsides work, you could not be out past a fair curfew, as if you were in middle school.

Another exception that was made was going to church, which was on the top of my list of important things to do. There was not a doubt in my mind that I was going, but I did struggle with the decision of where I would go. My instinct was to go back to Now Faith since that had been the last church I was a part of. I had written to the pastor from prison but had not gotten a response from him. Was that a sign that I was no longer welcomed there? Was he upset with me because of my sudden departure, which put the church in a position to have to look for a new lessee for the building? I finally decided that I would, at the very least, visit the church. If I got the cold shoulder, then I would know that I was not welcomed. I knew the church had a shuttle, so I called and arranged for the driver to pick me up. Brother Ron T showed up in the white van that had "Now Faith" printed on each side in purple letters. He greeted me with a smile that said he was really happy to see me. He spoke with me during the ride as if I hadn't been gone for years. I observed this man with his Hershey complexion and teeth as white as snow. His hair was sprinkled with gray, but only at the temples. He was quick to remind me that I had no idea what his life was like before he gave it all over to God. He then told me that he believed God had great plans for me and that was why the enemy was going to continue to fight me. He encouraged me the entire ride with his huge smile and uplifting words until we arrived in front of the church. I sat for a second and took a look at the place. It was where God had led me shortly after I arrived in Colorado. Now I was returning in a whole different state of mind.

The passenger doors opened and I climbed out of the van wearing my white Air Force One sneakers, blue jeans, and printed navy T-shirt. I was by no means dressed like it was Easter Sunday, but I didn't have the chance to go through my clothes or make it to the store to buy some. Oh well, I heard the words "come as you are" many times at church and I often wondered if they were referring to your heart or your attire. Today I was hoping that they meant attire, because I did feel my heart was right. I expected people to look at me like I was a ghost when I entered, but several people who remembered me approached me immediately. Their greetings were warm, but I could not tell if they were simply being formal or really genuine. As easy as it may seem, that was a very difficult thing to interpret from church folks. They could smile at you with the glory of God on their face, but as soon as you passed them that glory could turn to shame on you. The service was great, as the praise team seemed to have the whole church on their feet. Caroline, the pastor's daughter, had a voice that could bring the dead back to life. The band was in sync as Dr. Ham orchestrated the moves of God.

I had been gone a long time, but I was beginning to feel like I was right at home. Sister E, the pastor's wife, sat in the same seat that she had the last time I was there. And the shine from this woman of God had not dimmed one bit. I could have easily said it was from the boulder-size diamond that complemented her hand or the earrings that grabbed everyone's attention, but the shine that was coming from her had little to do with material or temporal items. You could just tell that she wore the glory of God all about her.

I stood on my feet as they introduced Pastor E, the set man of the house. He walked in and greeted several people on his way to the pulpit. He was dressed immaculately. What I liked even more was that when this man got in the zone, you didn't know what to expect, but you could be sure that you would feel the presence of God. After the service he invited me into his study. We had a talk about how I was doing. He never brought up breaking the lease or bringing shame to the church. His concern was how my family and I were doing considering the circumstances. I didn't have the guts to tell him about the real situation. With a pride-filled tone, I told him we were doing fine. I wondered if I was still in a state of denial about the whole situation. I figured that I would cover that complex subject at a later date. I asked him about the letter I had written him. I had yet to get a response. He told me that he had never gotten the letter. I had no reason to believe that this devout man of God would lie to me, so I then asked if anyone had tried to reach out to me to make sure I was okay. He said that he had sent in a visiting form, but found out that I was no longer at the facility and was sent to another state. We talked for a little while longer before I had to get back to my regulated living arrangements. I told him that I would definitely be back and was serious about the work of the Lord. He then told me that he would love to have me back and that he really cared about me.

I left his office feeling like I had gotten a big load off my chest. One thing that I always liked about Pastor E was that he was a very genuine man. What you saw was what you got, and what you got was a man who had the heart of God. I made a decision that Sunday that I was going to continue to go to Now Faith. I felt that God had directed me there for whatever reason from the very beginning. I made plans to attend every Sunday in hopes of becoming whatever God wanted me to be.

During the next couple of weeks, I found out how much of a superficial life I had lived for so many years. Being a drug dealer gave a person the impression that life was simple and money was easy to come by. But now that this façade was behind me, I was faced with what we call the "real world." In the real world, people worked hard for everything they got and nothing was simple at all. Purchases had to be carefully thought out or budgeted ahead of time. I also had the awkward experience of catching a bus to search for a job. I hadn't ridden the bus since I was a kid, and had driven my own car before I even had a license. It was all brand new to me, but I was determined to do whatever I had to do to get my life in order.

I filled out several applications but had not gotten a call back, so I just continued on my search. I needed to lower my standards as I realized that I wasn't going to get a Fortune 500 job with my record. The funny thing was, the last time I had worked for anyone other than myself was during my summer stay in Colorado when I was a teenager. I wondered, "Since my last real job aside from running my own businesses was Wendy's, should I lower my standards to fast food?"

I was in a very tough situation, but I had to remember that whatever I had to do at this point would only be a stepping-stone to something so much greater. I felt that I was in excellent shape, so I applied for a couple of jobs doing manual labor. The pay was not that great, but I figured something would be better than nothing at all. Eventually, I got a call from a man named John, who was a warehouse manager for a tile company. He asked me a couple of questions and then invited me for an interview. I walked into his office fifteen minutes early. Before he spoke, I already knew that I would score a few points with him because I was a diehard Steelers fan and he had a Steelers snow globe on his desk. If he knew I grew up in Pittsburgh, he would probably give me a shot.

I watched the tall, relaxed man with an Italian demeanor take a seat across from me. He immediately leaned back in his chair, folded his hands behind his head, and asked how I was doing. The thick lenses of his glasses prevented me from having a clear shot of his eyes, but I was reading his body language. I told him that I was doing okay but was trying to make things better. He seemed to have liked my response by his tight smile. He started off by saying that he noticed on my application that I was from the Steel City. I confirmed this with a nod, not knowing which direction he was going with the conversation. However, when he said he was also from there, I felt I had added even more points to the scoreboard. As crazy as my life had been in Pittsburgh, maybe it was finally going to pay off for me. Or was God again directing me to the right people? I already knew the answer to that, so I just whispered another thank you to Him. After the small talk, John got right down to business. He wanted me to be clear that he was intrigued by the connection, but we still had an interview to conduct. He continued by going over the job description details. He may as well have been speaking Chinese since I really had no experience in this kind of work. He explained the forklift certifications that would be a requirement. I sat patiently waiting for him to finish his spiel before I spoke a word. While he was talking, I told myself I couldn't pretend to have any experience with this sort of job.

He asked if I had any questions or concerns, and I decided to go with the truth.

I sat up straight in my chair and looked across at him. I said that I honestly had no warehouse experience and had never even sat on a forklift, but what I do have is a willingness to learn just about anything. I said that I was a very hard worker who catches on really fast, and most importantly, I was very dependable and would not miss work. He then sat up in his chair and picked up my application as if he had seen it for the first time. He studied it for what seemed like an eternity, and then chose his words. When he asked the next questions, I knew right away why he hesitated. He looked across at me and said that he noticed I had been convicted of a felony but I didn't explain it on the application. I took a deep breath. I thought about how I had already been completely honest about my qualifications so there was no reason to lie about my disqualifications. I picked my head up away from my church socks and looked straight into his lenses. I said that I had put myself in a tough financial position and made a choice to break the law to try to fix the situation, which unfortunately just made everything worse. I told him that I was convicted of possession of a controlled substance. I told him that I took full responsibility for attempting to sell drugs to obtain some extra money, and was anxious to get that part of my life behind me. Right after I finished speaking, he immediately stood up and said he had one last question. With an even-toned voice I said, "Sure."

He smiled, looked down at me, and said, "So, when can you start?"

I looked up at him and said, "Yesterday."

The job was going really well. Within weeks, I was already operating a forklift. The physical part of the job was indeed as physical as John described. We had to build 10,000-pound pallets of very expensive tile. There was no need for me to find a gym as I was worn out by the time I left there every day. I showed John my appreciation for giving me a shot by not missing a day of work and staying late if he needed me.

Things had also gone extremely well at the halfway house as I had done every thing that was asked of me, and I was approaching the end of my stay. Since I had no place to call home, I went on an apartment search. I ended up teaming up with my cousin Maud, who had come out to Colorado years prior to help me with the business. He eventually decided to make it his home. We found a very nice two-bedroom apartment that had granite counters and wooden floors. Compared to what I had just left, it felt like a royal palace. Maud and I had always been pretty close, as I had treated him to the same luxuries as my uncles did for me, but he had never fallen for the temptation like I had. He was several years younger than me, so he actually looked up to me like I was his older brother. There was no doubt in my mind that we would get along just fine. We slowly furnished the place, and could say that things were really starting to come together.

Things were really awkward between Tracy and me, but I made it a point to get the boys every weekend. They seemed to be very happy that I was back around. I noticed there were times when we were together that they were really quiet, but I had to let them adjust to me at their own pace. It was not their fault that I had disappeared, so it would be unrealistic for me to think I could show up as if nothing happened. Tracy dropped them off faithfully. When she stopped by a few times without them, I realized that we still cared about each other. But she was still bitter about my past life and how things had turned out, and I was still bitter about the white and green envelope that I had received in prison. We had gone to lunch a few times while I was at the halfway house. She also insisted that she drive me to a few interviews during my job search so I would not have to catch the bus. We tried our best to function as parents and just friends, but the more we were around each other the harder it seemed for us to be apart.

We had a few tough conversations and came to an understanding that it was time to move forward. That's until one day when she threw me totally off guard and told me that she really missed me and wanted me to come home. This put me in a very tough position. I still loved her and the kids, but she had just sent me divorce papers. I was not sure I could trust this person again. She probably felt the same way when she sent the papers in the first place. Could I forgive her? I felt like she had turned her back on me when I was at my lowest point. This was a question that I could not answer right away, so I prayed and asked God what I should do. I couldn't help but weigh all the negatives, but when I thought of the positives of actually being there every day for the kids, along with the thought of being a normal family, it made things tough. I also thought about the fact that all she knew was this drug dealer and had never been introduced to the real man of God I was becoming. Would she even like that person? Or would she crave the personality that she had actually fallen in love with from the beginning?

We finally continued the conversation. I decided that I would try to forgive, as I knew I was not innocent in our situation. I told her that I would come home. She then informed me that she was not the same woman as when I left. For some reason, I did not pay attention to that very important warning. I decided that I would put everything in God's hands and try my best to make things work. The boys were ecstatic. They instantly started warming up to me more and more. I was able to help them with their homework every day, and I made plans every weekend for us to do something fun together. We also started going to Now Faith together as a family. I got more involved with the church and felt that God was leading me somewhere in the ministry.

I had also volunteered to coach my sons' football team. Now this was a real learning experience. The last time I had coached was in Duquesne, where we had reestablished the league. Now we lived in a middle-class neighborhood where the kids had everything they wanted and more. At the practices years ago in Duquesne there weren't any parents. Some kids were dropped off, but mainly they walked by themselves to practice. These privileged kids in the middle-class neighborhood played because their parents wanted them to play, but the kids years ago played because that was all there was to do. I had loved coaching back then, but this new coaching job was a little uncomfortable for me. There were two kids in particular who wanted to do extremely well. But I had to separate being a dad from coaching, which was very difficult. I knew other parents were waiting for me to show favoritism, but I found a way to avoid it. Sometimes I felt I was naturally harder on my kids. Fortunately, I was able to find a balance with the entire team. I would joke and play with each player during every practice. I had to admit that it was a very big commitment, but I enjoyed every bit of it. I was essentially volunteering my time to again help a group of kids create memories that they would never forget.

Things were going really great at home and everyone seemed to be adjusting pretty well. It did bother me a bit that Tracy and I had not really sat down and discussed our past mistakes. Nor did we formulate a plan that was going to help us succeed in the future. Were we again depending on the word "love" by itself? Neither one of us had grown up in a particularly happy family, but I knew that I had a strong desire to be the man I needed to be for her. I also wanted to be more than just a biological dad to my children. Speaking of which, I had been talking to my real dad over the phone lately. After so many years of not communicating, we were finally having some very interesting conversations. To my surprise, he was very knowledgeable about the word of God, which instantly became what we had in common. He would quote Old Testament history and New Testament Revelations at the drop of a dime. I also realized that he was a very intelligent man. And just like my mother, he had been totally delivered from the use of drugs, never to turn back.

I couldn't believe that I never recalled having a conversation with this man during my childhood that went beyond a normal greeting. However, we were now on the phone with each other almost every day. I was glad that I was getting comfortable with him. I eventually mustered up enough courage to get some long awaited answers to questions that had been bugging me. The questions I had were rather sensitive, so I had to be very careful with my approach. Then I thought about how I was able to express myself completely and uninterrupted when I wrote letters in prison, unlike with a conversation. The addressee would be forced to digest all of my words before they were able to respond. I gave it a little thought and decided that I would send him an email, and I would lay it all out there to clear my conscience.

The first thing I addressed was the fact that he had made no real attempt to be a part of my life. He had never inquired about my grades from preschool to college. He had never attended one sporting event from little league to high school. I couldn't even remember him showing up to one birthday party of mine. I needed to know if there was a reason that I had been just too young to understand. Did something happen between him and my mother that made him want no part of my life? I knew one thing for sure. It wasn't my fault. I had done nothing except live my life, which happened to be a life he created. And I couldn't ever say that I missed him, because you can't miss something you never had. But at this point I was willing to give my ear to him in hopes of some kind of clarity. Everything that I had learned as a man I had to learn from negative influences, the streets, or by trial and error. I had no one who could be the life coach necessary for a young man to develop into something productive. I could say that he never gave me the privilege of using the word "dad," but I was very happy that my boys had already learned to use that word religiously. I was determined not to let them feel the void that I had felt growing up. Yes, I would make mistakes and it wouldn't be easy. But no matter what I had to go through in my life, I would never, ever lose the bond with my children.

My first question was very important to me and extremely personal, but my second question would have way more sting to it. In fact, I wasn't even sure if I could have asked the question face to face. It wasn't out of fear of the reaction I would get. It was more that I wasn't quite sure if I was prepared to hear the answer. I went into detail about every thing that had happened to me in the fourth grade. I told him about the blond-haired little girl who sat next to me, how all of a sudden she disappeared and I found out that her project apartment had been broken into and the suspect was also accused of attempted rape. I told him that I had been ridiculed by all of my classmates and friends. They were calling me a rapist, and I had absolutely no idea why until Bear told me. I told him that my grandmother had also informed me of everything she found out about the incident. I let him know that I thought it was unfair that I had to suffer because of his mistakes, especially since he had not even been a part of my life. I wanted him to know that I had been holding this in for years. I also remembered his promises when Mr. Mangrum had taken me to visit him in jail. I wasn't quite sure what kind of response I would get, but I was ready for the talk or explanation. I was hoping that it wouldn't put an end to our communication, but I had to take the chance. If seeking the truth caused him to disappear, then maybe our newfound relationship was not really valid.

It took a couple of days to get a response. In the meantime, I did not receive a phone call from him. Each day that passed I was trying to predict what would happen. I had been waiting all these years, though, so I had to give him time to respond. Then I got an alert on my smart phone and quickly noticed it was a reply from him. I decided that I would wait until I got home, sit at a desk, and read it on the computer. I figured this email reply held the key to a chest full of emotions that had been locked away for a long time.

I sat at the desk clutching the mouse with my thumb and finger. I was hesitant to pull the trigger. I was staring at the screen that notified me of my new mail. What was I afraid of? I took a deep breath and closed my eyes while pressing down on the button. There was a very lengthy response. He began by thanking me for having the courage to confront him with these issues. He admitted that he, too, had wanted to have a conversation with me, but also struggled with the approach. He went on to tell me in detail about his life of crime and drug abuse.

He said there were times in his life when he didn't care about himself, so it was impossible to care about anyone else. The heroin addiction had gotten so bad that he began to do things that he could not understand himself. He told me that if he had been in my life during those times, he would not have been any good for me anyway. He went on to say that he cared about me very much and had thought about me quite a bit. But as time went on, he had gotten so far away from me that he had no clue where to start. He expressed how appreciative he was that we were finally in touch with each other. He said he hoped we would continue to build our relationship.

He then began to explain the answer to the question that stung. To my surprise he was very open and detailed about the whole event, as he remembered it just like it was yesterday. The truth was that he had committed a few crimes to support his addiction, but this was not one of them. He explained that he was at the apartment that night. They were apparently getting high. However, he did not touch anyone, and was accused of something that he never did. He said that he was so confident about the case that he even represented himself in court. The truth was revealed, and the whole case was dismissed. He apologized for the embarrassment that he had caused me and hoped that I could forgive him. He acknowledged that, had it not been for the life he had been living, he wouldn't have been in that position in the first place. Again, he thanked me for the email, told me to feel free to ask any questions that I had on my mind, and said he would be completely honest with me.

After that email, we continued to talk regularly. I even got the opportunity to bond with my half-brother and half-sister. My sister had graduated from Michigan State and was still living in Detroit, and my brother had graduated from acting school and was residing in Hollywood, California. I was glad that I had dealt with a part of my life that had been a mystery for so long, and I was prepared to move forward and leave the past far behind me.

Things got better and better at work as John was an excellent boss to work for. It was not just because he was a Steelers fan, but also because he understood my situation and was willing to take a gamble on me. I continued to show up to work every day on time, and I completed every task that was put in front of me. I began in the warehouse totally unfamiliar with the job, but had mastered everything there was to know. I even got so good on a forklift that I could literally pick up a coin off the floor with the forks. This may have been a very small thing to someone who sat in a plush office and had a very healthy salary, but for me it was huge. I had previously only mastered the game—or at least I thought I did. (I found out that the only thing you could master in that kind of life was a trip to prison or death.) I was rewarded for my hard work. Within a short time, I was given a raise and promoted to shipping and receiving supervisor. It was an easier job physically, but it required more thinking and paying attention to detail. I was even given my own desk and area to work from in the back of the warehouse. The last few years I felt like my life had sunk so far down. Although I wasn't close to where I wanted to be, it felt good to start seeing some kind of progress.

During my time away, Mr. Faison had found a way to stay in touch with Tracy and the boys. He got together with them whenever he could. I had actually lost touch with everyone except immediate family. I felt that my time away needed to be extra focused so that when I did get past it, I would be mentally prepared. Now that I was out and things were getting better, I felt that it was okay to reach out to some people for moral support with whom I had had productive friendships. I decided to give Mr. Faison a call. To my surprise, he didn't hang up. He was actually very glad to hear from me. I told him that I had been free for a little while but wanted to get some things together before I reached out to people. I informed him of my employment situation and how well things had been going. He then told me a little about a home care business that he and his new wife were attempting to launch. That was a surprise to me! Before I left, I couldn't remember him saying that he was even dating. He sounded really excited about the marriage and told me how great things had been going. He then told me that I had been in his thoughts and prayers. He said he would like to sit down with me as soon as time permitted. I agreed as I thought very highly of this man. He had always seemed to be really genuine to me. Had I had a little patience and really discussed the true problems of my business, I probably wouldn't have been in the position that I put myself in. Oh well, hindsight was really 20/20. But I was determined to learn from everything that I had been through.

We finally met up a couple of months later and I was definitely caught off guard by the direction our conversation went. We somehow arrived at the topic of possibly launching another clothing store. Mr. Faison told me how much potential business I was developing when he met me. He said that if he had known the truth about how things were going, he would have been able to help me. He told me that he wished I could have been more up front. I explained that it was rather difficult, as we had not known each other long. And even more difficult to explain would have been the life that I was trying to escape from. I wasn't quite sure if I would have ruined our relationship before it even began.

He then told me that he did have his suspicions, but did not want to assume, even though that assumption was confirmed when he heard that I had gotten arrested. He then went on to explain that he understood that way of life, as his father had been a mover and a shaker. He himself had never indulged in that kind of lifestyle and instead gravitated toward a life of sports. That's how he received a college education, and the rest was history. He was not judgmental of my mistake, but made it very clear that he hoped that I had really learned my lesson. We met several more times, and before I knew it, we were making plans to open another clothing store. I had to be honest in saying that I was very nervous to leave the warehouse. I had worked my way up and knew that there were even more potential opportunities, but I knew in my heart that I had a passion for business. I grew to love the one I had started years ago. I had a long talk with John. He was not surprised at all as he told me that I had way more potential than a warehouse job. I put in my two weeks notice, and in the blink of an eye we were having a grand opening for a new store in downtown Denver.

Unlike years ago, this was a very different situation for me. Before, I had taken care of all of the finances for my business. I had learned everything I needed to know from Morris. But now Mr. Faison was taking care of all the finances for the business. He also hired a business consultant and brought on his wife as part of the operation. Things seem to be going really well at first. I was back in Vegas attending the Magic shows, and I was opening up a business that I absolutely loved. To our surprise, this business was a little different than the one I had years earlier. We were on the back end of downtown, thus foot traffic would not be something we would benefit from. We also had a major parking issue. It was hard for customers to find a spot, and when they did find parking, they were often hit with a ticket after they shopped. We hoped that we would immediately create a decent cash flow and attract some of the high-profile clientele that I had years ago, but this location seemed to need more time to develop. Things got a little rocky between the business consultants and Mr. Faison. It became a tug-of-war for him, his wife, and me in terms of making decisions.

To make a very unfortunate story short, we pulled out of the business before it had a good year run. With overhead so high and everyone suddenly being on a different page, along with the large amount of inventory that was not moving fast enough, we made the decision to shut things down. I was very disappointed. Not only was the business closing, but during the end, I also felt as if I was left in the dark about many things. Oh well, nothing beats a failure but a try.

So now I was suddenly back in the market for a job. My first thought was to call John and see if I could go back. I knew he would want a long commitment from me, though. I needed money fast as a lot had taken place over the last month. I found out that Tracy was pregnant and we would be having another son, and I had just traveled back to Pittsburgh for an emergency when my mother had a stroke. When I got the call from my sister Ashley, she was so shook up that I knew it had to be really bad. My mother had been clean from drugs for many years, but she was somehow still affected by her stint of abuse. She was only in her late forties, but her heart was that of a seventy year old. Although her physical heart was in bad shape, I was still very thankful that her spiritual heart was like new.

I jumped on a flight immediately. I feared the worst. I remember praying all the way home. When I got there, I found out that she would be getting a pacemaker. I knew, however, that God could be the only one to set the pace of her life. I stayed in Pittsburgh to make sure everything was okay. As soon as my mother was coherent, she told me to get back to my family and business, and that she was okay in God's hands. It was not the time to tell her that things weren't going particularly well with the business and I would probably be looking for a job really soon. After I saw that she was going to be okay, I headed back to the Mile High City.

I had been delivering newspapers in the wee hours of the night to supplement my income from the clothing store as I had made an agreement with Mr. Faison that I would accept a minimal salary until the business picked up. I continued to do so while in search of a new full-time job. I figured worst-case scenario I would give John a call and go back to my old job. One thing I was sure of. No matter how bad things got, I could never go back to my former life. Well, things got worse before they got better. I even called John, and he was actually about to leave the company as he had found a new job. I was familiar with the new manager who had been promoted, but he told me that it would be a month or so before he could bring me back on.

So now I found myself in a real state of panic. Not only was it a struggle to pull my half to take care of my home, but people were also calling me with threats of repossessing my car. I had never been in that position as I had never really had car payments. I just bought what I wanted off of the showroom floor. But I was now learning that this was the real world that people dealt with every day.

I remember driving early one morning and tossing the Denver Post newspaper out the passenger window of my platinum Nissan Maxima, thinking that it would be taken from me really soon if I didn't figure something out. I turned off my music and just began to pray. I told God that I was doing my best, but I really needed his help. I told him that I was at a point where I didn't know what to do, so I was depending on him. I had been praying out loud in my car. My eyes were obviously open as I was driving, but I somehow was not paying attention to the delivery truck that was cutting right in front of me to make its delivery. I slammed on my brakes, interrupting my prayer. I gave him a look that might have caused many deaths if it actually could kill. The driver never even acknowledged me as he stayed in sync with his route. He would pull up to a house, slam on the emergency brake, and was out the door in a flash with gallons of milk in both hands. I sat for a couple seconds. I noticed my headlights shining directly on the side of the truck where it stated the name and phone number of the dairy where the driver worked. I was not going to call to complain about his hazardous driving, but I thought that maybe there was a purpose that my prayer was interrupted. That same day I went to the company to fill out an application. I felt good about my chances because I thought the whole incident was a sign.

Right after I finished my paper route that morning, I made my customary phone call. I had gotten into the habit of calling my grandmother every morning after I finished my route. I knew she hadn't been feeling very well lately, but every time I called she became excited, as if she hadn't spoken to me in years. Even though we talked almost every day, there was never a dull conversation. The topic would pretty much be the same. She would encourage me to keep going and to trust God. She would also tell me how proud she was that I had really made an attempt to change my life. She said that she knew it wouldn't be easy for me as the enemy was going to always fight me, but she knew that God had something special in store for my life. I would play music for her over the phone, we would share scriptures, we would laugh with each other, and most of all, we would pray. And on this particular morning, she had prayed that God would give me favor with my employment situation.

Within the next couple of days, I received a call from the dairy to come in for an interview. Here I was at yet another interview in which I had no experience in what the job required. I had never delivered anything except for the newspapers part-time and, well, the forbidden fruit years ago. I was also clueless when it came to operating the handheld computer that would process each delivery. During the interview, I sat across from an older version of Dennis the Menace. His thick mustache suggested a background in some kind of law enforcement. His description of the job was pretty much the most difficult that I had ever applied for. He explained that many people did not even make it past what they called a "trial ride." It was actually the second part of the interview. You had to ride in a truck with a veteran driver who would evaluate your physical condition and report back to the hiring manager. Then, a decision was made.

After drilling me on my work experience and having me explain my criminal background, he played with his thick mustache with his thumb and finger before he said that he would give me a shot. He explained that if I did well on the trial ride, then he was willing to give me a chance. He set me up with a guy name Blake. From the first look at this guy, I felt like if he could do it, then it should be a piece of cake for me. His wiry frame and glasses made him look more like a computer geek or history teacher than a delivery driver. To my surprise, this guy was a real machine. He would dart in and out of the truck at lightning speed. It seemed like by the time the emergency brake was pushed down, he already had the dairy product in hand for delivery. He stated that the goal was to deliver to thirty houses per hour, but he had to be doing at least forty or maybe even fifty. Whether he was trying to make an impression or not, he did. I could not believe how physical the work was. He did a really good job explaining everything that I needed to know. Due to my current situation and my refusal to back down from a challenge, I had made up my mind to accept the job by the time we finished emptying the truck.

I was officially part of the company that very same week. To my surprise, the pay was more than I had made at the warehouse or the clothing store. I thanked God for the opportunity. About a year passed and I had totally committed myself to this company. Not only did I perfect my own route, but I was also covering an extra one after I finished my assigned neighborhood. As challenging as the job was when I began, my mind and body seemed to adjust to it pretty quickly. A supervisor named Bob noticed my hard work and dedication and pulled me aside. He was the polar opposite of Blake. His physical condition implied that he was too out of shape to do this kind of job. However, I had quickly learned not to judge a book by its cover. He was excellent at what he did. In his younger days he was actually a blond-haired quarterback phenom out of Texas. He had just allowed the "I don't care" diet to take over his body. Bob told me that my work ethic had not gone unnoticed and that there was another supervisor position opening up soon. He thought I should apply for it. I was all eyes and ears when it came to a raise, so I told him to keep me posted.

Before I knew it, I was promoted to supervisor in the department. I was not assigned to a particular route, but I would be on call to cover if needed, which seemed like an everyday occurrence. Sometimes I was even doing sixteen-hour shifts. So between work, church, and coaching the boys, I really didn't have any free time. And that was okay with me because I needed to make all the money that I could, considering I had a new son coming soon. I was starting to feel really good about myself. I had been knocked down so many times within the past couple of years, but like a determined prizefighter, I continued to get up off the canvas. Except this next blow would hit me so hard that it would probably take a whole ten count to gather myself.

I had still been making morning calls to my grandmother, as it had become part of my daily routine. I enjoyed talking to her. She always made me feel good no matter how bad a situation may have been. When I got a call from her one evening, I automatically knew something was wrong. I had already gotten word that she was not feeling well, but I did not hear it from her. When we talked, she would laugh and speak as if she were perfectly fine. I quickly remembered how years ago she was so determined, along with my mother, to convince me to go away and straighten out my life. So when she prompted me to come home, I knew it was serious. I also knew that since I had moved to Colorado, she had never once asked me to come home to see her. Yeah, I had surprised her several times by flying home and sneaking into her house to scare her, which was always a very comical event. She was always the first one up in the house, so I would be sitting at her kitchen table when she came downstairs. She would jump as she was not paying attention until she got close to me. Then she would automatically put her fist up in front of her face like she was ready to fight. Even though I caught her off guard, laughter would follow, along with the biggest hug and kiss. I loved this woman so much, and I knew that she was so crazy about her first grandchild. She had been in the hospital a few times of late, and it had gotten to the point where a hospital bed was put in her living room so that nurses could come by to care for her. I was aware that she no longer had the strength to move her body around as much, but her spirit never changed one bit.

The call was coming from a number I didn't recognize, but the 412 area code was enough for me to answer right away. At first, I could barely hear the person on the line, but then realized it was my grams. She said in a very soft, yet demanding, voice that I needed to come see her right away. I instinctively asked if everything was okay. Her response was that she was calling from hospice. It was a place where you went when the hospital had given up on your survival, but she was someone who was still able to say she was doing great. She had always talked freely about going home to be with the Lord. I dismissed her remark every time, but this time her words really got to me. And it wasn't her command to come see her that bothered me. I would do anything this woman told me to do. It was the tone in which she said it that told me that I had better react.

The next morning I was in the friendly skies on my way back to Pittsburgh. I opened my window shade. As I passed through the clouds, I figured that I would talk to God since I was pretty close to him. I was not referring to being physically close, but that my spirit had gotten so much stronger toward the things of God. At this point, I was beginning to have confidence that His ear was open to me. I was filled with enough reverence to understand that His will was always going to be done.

I arrived in Pittsburgh and my ride was already waiting to immediately take me to the hospice. It was a small, red brick building that looked more like a doctor's office than a hospital. I approached the receptionist with a forced smile as the place had an air of discomfort. Was it because the people who stayed there understood that it would probably be the last place that they dwelled here on earth? The heavyset lady smiled while pushing her glasses off of her nose. I told her whom I was there to see. She instantly brightened up and dropped the pen that she had been writing with. I had not told her who I was or where I was from, but she immediately said that I must be her patient's grandson from Colorado. She walked from around the desk and escorted me to a room down the hall. On the way, she informed me that my grandmother had talked about me every day that she was there.

I walked into the room where she was lightly dozing and it didn't take long for her to open her eyes, although the task seemed to be rather difficult for her. By the time she got them open, she immediately perked up and lifted her fists up in front of her face. She spoke with a very tired voice and said, "You caught me off guard again." She kept her hands up for a few seconds like she was ready to fight, but I pushed in between them and gave her the biggest hug and kiss.

This woman was so amazing. Here she sat in a place where all of her organs had begun to fail, yet she still kept her spirit alive. I looked at her body that seemed weak and feeble, but I knew that this was one of the strongest people that I had ever known. She had practically raised me. She was also the reason that I was able to succeed at new jobs. Although I did not have an extensive work history, it was she who made me work in the blazing heat down in the fields of the South. It was she who showed me how to thoroughly clean as I was her assistant when she changed around her entire house. She had instilled qualities in me that made me a better person. Yeah, the streets had changed me, but I never lost the respect that she demanded I have for people and things. And because I had never heard her use one single curse word, I had followed suit and not allowed it to be a part of my language. My friends would tease me all the time and say that they could not believe they had never heard me use foul language.

What they didn't know was that I understood there was another side to my sweet grandmother. There were things that you just didn't do or else there would be consequences. And sometimes she didn't take the time to go find a belt——you might just become a victim of whatever she had in her hand at the time of your transgression. She would also send you out to a tree to pick your own punishment. Once I tried the method of picking the smallest switch off the tree, only to find out that it would earn me double the lashes. So I became smart and picked the medium. She would also advocate for you if she knew you were right. Her favorite saying went, "Right is right, and wrong is wrong." If you were wrong, she would be the juror who voted for your execution.

I remember a time when I was put on punishment for neglecting my schoolwork. There was a big skating party that all of my friends were going to. I was very disappointed that I couldn't go, so I decided that I would play the pity party card. I connected about 100 rubber bands of all assorted colors together and decided to wrap them around my neck, pretending that I was attempting suicide because I couldn't go to the party. Grams happened to walk in the kitchen just as I was preparing for my act. She took one look at me, and instead of running to my rescue and feeling sorry for me, she did the total opposite. She grabbed her miniature wooden paddle-like cutting board and lifted it over her head as if she was going to hit me with it. She check swung a couple of times to make me flinch. Then she uttered, "If you were really serious about killing yourself, then I will help you do it." That was a moment that my aunts would never let me forget. They teased me for a lifetime about it. And I would never forget game nights when Grams took the time to play Monopoly and Sorry with us.

I looked at my favorite woman on the whole entire earth and fought back tears as I saw tubes coming from her face and IV needles stuck in the top of her hand. I did not get a hotel room or stay at a family member's house. I just asked the nurse for a pillow for the reclining chair next to Gram's bed. I stayed there with her for three days. During that time, we had a moment I would never forget. It was as if she were giving me instructions that I needed to get through the maze of life without getting too lost.

She reminded me of the Golden Rule, stating that I should never treat people like they treated me, but instead always treat them how I wanted to be treated. She shared her secret of never really wanting for much because she always gave to people with a pure heart. Most of the time when she spoke during those three days, she had her normal, happy demeanor despite her condition. However, I remember on day three how her face turned serious when she struggled to look over at me. She said God had a strong calling on my life and I should not be alarmed that the enemy was going to fight me tooth and nail. She told me that it wouldn't stop, and to be strong and of good courage because God was going to continue the work in me that He had begun no matter what I had to go through. I sat and listened to what she had been telling me my whole life. For three days we sat next to each other, laughing and enjoying what were our last moments together. She was quoting scriptures and I was reading to her from the word of God.

She did not have a written will as she didn't have a lot of material items to leave behind. Her desired will was that her family would come to the knowledge of Christ, which was far more valuable than any amount of money. She would also leave behind a legacy that would be very difficult to duplicate, but very profitable to imitate.

It was day three and time was approaching when I would be traveling back to Colorado for work and family. I looked at her and asked if there was anything she needed from me. I halfway expected her to give me some difficult task that needed to be taken care of, but what she asked for was very simple. She told me that she wanted me to look out for her baby. Most people understand that a baby could be grown in age, and that the very last child born would be described as such. In my grandmother's case, it had been many years since she had given birth to a child. Despite that, she had practically raised most of the kids in our family, along with several kids that had no relation by blood. You would not have known that they weren't blood because of how well she treated them, and that she demanded we do the same. When she asked me to take care of her baby, she was referring to the last child that she had raised. Her name was Antoinette, and she had been given to my grandmother as a newborn because her biological mother was not in a position to raise her. All I could do was smile at a woman who lay in her final moments, yet all she could think about was someone else being taken care of. But that was just who she was.

After giving her my word that I would do my very best, she perked up and gave me her second request. She then made me laugh as she told me to get her favorite drink for her. I knew that she was referring to a strawberry milkshake. I would surprise her with one all the time. I instantly jumped up, put my feet in my boots, and went to my aunt's to take a quick shower. I picked up her request on the way back to the hospice. I had not been gone long as I did not want to leave her side for fear of the worst. By the time I arrived, she was sitting up in bed with her eyes wide open. I put the straw inside the disposable cup and put it to her mouth, but she would not take a drink from it. Instead of asking if she was okay, I just asked if she still wanted it, and if not, that was okay. She opened her lips, not to drink but to ask in a soft voice, "Are you leaving me?"

I had never told her that I was flying back to Denver that night because my plan was to never say good-bye to a woman who would be in my heart for as long as I had breath. She had caught me off guard. Somehow she just knew. So I smiled, looked at her, and whispered, "Never." It must have been sufficient as she reminded me that I always knew the right thing to say. I kissed and hugged her for what I knew was the very last time. As I was leaving, the nurse pulled me aside and told me that my grandmother was one of the most amazing women she had ever taken care of. She went on to tell me how much Grams loved me. She said Grams' grandson was her topic of conversation every day that she spent there. Enthusiasm went south as she seemed like she was choosing her words carefully when she spoke. She explained that my grandmother's organs had already been shut down for days and that it was a miracle she was still holding on. She went on to say that she had learned that people were able to hang on to life somehow no matter how bad the body may be until they were able to see someone who they really loved and wanted to get a message across to before they made their ascension to heaven. Her last words were to not be surprised if my grandmother now passed, as she believed that I was that person.

I sat on the runway at Pittsburgh National Airport, watching the heavy raindrops beat against my window. I had not spoken a word to anyone during my whole check-in process. In my periphery vision, I saw a plane taking off, along with a ton of lights, but my mind was unable to see any of it. And then suddenly the thunderstorm began. The water was falling uncontrollably and the thunderous noise was continuous. This storm was not outside of my window, however. The rain and thunder was coming from me, as I could not control my crying. I knew in my heart that it was the last time I would see her on earth. The next day, as the nurse predicted, Grams went to a way better place.

Chapter Twenty-One

Enough Is Enough

Grams was gone, but I had promised myself that I would honor her every day by trying to practice all the good qualities that she had instilled in me. I had taken it pretty hard as I would miss my morning calls and never forget our early morning breakfast times together. After traveling home for a very difficult funeral service, I was back in Denver committing myself to a job that just seemed to be getting better and better. And although God had taken a very special life from me, before I knew it he was blessing me with another one. My third son was born and he brought a new excitement to our home. It had been several years since we had cared for an infant. Nevertheless, our instincts went into overprotective care mode.

Having twins the first time around had its advantages and disadvantages all at the same time. It was an advantage this time to have only one child because it would obviously be easier to care for. However, one disadvantage of having just one child was that he would demand more of our attention, as he would not have a counterpart to play with. Another advantage was having two older brothers who would lend more than a helping hand.

Things would also be different this time around financially. When the twins were born, I was the breadwinner, and Tracy did not have to worry about anything concerning her or the boys. She was the bread maker, which was as vitally important. She returned and physically took care of the boys and me. Now, at this stage of our lives, both of us became the breadwinners, as it was necessary to make ends meet. She was working full-time, along with extra work on the weekends, and I was working way too many hours at the dairy. Fortunately, I typically worked the graveyard shift as a route supervisor, so I was able to take care of our newborn son during the day. Unless his sleep schedule got mixed up, Tracy had the luxury of watching him while he slept peacefully. And after a long ten-hour graveyard shift, I rushed home so that I could be a primary caregiver.

Although this was very challenging for me, I really got a chance to appreciate a mother's strength. I changed diapers, made bottles, gave baths, and as tired as I usually was, I still had to keep from dozing off so I could play with him. By the time Tracy and the twins got home from school, it would be hard to keep my eyes open, so I would take my three- to four-hour nap. Then I was off to the dairy for my night shift.

This also gave me an understanding of why a mother's bond was so strong with her child even more so than the father's. Not only was that child a part of their body for nine months, but they also took such good care of the child during that critical developmental stage. I would never be able to form the bond that was created while the child was in the womb, but I was happy to be creating a bond with my son that would probably never be broken.

In warp speed he went from drinking out of a bottle to asking for his sippy cup. And from the sippy cup...well, he went to spilling juice all over the floor. He had brought a new joy to the house, but I was starting to fear that Tracy's and my work schedules, along with the fact that we seemed to have started to live separate lives, were starting to affect us. She started to focus more on her career and the friends she had established during my time away, and I devoted more of my time to the dairy and volunteering my time to the church.

A year or so had passed and there was an unexpected shift at the company I worked for. The long-time president had gotten fired and that initiated some changes in the company. His firing was one that I would learn a lot from. One, I learned that everyone was expendable, depending on the performance of a company. Two, I learned it didn't matter how many years you had been with a company. If it came down to the survival of the company, you were out of there. In this case, the department manager had actually been a part of the company for about twenty years. When the foundation of any building was affected, then it was obvious that it would affect every part of the structure. In our department, there were a few people who lost their jobs, opening up opportunities in management. I had really excelled at the supervisor position, which in turn taught me a whole lot about myself. Whether it was my years of illegal activity, my small business, my time at the warehouse, or my new career at the dairy, I learned that my biggest challenge was to make up my mind to do something. Once my mind was made up, then there was no halfway for me. If I was in, then I was all in. That had been my approach for most of the things I had done. Fortunately, that attitude of determination was now starting to pay off in a positive way.

Mom had preached to me over and over again that I should be a leader and not a follower. I remembered the lessons she had taught me as a kid. I even recalled the time she locked me out of the house so I could fight because I had put myself in a position where I was following someone and gotten myself in trouble. I had taken her words to heart, and being a leader became a part of my personality. Unfortunately, I had wasted some valuable years being a leader in a lifestyle that was destined for destruction. But more importantly, it was a lifestyle that was holding me back from a life that was productive. Many people had depended on me and looked up to me for all the wrong reasons. Money was power no matter how you obtained it, but in that world, your power was synonymous with that of a superhero. Superheroes couldn't really fly at the speed of light. They really couldn't swing from building to building. They did not really turn green and become the strongest person in the world. Each one was actually a normal being until something kicked in and gave them the supernatural powers that enabled them to try to save the world. Not only was a drug dealer's power a thing of fairy tales, but it also destroyed the world instead of saving it.

It was such a good feeling that I could work hard at the bottom of a company and move up. Now, all of a sudden, I was being considered for upper management because of my ability to redirect my leadership skills into a real work environment. They posted the position throughout the dairy and our immediate manager informed all of us supervisors that we were encouraged to apply for the open position. A few weeks had gone by and I had not applied for the position. I was called into the office of the department manager who wanted to know why I had not put my name in the hat. As he leaned back in his chair twiddling his thumbs, I sat on the edge of the hard wooden chair. I decided that honesty had always done well for me, so that was the only approach I took.

Chris was one of the additions to the new structure of the dairy, but he was a veteran when it came to how things worked. He had worked for the dairy for close to twenty years and then left to pursue other opportunities. He was brought back to help get things in order. His management strategy was simple: track every single thing we did so that we could improve all the numbers.

He sat across from me with one of his legs folded onto the opposite knee. His sandy brown hair was immaculately cut into a rounded version of a boxed fade. I watched his face turn beet red as he was anticipating my response. I looked him straight in the eye and told him that I felt that if they had the confidence to fire a manager, then they already had in mind who would be able to fill his shoes. And since I was not the supervisor with the most tenure, I figured that I probably didn't have a shot. He encouraged me to put my name in the hat anyway. After a series of interviews, not only was I considered, but I was also the person that they already had in mind. I accepted the position and everything about my job changed instantly. I had started as a delivery driver and within a few years was now in management. I was partially responsible for close to seventy employees. I was given my own office with a computer, extension, and the works. My dress code changed to business casual, and I was now invited to board meetings where the real numbers of the company were discussed. I was also required to have a report prepared for everything that was happening in my department. I had clearly been the go-to guy in the streets, and it did not take long for that to happen in one department. I began to get frequent visits from not only our department manager, but also the president, vice president, and owner of the company. They would sit across from me in my office in search of answers that I would always have available when they arrived. I spent countless hours dissecting the computer program that held all the information. My customer service had become impeccable, as even the customer service manager would transfer the most difficult calls to my office. I also had a great rapport with all the drivers. In no time, we were seeing some good results in the company.

The management team knew that my work ethic was above and beyond the norm, but what they didn't know was that I had come from the very bottom in life and had grown to appreciate a real career. I also found myself conducting interviews with guys that had criminal backgrounds. Because of my past, I had the ability to look at the person's desire to succeed and not be judgmental of their past mistakes. This company had clearly given me a chance, and I would be a hypocrite if I slammed the door in someone else's face that may have had some of the same struggles that I had in my past. Needless to say, I handed out many opportunities. Most of the people who I gave a shot to really made the best of it.

I was given a very healthy salary, one that most people with a college degree would have really appreciated. This was very tricky for a guy with my past. It was difficult not to think back to the days when I made the yearly salary in a week's time. But I also had learned the consequences of earning large amounts of cash that way. Regardless, I still had some mental adjusting to do. I kept telling myself that my past life was just a fairy tale, or more accurately, a nightmare, and I was now living the way a productive citizen lived. I had a 401k, vacation time, and insurance benefits for my family. I also saved money by having access to all our company's dairy products at a discounted rate. I was starting to get invited to company events and functions, too, as I was now a part of the team.

There was one particular event that would stick with me forever. I couldn't figure out if it was more comical or frightening. Since my life had changed drastically, I was leaning more toward the comical side. I had taken up a new hobby during my spare time: golf. It was also something that the boys and I did as a bonding exercise. It was not something that had been popular for African American kids where I was from, but my goal was always to broaden the horizons of my children and myself. My manager Chris invited me to a golf tournament that was being held at a private country club. The dairy did not sponsor this event, but I decided that the tournament would be very exciting to go to. Not only was my golf game drastically improving, but Chris was also able to pull some strings to get a paid day off of work for us. I was definitely all in on this event.

We were scheduled to tee off at 7:10 a.m. We all arrived about 6:00 a.m. so we could hit a few buckets of balls to make sure our swing was up to par. They had a continental breakfast already prepared, along with a bunch of free souvenirs. Well, they were not really free, as we had to pay a fee of $150 just to enter the tournament. It was a best ball event, which meant that your team of four players would each hit a ball and you would use the ball that was in the best position or closest to the green. I hadn't paid any attention to the marketing materials for this event, but I had taken a peculiar notice of all the other players. Not only was I the youngest player, but I was also the only minority. All the other players had a certain demeanor as they passed us on each hole and said their hellos. It wasn't until I was on the seventh hole that I finally realized whom I was playing golf with. Chris's wife pulled up to us in a golf cart and introduced him to a guy who she worked with. She then introduced him to another guy who she stated worked for the Denver unit. I then took notice of the title of the tournament, which was a DEA (Drug Enforcement Administration) golf event. I had been on the other side of them my whole life. I had been the guy who they spent their careers looking for, yet I was playing golf with them. I immediately lost all power in my swing and began to hit every ball in the rough. This was a very awkward situation for me. I had a dislike for all law enforcement simply because I had been breaking the law. These guys from the drug enforcement agency had not done anything to me, but because of my past, they automatically made me uncomfortable.

I then thought about something that had happened a few weeks earlier. It was well after two in the morning and I heard a very strong knock on my door. From the landing at the top of the stairs, I could clearly see red and blue police lights flashing. If you were to rewind my life to years earlier, I would have been in a complete panic, as I would have probably had something inside my home that wasn't supposed to be there. But that night, without hesitation, I immediately went to the door to see what the problem was. I opened the front door to see a tall, white officer standing alone, waiting for me to answer. He let me know that he had been patrolling the neighborhood and noticed that our garage door was halfway open. He wanted to make sure that everyone in our home was safe. I told him that one of the boys had probably forgotten to close it all the way. I thanked him for checking on us. Years ago, I felt that the police's only job was to serve me some kind of warrant, but this time they were actually fulfilling the other part of their slogan, which was to protect me. It also made me realize that if I was not doing anything wrong, then there was no need to be afraid of law enforcement. As the scripture says, if you want to be unafraid of authority, then do what is good. I was now a hardworking, productive citizen. So why did I feel out of place? I thought about this for a moment and decided that there was absolutely no reason for me to feel this way at all. I shook it off, tightened up my grip on my 1-wood and ripped the tiny white ball about the length of three football fields. And I enjoyed the rest of the day.

I had both of my arms extended above my head, and one of my knees bent up toward my abdomen while my other leg was starting to climb the ladder of corporate America. I had heard the term many times, but previously did not have a clue what it looked like or what it felt like. There were meetings after meetings, and I enjoyed learning how a really big company operated from a management standpoint. My small business ventures seemed to depend solely on the skills that I possessed, while teamwork was very critical in a company of this size. I had been very dedicated to the street life years before, but now my dedication was starting to pay off without the nagging thoughts of consequences and repercussions.

As proud of myself as I was for my accomplishments at the dairy, I was even more ecstatic about the efforts that I had put forth at my church. I had totally committed myself to the ministry. I attended every service, along with the meetings and studies that were required to become a fellow worker of the ministry. There was a mandatory meeting that took place every Sunday morning before service, where the pastor would review any current events that the staff needed to be aware of. This meeting was very similar to the ones we had at work. The difference was that the dairy wanted to improve its customer accounts and use marketing strategies to sell more product, and the meetings at church were to add more numbers to the membership and use marketing strategies to get more exposure for the church.

One of the keys to both of these meetings and goals was the word retention. No matter how many people signed up for the dairy or walked inside the church, if there wasn't something that caused them to remain, then true growth would be very difficult. My duty in both meetings was simple and very much the same: help improve the numbers. So I spent many hours in my office at the dairy, and I rarely missed anything that was scheduled at the church.

After a couple of years of dedication, I was offered the position of youth pastor. This was perfect for me as my twins were a part of the youth group. I also had a passion for young people. I realized that it was the youth group that Mr. Mangrum had started back in Pennsylvania years ago that had introduced me to God in the first place. Although I may have strayed far away, I believed that the seeds that were planted at an early age would always draw me back to God.

We were assigned to meet in the theater of the church every Tuesday evening during regular Bible study. It did not take long for me to get attached to this group of kids. I quickly realized that they had a hunger for the things of God and just needed some direction. These Tuesday nights became very popular as we played games and practiced for plays that we would perform. Most of all, I made sure that the word of God was delivered at a level they could appreciate. We started a chess club on Saturday mornings, and we also went on many field trips. Whether it was snow tubing in the mountains or paintballing in the city, we always scheduled something fun for them to do.

One of my favorite field trips was when I would take the whole group on a hike to a place called Hanging Lake. I remember telling each kid what they should bring along, not realizing that most of them didn't want to walk the distance from the car to their house, let alone go on a hike. I had to admit that hiking was something that was not on my list of exciting things to do as a teenager, but I figured it would be something different and a memory that would never be forgotten. I had done a little research on this particular hike so I was confident that it would be pretty safe. There were no dangerous cliffs to climb and it was described as a mountainous hill at best.

To my surprise, almost the entire youth group showed up for this event. We loaded up the church van with backpacks and water jugs and were on our way. After about an hour and a half drive, we finally reached our destination. We got out of the van, got in a circle, and prayed that God would protect us from any hurt, harm, or danger. Then we were ready to go. We put a chaperone in the front and I stayed in the back so we could make sure that everyone was safe and no one was kidnapped by a mountain lion. We hadn't gotten a good fifteen minutes into the hike before I started hearing whining and complaining about how hard the hike was, and how tired they were already. I thought about how this generation of children was so different as most of their exercise came from pushing buttons on a video game controller. When I was younger, we rode bikes all the time, and there was a pickup game of football or basketball going on every day. Now, most of these kids would only challenge each other on Xbox or PlayStation.

We stopped for a couple of small breaks. I had taken a backpack of extra water for the journey. I wasn't sure how difficult this hike would be, but I knew it was my job to keep them motivated. I figured there would be several times where they would want to quit, but I had to keep pushing them. The farther we got, the more it made sense to keep going. There were kids who even suggested that they wait right where they were until we were on our way back down. I had looked at the end of this hike online, but I had not disclosed what they would see when we reached the top. So after all the complaining that I had to hear on the way up, by the time we reached our destination, all I could hear them say were *ooooh*s and *ahhhh*s. They were so amazed by the view in front of them that they had totally forgotten how hard the journey was.

I had to take advantage of the lesson that was right there in front of us. I got the kids in a small circle and I told them that life would be so much like this hike. I told them that there would be times where they would want to give up. There would be times that they were so fatigued that their body would tell their mind to quit. However, if they just kept pushing, ignored the pain, and moved forward, the reward would be so much greater than the pain they had to endure. We looked at the waterfalls that were gushing out of the middle of the mountains into a small lake of the clearest water I had ever seen. I could see smiles of satisfaction on all the kids' faces. The journey down seemed to have been a piece of cake, because they knew that what they had just witnessed at the top of this hike was well worth the journey. No matter how beautiful something may seem in this life, nothing compares to the beauty of God's creation.

I also found that most of the times that I had prepared a lesson or message for these children, that very same lesson applied to me in so many ways. I strongly believed that I was not able to give anything away unless I first obtained it myself. In this particular case, I had not realized that the profound message I had given to our youth group at the top of this hike was something that they would never forget. This message would be one that I myself would need to remember, too.

As well as things had been going with my job and my church, there was a very important area of my life where I seemed to be struggling: my family. Life was a very interesting road to travel. Just when you thought you had a firm grip on the steering wheel, that's when you suddenly slid on some black ice and had to do something to avoid a fatal accident. The boys and I seemed to be inseparable. Besides going to work and school, we did absolutely everything together. The twins had their group of high school friends that they hung out with, so it was the little guy and me who became regulars at the local movie theater. The twins were way too cool to watch animated movies, so I was stuck trying to figure out the real storylines of cartoons. I was heavily involved in all of their schoolwork, too. I realized that most kids were punished for bad grades, but if the parent did nothing to help prevent them, then it was very difficult for them to improve. I also knew that if the kids knew that you were paying close attention to them, they were less likely to neglect their schoolwork.

Something else that made me really happy was that I was also raising my sons in the fear of the Lord. They attended every service with me and really enjoyed being a part of the youth group, and it wasn't just because I was the youth pastor. I could tell that they were developing their own relationship with God. Train up a child in the way he should go, and they will not depart far from it. I figured that if I helped build a foundation, no matter what winds may blow in their life, they would be able to withstand them. I had given my children the most expensive clothes and the latest toys most of their life, but I was now realizing that I had to give them something that was actually of worth. And that was my time. But more importantly, I needed to give them an understanding of who God was. Our bond became stronger and stronger.

Unfortunately, as the bond strengthened between the kids and me, it seemed to be getting weaker between Tracy and me. There was not a doubt that we both really loved each other, but there was no real relationship without companionship. We lived under the same roof, but it was like we lived in two totally separate houses. And although we did have moments of excitement together, they became few and far between. It became a tug-of-war for her separate life and me, and it became a tug-of war for her and my church involvement. Our communication became strained, as things got worse before they got better. Before I knew it, we were talking about a separation.

The word divorce did not become part of the conversation as we had not yet had the courage to take our vows again since I had gotten the white envelope in prison. I wasn't really sure if it was fear that prevented us from doing so, or if it was the fact that neither of us was really sure if we were ready to make that commitment again. I thought about the words she had spoken to me when she had asked me to come back home. She clearly stated that she was not the same person who I used to know before my incarceration. Although I hadn't spoken those words to her, I had actually been feeling the same thing. I was heavily involved in the streets when we met and continued to live a crazy lifestyle throughout most of our relationship. Now I had become a man of God. No, I was not perfect and would still struggle with human temptations, but I now made a conscious effort to do the right thing, whereas in times past I did not.

I couldn't help but wonder if we had gone through the motions of a long relationship and marriage with no real clue of who our mate really was. He who fails to plan, plans to fail. We had many problems in the past, but we had gotten back together without formulating a solid plan that would prevent us from failing again. Yeah, there were warnings of the obvious things that we should and shouldn't do, but unless two people were willing to work together to make things work, then success would be impossible. The only things that became common ground were the kids and bills, which would remain even if we were not together. I also felt like God wasn't the head of our relationship. We were together for years before we figured out that there was a conflict of religion. She would still attend her Catholic services at times, while the boys and I would go to our church.

After all of my hard work and dreams of having a solid family, I was eventually searching for my own apartment. I thought my life was finally coming together, but I was starting to feel like it was slipping away from me. I thought about the children of Israel. When they left Egypt and found themselves in a tough place, they were quick to remind God that they could have just stayed in Egypt rather than go to a new place only to die. I was feeling like I had taken the journey to a new place in my life, but I was still finding myself in a struggle. Was my relationship better when I was living my former lifestyle? It seemed like now that I was trying to live for God, everything was falling apart. I also remembered when I was in prison that I had not gotten divorce papers until I had actually made the choice to follow God. Was this the area that the enemy knew would affect me most? I had many questions for God because I could not figure out the answers.

I thought about how this would affect the boys since we had gotten so close over the years. Then I thought that it would probably affect them more if they had to watch their parents in a relationship where happiness was invisible. I cried out to God for many days asking for His help. This was a very difficult dilemma that I had found myself in.

They say an injury to one part of the body can affect the whole body, especially if the injured part is very important. My family structure was injured, and now it was starting to affect my job as well as my commitment to the church. I tried to stay poker-faced every time I went in the office because I knew I had to separate my personal problems from work, but there were many days where I found it very difficult to stay focused. I had worked so hard at this company that my lack of focus was starting to stick out like a sore thumb. And then there were days where the constant challenge of work kept my mind from dwelling on the obvious. And to complicate matters, Mom's health became worse. Therefore, I found myself traveling back home to make sure she was doing okay.

One of the keys to my success was that I had totally separated myself from my past friends and associates, but during these trips home, I began to communicate with friends from my past lifestyle. There was something inside of me that said I was strong enough to withstand the temptation of the streets. Another part of me knew that this particular temptation of the fast life would be something that I would have to fight off for the rest of my life.

I had been totally free of the street life for many years, but was I now setting myself up for a relapse? This was especially concerning since I was also considering taking on a new business venture that would add to my salary at the dairy. I had gotten a call from the former landlord of my first business. He had made me aware of a business that was going to shut down and wanted to know if I was interested in trying to save it for a reasonable amount of money. Most people would have been content with the job situation that I had, but my dream of having my own successful small business again was all of a sudden brought back to life. I took some time to think about this decision, but I was not confident enough to walk away from a great job to take on a struggling business. I continued to work as hard as I could at the dairy, considering the issues that had arisen with my family. I found myself spending more time at the office and less time at home so that I would avoid an argument. Better yet, I could avoid dealing with a silent argument where words were not spoken but there was an air of discomfort.

After one particular argument, I decided that I would jump in my car and go to a pool hall by myself to let off some steam. I hadn't shot pool for many years, but I still had the same passion as my Side Pocket gambling days. I took the first open table and began to work on my game. A waiter approached and asked if I wanted a drink. While chalking my stick, I decided that I would also do something that I hadn't done for many years. I looked up at her and asked her to bring me something strong. After a couple suggestions, I decided to go with smooth and brown liquor. After the first drink, I could feel my whole attitude shift. By the second drink, you could tell I hadn't picked up a pool stick for a very long time. Even in my years of drinking, I always had enough after the second drink since I was very serious about being in control of my faculties. Due to my tolerance being very low, I decided that the second drink that day was more than enough. I also knew that I was only there trying to avoid the issues in my home. Our argument had been very intense, and we had actually discussed how soon I would be moving to my own place. All the years we had been together, we could probably count the number of arguments we had on one hand. I wondered if that was because we were nonviolent people, or if we were just that good at avoiding problems.

I paid the tab, got in my car, put the seatbelt on, and prepared for the drive home. The alcohol made me want to call her right away, but I went with the option of just sending a text. I would talk to her when I got to the house. I had only gotten halfway through the text when I noticed the red and blue lights flashing behind me. I immediately pulled over to the right side of the road in hopes that they were on their way to an emergency. I had no such luck as the police car pulled directly behind me. I took a deep, intoxicated breath as he approached my window. I knew I had not been speeding as I unconsciously always drove the speed limit. In fact, there were times when I often drove under the limit. The officer walked up with his state trooper attire and asked for my license, insurance, and registration. I asked him what the problem was. He ignored me until I gave him the items that he had requested. He then told me that he had pulled me over because he noticed me swerving in the lane and he thought he had seen me texting while I was driving. He then asked me to step out of the car as he had noticed a light smell of alcohol when I rolled down my window. After walking the straight line by putting each foot in front of the other, standing on one leg, and a series of other tests that may have been awkward even if you were completely sober, I was cited for a DWI. It meant that I was not totally drunk, but I had exceeded the limit of alcohol and shouldn't be behind a wheel. The funny thing about this situation was the fact that there were times where I had a few drinks and drove home without a problem. I knew the truth was that my swerving was due to the angry text that I was sending while driving, which was just as bad because there are many people who have lost their lives because of texting. I was taken to the police station and had to make a phone call to Tracy after all. And this time it was to come pick me up from the police station. We spoke very little on the way home and this did not make things better at all.

As far as my job went, this was the absolute worst thing that could have happened to me. I was a manager in a route department. I sat across from potential employees every day and made it clear to them that their driving history was one of the most important factors in their hire. If you had a DUI or DWI within a certain timeframe, then you were not able to work at the dairy. This also included management, and there were times when we would have to bail out a driver if they got sick during their route. With this new development, I knew I had now put myself in a position where I would lose my job. I had even more now to figure out. I could not believe how my life had done a complete 180. Just a short time before, everything seemed to be going excellently. Now, all of a sudden, things were out of control. I was losing my family, I was losing the job I had worked so hard for, and I was starting to lose faith that God was really looking out for me.

I went to my pastor and told him that it was best that I resign as youth pastor. I was not in a position to be a good example for young people. He encouraged me to keep moving forward no matter how hard things seemed to get. I tried thinking of the beautiful waterfalls at the top of the hike, but the clear water now seemed to be polluted. This was very hard for me. I really loved working with young people. It really hurt me when I was approached by one of the kids from the group who told me that since I was resigning, they did not want to come to church any longer. I had put so much effort into making it exciting for young people to learn about God, and now I was just walking away.

I also made a decision that it would be easier for me to resign from the dairy before they found out about my DWI. That way I was leaving the door open for when I got my life in order so that I could possibly return if need be. I knew that if I got fired, then there would be no hope of ever returning. I did have a little time on my hands before my big mistake was noticed. Since I actually hadn't operated a vehicle in such a long time at the dairy, my driving history was not an important factor at that point. Most of my work was mostly paperwork and employee development, but I knew there would be a point where I would be required to drive. So in the meantime, I had to get my ducks in order so that I could still pay the bills. I decided that since my career may be short-lived at the dairy, it would probably be a good idea to take on the new business venture that was offered to me. At least I could build it to the point where it could compensate for the loss of my salary at the dairy.

Within months, my whole life had changed. I had finally moved into my own apartment. To my surprise, the boys and I continued to maintain a very strong bond. In some instances, I believe it had gotten even stronger. Tracy and I remained cordial to each other. We had spent so many years together that it was difficult not to care what happened to one another. We functioned as parents, although there were times we did cross the line. We had made up our minds that we were approaching the end of the road.

I scheduled a meeting with our company vice president who had grown to really like me. I informed him of my resignation. He looked like a clean-cut Woody from *Cheers*. He had a smile and laugh that could change the temperature of a room. If he meant business, then that room would turn into a furnace. His counterpart, the president, had no desire to adjust the temperature of a room. Every time he walked into the room there were very few smiles as he was all business. The vice president sat across from me with a caring look on his face. He told me how valuable I was to the company. He said if I ever had a change of heart, there would be a place for me there. I wanted so badly to just tell him everything that was going on in my life, but I somehow felt that it wouldn't matter. Even if he made an exception, what if I wasn't able to get things under control? So I made the decision to walk away and possibly return when I figured some things out.

I had already taken on the new business venture before I resigned from the dairy. Things seemed to be very promising. It was a different kind of business than I was used to, but my past failures and the many things I had learned as a manager at the dairy would be a great help to the business.

Unfortunately, within a year's time, the business began to struggle due to my wanting to develop it faster than it would allow. The difference between it and some of my earlier business attempts was that I had more than enough capital during the beginning stages. But my livelihood was solely dependant on the growth of the business, considering the fact that I did not have a source of income and wasn't getting compensation from street life. Lessons are repeated until they are learned! I found myself once again under extreme pressure. My biggest mistake was to think that once I got my life in order, the enemy would just let me be. I was wrong about that!

I had not been to church in months, but I would still get frequent calls from my pastor, checking to see if I was okay. His rhetorical question was only to let me know that he was concerned. He would say that he was praying for me. Through wisdom, and the way he operated spiritually, he knew that things were not going well at all.

A very common mistake is when people separate themselves from God or the church when they feel like they are making bad choices in life. People feel like they have to get their lives in order before they could show up on the church steps again. But that was such an unrealistic expectation. If your car was not running correctly, then there was no way it could get fixed before you took it to the shop. The key was getting it to the shop. More importantly, you should have been making regular visits to keep up with maintenance. The same thing applied to the things of God.

I had felt myself slip away. I found myself trying to hide from a God who sees all things. I was totally separated from the church, but one day I received a call from my pastor that I thought was a routine checkup. Instead of asking me how I was doing, he asked me how my schedule was looking for Friday morning. A little curious with his question, I told him that I was pretty much free besides the regular duties of the business. He then went on to tell me that he had a big favor to ask. A well-known pastor was flying to Denver for a funeral service. My pastor wanted to know if I was available to pick the other pastor up, take him to his hotel, and drive him to the service where he would be preaching. I felt this request was very odd. One, I had not been to church for quite some time. And two, I knew my pastor had many men around him who could have handled this request without a problem. Most of all, I was confused about why he would trust me to accommodate a preacher who he described as very well known, yet he had not seen me in church in a while. I reluctantly agreed to take care of his request. He had not given me the name of the person who I was picking up, only the exact time to arrive at Denver International Airport to pick him up. He informed me that he had let the other pastor know what I would be driving and would be expecting me upon his arrival.

I had never discussed all the details of my incarceration with my pastor. I never told him what the turning point was that caused me to commit everything to God, and how it happened during a time I felt I had nothing to give. I had been almost at the same place where I was right now, where it seemed that all hope had been lost. I had been shipped off to a prison far away and had received the white envelope with the divorce papers. Yet, somehow, I was able to gain strength from devoting all of my time to studying the word of God. I was also being ministered from a distance. Those tapes that I had found in the chapel were the very things that motivated me to dive a little deeper into the word of God. I had made it through all the tapes of T.D. Jakes, and by the time I got to the tapes of Noel Jones, I had begun to formulate a real pattern of how I needed to study. Most of all, I realized how much I needed to learn. I remembered putting my head down, trying to hide the tears. I had to remember that I was in a place where being weak was unacceptable. Bishop Noel Jones had tapped into my spirit. Although the tapes were outdated, they seemed to be speaking to my current state. I had gotten through every tape that they had of his, and I had also gotten used to watching *Fresh Oil* every Wednesday morning. I could not believe how God was using this man to speak to me and teach me from a distance, but his words were so close to my heart. I had studied the tapes of T.D. Jakes. He had an elite ability to paint a panoramic picture with the word of God. I had fallen in love with his message titled "Developing the Negative," and then shortly after he had showed up to the prison where I was a resident. After watching Noel's tapes, I then made a promise that I would visit him at his church in California at some point. Now I found myself physically free, but I was in a state where I became spiritually bound. Everything seemed to fall apart again. I was at the point of once again making some very poor decisions.

Friday morning arrived and I prepared myself to take care of my pastor's request. He had many pastor friends who traveled to Colorado to speak. Even when I was active in his ministry, he had never asked me to do a favor like this. I was thinking it was his way of just keeping me involved to some degree to let me know that he had not given up on me. I met up with one of the brothers from the church who would be helping me make sure the guest pastor's visit went smoothly. Dee was a brother who I really liked as he had a real commitment to the ministry. His had dreadlocks pulled back into a ponytail and the build of a linebacker, which together automatically implied security.

We arrived a bit early at the passenger pickup area of the specified airline, but within seconds a tall, dark man approached our vehicle. I watched him as if he were in slow motion. Each step that he took was one of purpose and surety. His salt and pepper hair and beard spoke pure wisdom. I sat with my mouth wide open, looking as if someone had hit the pause button on the remote. I guess there wasn't a need to get the name of this pastor. I instantly recognized him as the great Bishop Noel Jones.

Dee jumped out of the vehicle and opened the rear door. I seemed to still be on pause. Suddenly, I snapped out of it and pulled away from the curb. If there had been any doubt in my mind that God was real, all of that doubt was erased that day. My pastor had no idea of the experience I had had during one of my worst times. I had watched this man, who God used to speak to me through a television screen, and now I was riding in the same car with him. What made it so incredible was the fact that I was again at one of those low points in my life. We dropped him off at his hotel and arranged to pick him up again about an hour before the scheduled service. He had not spoken many words on the way to the hotel, but the ride to the church was quite different.

We picked him up at the exact time of the agreement and the conversation on the way was very interesting. The very first words that this man spoke were the most important that he would say during our encounter. He spoke of philosophy, and how Charles Swartz was quoted as saying that death was the "great equalizer." No matter how much material a person had acquired during their life, when we died, we were all equal and had to answer to God. I pulled out of the hotel parking lot and made a left onto the main road. I had looked up the church where we were going to figure out an easy route. Once I got to a certain point that I was familiar with, I felt that I could take a shortcut. To my surprise, the roads did not connect and I found myself in an unfamiliar area. I remember being at a stop sign and looking over the steering wheel in both directions. It was very apparent that I seemed to be lost (a life lesson). During my hesitation, the bishop spoke his first words to me. He cleared his throat and said, "Man of God, you cannot go wrong going right." I took a right turn and within minutes I was on a highway that I was familiar with. We made it to the church in no time. Although it was a funeral service, I listened intently to this man preach in person. Somehow he had traveled to me without the need of me going to California. And to top it off, it was at a time when it was really necessary. Everything else went perfectly. We got him back to the airport and he was on his way. That would be a day that I would never forget.

Corinthians 2:14 reads, "But the natural man receiveth not the things of the Spirit of God: for they are foolishness unto him, neither can he know them, because they are spiritually discerned." I had been in the company of one of the greatest preachers of our time, yet I had not been in a place spiritually where I could hear anything that was said. I was still amazed that the meeting had actually taken place, but at that point it didn't seem like it was enough to shift me back into the right gear.

I traveled back to Pittsburgh to attend my Aunt Debbie's funeral. It was unbelievable that both she and my uncle had passed before the age of fifty. She had a stroke some time ago and it had really affected the person that she was. I always remember her as one of the strongest and smartest people in our family. She was a person who everyone loved to be around. After her stroke, her health deteriorated. Then her life was gone at a very young age.

After the services, I stayed home for a couple of days. During that time, I had a few conversations with some friends from my past life. I knew that I was in a financial struggle, but I could not believe that after all those years of hard work, I was now thinking the unthinkable. What I was thinking about was the Hail Mary. In Catholic terms, Hail Mary meant a prayer or salvation to the Virgin Mary. In football terms, a Hail Mary was a last second pass that would give the team one final chance of victory before the clock expired. A Hail Mary in street terms was very similar to football. You had to cover a lot of distance when there wasn't a lot of time left. I was now thinking of throwing this long pass from Denver to Pittsburgh. Only instead of a football, I was now gripping the forbidden fruit in my hand. The biggest misconception of crime was that you could get away with it on the second or third try. You believed that you had gotten smarter and that there was a better way you could do it to prevent getting caught again. The reality was that the only way you could prevent getting caught was to not do it at all.

I formulated what I thought was a foolproof plan, but I had to know that at this point in my life when God had been so good to me, anything I did wrong would be exposed. I thought about the friends who had lived a daily life of crime, and whenever I would sneeze too hard, it seemed I would be in trouble. My foolproof plan ended up backfiring, and I found myself in trouble once again. There is a scripture that says, "When sin aboundeth, grace the more." I was clearly out of line, yet God still continued to show His grace toward me. Although my situation wasn't nearly as bad as it was years before, there was clearly another lesson that I needed to learn. Many times I felt like the enemy wouldn't leave me alone, but I was also now realizing that God would never give up on me. It was just as important that I stop taking His grace for granted.

It had taken me to bump my head again to get back to where I belonged as a man of God. I then thought about those words that were spoken to me by the Bishop Noel Jones. God had sent him to give me a message in person that I somehow wasn't able to understand. The message was now crystal clear. When I was at that stop sign peeking over my steering wheel in an obvious state of confusion, he had given me advice that I thought was pertaining to the direction I was driving. However, his advice was the word from God that was giving me direction for my life. He had simply stated, "You can't go wrong going right." Although I had made the right turn in my vehicle and had gotten on track, I had made the wrong turn when it came to my life. If only I could have discerned the message from God, I would have avoided getting myself in trouble again. Warning always comes before destruction, but you had to take heed to the warning.

There was so much validity to the statement that you reaped what you sowed. I would have to deal with the consequences of my current actions. I was very fortunate, or better yet blessed, that although those consequences were very painful, they were not fatal. I was sent on a mini vacation back to a place that I had promised myself never to return. I couldn't help thinking about the many years I had spent transgressing in the city I was from but couldn't tell you what the inside of a jail looked like there. I had moved far away for change, but now I would be on grown-man punishment for the second time. During this short stint, I had a lot of time to think about my life. It was imperative that I figure out why I continued to make bad choices. You could spray the weeds in your driveway with weed killer, but those weeds would continue to grow back unless you got the proper tools and dug up the root. I knew I had a lot of surface issues, but now it was time that I finally took a look at the roots.

I thought about my childhood, my family, and the friends that I grew up around. I thought about the places where I had lived and the things that I had seen at a very young age. I wondered if there was a possibility that I could have avoided prison bars despite these powerful influences? I thought about my kids and how they were on their way to college and had not seen a fraction of the things that I was exposed to in my childhood. I had made a huge sacrifice moving away and trying to escape the game, but I still had to deal with the residue. Although it had been a constant battle to escape my past, it was a sacrifice that was actually paying off for my children's future.

I had friends back home who had kids the same age as mine. They were already in the judicial system. I moved away into a middle-class neighborhood, and my boys were now off to college. If people thought that an environment didn't have an effect on how a person's life ended up, then they were wrong. Yeah, there were people who were strong enough to rise above the living conditions of the projects. However, most of the people bumped their heads a few times until the light turned on and they were forced to find a better way.

I thought about my uncles who had been very popular drug dealers during my childhood. They seemed to have had the best of everything until the police came knocking on their doors. They had been sent off to prison a few times. Then finally, by the time they were well into their forties, they decided it was time to try to build an honest career. I was very proud of them as they had finally given up the game, but had they started building their careers in their twenties instead of selling drugs, then they would probably be getting ready for a very good retirement.

I thought about each of my childhood friends who I had played tackle football with down at the field in Burns Heights. At a very young age we all had a dream to rise above the living conditions in the projects. Mo-Joe, Lump, and Bear carried the football skills they had learned in the Heights all the way to high school. They had become some of the greatest athletes that the city of Duquesne had ever seen. Mo-Joe, who was arguably one of the greatest running backs to carry the ball, would not make it to the level of college football. He would eventually fall to the temptation of the streets. After a few mishaps and some years of maturity, he was able to devote his time to teaching kids in the neighborhood the skills he had acquired at a young age playing football. Bear, who actually did go off to college, had become one of the best receivers to play the game, only to be influenced by the glamorous life I had lived. He turned in his books and picked up the forbidden fruit. It went okay for several years until he was sent off to prison to deal with the consequences. Lump had actually finished all four years of college and had gotten a big contract to play basketball overseas. But, go figure, it was not enough compared to the fast money that was coming from a different kind of game. He returned home and teamed up with a group of guys that were indicted by the Feds. Instead of getting his tryout for the NBA, he was now being recruited on a prison basketball team.

Damien, or the kid we called Grip, had separated himself from us by the time we reached middle school and before I had moved away. He had been our leader as kids. He was the one who we would follow everywhere around Duquesne. He now seemed to be following in our footsteps since he also ended up in prison.

Rodney had been the first of all of us to visit a prison cell. He didn't play any sports as a kid. His dream was to become a rapper. Before he had a chance to develop that dream, he was sent off to prison. Upon his release, he seemed to pick up right where he left off. He recorded a couple of albums and got immediately involved in the music industry. There was also something different about him. He started to acknowledge that God was real. He was very thankful that the prayer that he had said on my porch as a kid had finally been answered. He had been frustrated about the things his mother was doing, so I encouraged him to talk to a person who could help him. After all those years, his mother was totally delivered from drugs. He showed his appreciation by attending a church called Mount Arat. But just when he had started to get a grip on his life, it was suddenly taken. Rodney was the victim of a shooting. The bullet may not even have been meant for him. He seemed to be in the wrong place at the wrong time.

Ju-Ju had shown the first signs of becoming a drug dealer when we were kids. He was always dressed the best, and he also had a love of money before we knew what to do with it. I remember the day he pulled up next to me in his drop-top IROC-Z. From that moment on, we took the game to another level. He also spent time in prison. He seemed to be in and out for several years. Ju-Ju was affected by more than just the proceeds of the forbidden fruit. He had now become a consumer.

I could not believe, as I looked back, that not one of us could say that we had not been to prison. I also saw that not one single person who was involved with drugs had not been arrested, or even worse, lost their life. Why had it taken me so many years to come to this conclusion? The streets were a dead end. It was a game that you could never win. Most importantly, it was the only game that I could think of where there was not a winner. The user lost their health and spirit, the dealers lost their freedom, and their families, in most cases, lost their lives altogether.

I thought about my journey. How I was raised in the church only to fall victim to street life. I had enjoyed the luxuries that it had yielded, but it was the memories of my early childhood that had encouraged me to search for a way out. After walking away from everything, only to find that changing my address was clearly not enough, I then had to deal with the consequences of my actions. I had tried to escape the inevitable. All along there was a desire to do the right thing. I had attended business school, as well as church, during my life of crime, but a double life was always going to be overpowered by the stronger temptation. I had watched both of my parents struggle with addiction during my childhood, and then see them find the strength to overcome the temptation. They became totally clean, but then it was their son who had chosen to start riding dirty.

I tried to run away from the life rather than dealing with it head on. I traveled to another state across the country that had ten times the amount of drugs coming through it. I had no idea how available the forbidden fruit would be in my new destination. More importantly, I didn't know how cheap it could be purchased. I felt in my heart that God had led me to a new place where the temptation would be even stronger than the place I had left behind. I succeeded in giving my children a chance to grow up in a way better environment. Their mother had picked up the slack during the times of my incarceration. The end result had them enrolling in college on a quest to become productive citizens.

There were times in the game when I felt that I had everything—especially the things that money could buy. I had to eventually learn that wealth earned through vanity shall diminish, but he who laboreth shall increase. Every penny that you made in the drug trade would eventually be lost or taken away, but things that you worked hard for would always remain. I finally had to admit to myself that I was addicted to getting high. Yes, I had kept the vow of never using drugs, but I was addicted to the high that a wad of cash in a rubber band gave me. I was addicted to the power and the attention that it provided. People who were impressed by that life thought I was a hero, when in fact I had only been a villain. I cared nothing about how my lifestyle affected other people. I was clear of the effects since I had experienced them as a child.

I looked back over the many times that my life had been in apparent danger. In fact, there were times when I knew that I should not have been alive, and yet God had spared me. We ask God for a sign or to hear his voice, but when his grace is clearly manifested, we are somehow ignorant to the fact. I thought about so many miracles that were right in front of me—not only with my own life but also with both of my parents. I remember during my last visit home to Pittsburgh, I was at a gas station pumping gas. A man walked up to me with a humungous smile on his face. He gave me a hug that almost choked the life out of me. He had not known exactly what state I was in, but all he probably remembered was this drug dealer who used to sell to him many years ago. He also remembered me taking him to the hospital to see his dying mother before she went on to glory. He had been in a very bad state then, but somehow today he was glowing. His physique was one of great health, and his apparel was brand new and clean. I looked at the sparkling gold chain with a cross on his neck and he made me aware of what he now represented. He proudly announced that he was a child of God and had been delivered from the forbidden fruit. He went on to tell me how God had blessed him with a great job and a beautiful wife. This man was no other than the Mr. Chick Green, who had been one of my very first customers when I started to live the life of crime.

A short time after that I started to receive messages on Facebook from a lady whose name I did not recognize. She would always talk about God. Then one day she included a nickname that I had used in the projects when I first started dealing drugs. This woman was Ms. Tub. She had been bound by drugs for well over twenty years. She was proud to tell me that she, too, had been delivered.

I had lost everything. I was in bad shape financially, and my family was torn apart. However, God never gave up on me. I had finally dealt with the consequences of all of my bad choices. Not only was I now physically free, but I was also totally spiritually free. It had taken me years to overcome one of the strongest temptations of my past. There were many times that I had wanted to give up, but God would always throw me a life jacket. For the present, suffering was not worthy to be compared to the glory that shall be revealed. I was now a strong believer that there were so many great things ahead.

And as far as my past life, I had made up my mind. As my grandmother's favorite saying went, enough was finally enough!